The True Rudolph Valentino

by

Baltasar Fernández Cué

Translated by Renato Floris

Foreword by Evelyn Zumaya

Published by:
Viale Industria Pubblicazioni
Torino, Italy – May, 2019
viplibri@libero.it

Spanish Narrative
Copyright 1927
Baltasar Fernández Cué

Translation, Foreword & Layout
Copyright 2019
Renato Floris, Evelyn Zumaya

In Deposito Legale presso SBN

ISBN: 978-0-9987098-2-6

Una carta:

GAYLORD APARTMENTS
LOS ANGELES, CALIFORNIA.
———

19 de Febrero de 1927.

Sr. Don Baltasar Fernández Cué,
P. O. Box 403   Ciudad.

Mi querido amigo:

Tengo mucho gusto en confirmarle por escrito la amplia y sincera aprobación que verbalmente le expresé ya respecto de su proyecto de escribir una serie de artículos sobre la vida de mi querido y malogrado hermano Rodolfo. Asimismo le reitero mi autorización para que haga uso no sólo de los numerosos datos que en varias conversaciones tuve el gusto de proporcionarle ya, sino también de otros que usted juzgue necesarios y que yo le facilitaré tan pronto como usted lo desee. Además, puede usted contar con mi cooperación moral para llevar a cabo su loable proyecto.

Agradezco la leal intención de usted no solamente por la satisfacción que forzosamente tengo que hallar en cuanto tienda a representar de un modo honrado la personalidad de mi finado hermano, sino también porque considero necesario propalar la verdad acerca de él aunque no sea más que por refutar las falsas versiones que, sobre su vida y, más especialmente, sobre sus amores, reales o supuestos, circulan por el mundo.

Y nadie más indicado que usted para desmentir esas invenciones, ya que usted une a su habilidad y honradez la ventaja de haber sido buen amigo de mi hermano, de serlo todavía hoy, por fortuna, mío, y de contar también con la amistad de muchos de los que lo fueron de Rodolfo y que ahora le podrán ayudar a usted en su obra.

Finalmente, quiero también hacer constar el agrado con que veo la afición que los pueblos de habla española manifiestan hacia Rodolfo: afición que se adivina en las noticias que usted recibe respecto de la buena acogida que en esos países se daría a una versión fidedigna de la vida de Rodolfo. Corresponden así a la simpatía con que, como usted sabe, vió siempre mi hermano a esos mismos pueblos. Miraba con cariño cuanto a ellos se refería. Tenía predilección por los papeles que representaban tipos de esas nacionalidades. A estas mismas pertenecían algunos de sus mejores amigos, que lo son míos también. De un libro en español salió la película que le dió fama mundial. De otro del mismo autor se hizo otra película que muchos tienen por la obra maestra de mi hermano, y en la que tuvo orgullo en representar un tipo popularísimo en los pueblos de civilización hispánica. Y, como usted sabe también, cuando la muerte le sorprendió, estaba queriendo llevar a la pantalla otra novela del mismo idioma representando otra vez el mismo tipo tan popular en dichas naciones.

Independientemente de todas esas respetables consideraciones, a mí, por supuesto, no puede menos que agradarme cuanto tienda sanamente a mantener vivo el recuerdo de mi hermano en los corazones de sus innúmeros admiradores.

Le reitero, pues, mi agradecimiento, le deseo el mejor de los éxitos, y quedo suyo afmo. amigo q. e. s. m.

Alberto Guglielmi-Valentino.

Alberto Guglielmi Valentino's endorsement of *The True Rudolph Valentino* by Baltasar Cué[1]

---

1   As published in *Cine-Mundial*, April 1927.

3

"Take care, understand it well, to honor the memory of the one who was in life the most perfect of knights and remember there are women worthy to defend his name and his honor which is worth more than all worldly ambitions and richness."

A Rudolph Valentino fan living in Buenos Aires in 1927,
excerpted from a letter written to Baltasar Cué.

Translation of Alberto Guglielmi Valentino's
Letter of Endorsement

GAYLORD APARTMENTS
Los Angeles, California
February 19, 1927

Mr. Baltasar Fernández Cué
P. O. Box 403
Los Angeles, California

My dear friend,

I am pleased to confirm in writing, the sincere approval which I expressed to you verbally regarding your project to write a series of articles about the life of my dear and ill-fated brother Rodolfo. I reiterate my authorization for you to make use of not only the numerous materials which I had the pleasure to give you during our several conversations but also of other materials you deem necessary which I will provide as soon as you wish. In addition, you may count on my moral cooperation to carry out your laudable project.

I appreciate your honest intentions not only for the satisfaction it will bring me but as it will represent, in an honest way, the personality of my late brother. I consider it necessary to spread the truth about him even if it is only to correct the false versions of his life and, more especially, about his loves, real or supposed circulating around the world.

No one is more suited than you to refute these falsehoods, since along with your skill and honesty you have the advantage of having been a good friend of my brother, of being still today fortunately one of mine, and of also enjoying the friendship of many of those who were Rodolfo 's friends who can now help you in your work.

Finally, I would also like express my pleasure over the enthusiasm of the Spanish-speaking peoples towards Rodolfo: a true admiration you have witnessed in the response you receive regarding the positive reception in those countries where they report a true version of Rodolfo's life. This corresponds to the sympathy with which, as you know, my brother always felt towards those same people. He held affection for them and had a preference for screen roles which represented those nationalities.

To these same countries belonged some of his best friends; who are mine too. From a Spanish book came the movie which brought him world fame. From another, of the same author, a film was made which many say was my brother's masterpiece and in which he took pride in representing a very popular character in Spanish culture. And, as you also know when death surprised him, he was hoping to bring one more novel of the same language to the screen, again portraying the same character so popular in those nations.

Regardless of all those respectable considerations, I, of course, can not help but hope to keep the memory of my brother alive in the hearts of his many admirers. I thank you again and I wish you the best of the success. I remain your friend,

q. e. s. m. [2]

Alberto Guglielmi Valentino

---

2 Translator's Note, "t.n." - *que estrecha su mano* - (shaking your hand)- a formal courtesy.

Baltasar Cué's Time Capsule

A Foreword
by
Evelyn Zumaya

In the December 21, 1924 issue of the *Los Angeles Times,* an article was published titled, "Secrets of Rudolph Valentino's Life" written by Alma Whitaker. Ms. Whitaker's article was the result of her "modest" interview with Valentino, as she referred to it, on the occasion of the shaving of his infamous goatee. She posed many questions during the interview; inquiring about Valentino's films, his childhood and his recent and successful movie, *Monsieur Beaucaire.* Upon the completion of her interview, she presented him with a pen and one of his publicity photographs; asking for an autograph. Valentino thought for a moment before inscribing, "Hoping to be kindly remembered, Rudolph Valentino."

This endearing line is indicative of a prominent theme in Valentino's brief life; his desire for an accurate and positive representation of who he really was. He was tormented by his misrepresentation in the press, specifically in studio-generated publicity pieces.

At the time of his interview with Alma Whitaker, there is no doubt Valentino commanded the hearts and imaginations of his devoted fans worldwide. He was then box-office gold. But this pinnacle of success left him vulnerable to a conservative press campaign determined to impugn him and his influence. He was portrayed as a reckless and poor role model for America's young men and an unacceptable, if not indecent, target of American women's wistful gazes. In what would be his final days of life, Valentino suffered further torment in this regard from one defamatory portrayal presented as an editorial in *The Chicago Tribune.*

This editorial attributed his influence on the appearance of pink powder vending machines in men's bathrooms. The anonymous author of the editorial attacked Valentino's heritage and claimed he was effeminate. Those closest to Valentino blamed his early death on his rage over this attack.

Yet, unknown to his public at the time, he was doing something about his problem of being exploited by fiction. He was taking action to right the wrong and this effort brings us to the subject of this curious book.

❧❧

On August 23, 1926, Baltasar Cué listened in shock to news of the sudden death of his friend, Rudolph Valentino. The Spanish journalist not only faced a future without his friend "Rudy", but he was also left suspended in the literary limbo of a book interrupted; an important book, this book. At the time of his death, Rudolph Valentino was collaborating on this book with Baltasar Cué; determined to set the record straight and tell once and for all the true story of his life as only he could tell it.

Valentino left Hollywood with his manager George Ullman just a few weeks prior to his death, traveling east for the premieres of his movie *The Son of the Sheik*. Before leaving, he gave Baltasar Cué a few personal letters and articles he felt might be useful for reference and assured him he would return within three weeks time to devote his full attention to the completion of this book.

Cué had just spent a few weeks in Valentino's home, Falcon Lair, where he interviewed and observed the famous subject of his upcoming biography. He eagerly awaited Valentino's return to Los Angeles and was set to begin work immediately. This was not to be. When Valentino did return to California, it would be on his funeral train and sealed in a coffin.

In the days following Valentino's Los Angeles funeral, Cué remained determined death would not have its way again and deal a final blow to Valentino's book. But what raw data did Cué have to work with, now that his friend and primary source was gone? How could he proceed? Only Rudolph Valentino could accurately change his story and he did not live long enough to do so.

Yet, Baltasar Cué realized he could still write a rich narrative based on his friendship with Valentino and their time spent together during his last days in Los Angeles. Cué interviewed Valentino many times and was invited to accompany him on location of his last movie, *The Son of the Sheik*. They shared luncheons in Valentino's bungalow on the United Artists' lot and many evenings and week-ends Cué was welcomed as family to Falcon Lair. He witnessed Valentino's private world and would appear in photographs taken during the filming of *The Son of the Sheik* and at the wedding of actress Mae Murray and David Mdivani.

For a brief yet important while, Baltasar Cué seemed to be everywhere with Rudolph Valentino. Few people knew then it was because they were working on this book. In the mournful wake of Valentino's death, Cué's eye-witness accounts would become his most valuable resource but he would also be required to rely on other sources to complete his work.

Although for Valentino and Baltasar Cué, the writing of this book assumed an air of seriousness, it was conceived of initially as a joke. The concept was Cué's brainchild which he proposed to Valentino and his friend

Manuel Reachi over the three men's lunch in Valentino's studio bungalow. Valentino and Reachi found it an amusing idea; which went like this.

Cué proposed he write a fictional book about Valentino's life which was so scandalous and false the public would be outraged. He explained how the furor over such a book would inspire protests and he, as the author, would be threatened with lawsuits.

He envisioned that as the author of such a hit piece on Valentino, he might even be sent to jail. At that point, Valentino would stride boldly forward to issue his public statement saying he believed so strongly in the freedom of speech and the Constitution of the United States, that the horrible book should be allowed to stand and the lawsuits against its author terminated. This would endear him to the public and Valentino would be forever renown as a man who held the highest regard for all great American values.

However, when Cué and Valentino sat down to discuss the project, Valentino changed course. Lamenting the fiction about him already so prevalent, he expounded at length to Cué how this unfortunate situation came to be. He said his life story, as it was then known by the public, was an inaccurate one and generated solely as glossy prose to promote his movies.

Just prior to Valentino's leaving for New York on that fatal trip, he told his Spanish friend that this book would not be a joke to garner publicity, it would instead be the true story of his life; the one he wanted the world to read.

As Cué devised a way to complete this work after Valentino's death, he received a proposal from the editors of the Spanish language movie magazine *Cine-Mundial*. They expressed their desire to publish his biography of Rudolph Valentino as a series of ten articles, with the first lavishly-illustrated installment appearing in May of 1927 and the last installment published in February of 1928.

Cué accepted the offer and received the prompt endorsement of Valentino's only brother, Alberto Guglielmi Valentino. Cué began his work by interviewing not only Alberto Guglielmi but Valentino's friends as well; including the actor and director, Douglas Gerrard, producer and Mexican Embassy attaché, Manuel Reachi and Valentino's last love interest, actress Pola Negri. I also believe his anonymous source, he refers to as the "Latina", to possibly be the actress Marion Davies because of her positioning in the story.

In addition to first-hand accounts from these sources, Cué would complete aspects of his narrative by referring to those studio-generated publications; the very ones Valentino was eager to debunk. Still, Cué's most valuable source remained his eye-witness accounts of life with Valentino during the star's last weeks of life in Los Angeles. These included scenarios which took place while he was granted access to Valentino's daily life, whether on location during the filming of *The Son of the Sheik* or in Falcon Lair. In doing so, Cué created a perfect time capsule; a time capsule which would remain sealed from an English-speaking audience for the next ninety-two years.

To establish the historical context of this extraordinary time capsule, it is helpful to know just what was going on in Rudolph Valentino's life when Cué researched and wrote this book. I divide the following commentary into Cué's two distinct research time frames; the first being the spring of 1926 until Valentino left Los Angeles and the second which began with Valentino's death and ended some five months later in January 1927. This is when Cué submitted his completed manuscript to *Cine-Mundial* for publication.

When Baltasar Fernández Cué began work on this book with Valentino, he was forty-eight years old and had been living in Hollywood for two years working as a Spanish language translator and Hollywood correspondent. He was an ambitious self-promoter and charmed his way into professional acclaim by contributing articles to many Spanish motion picture periodicals; not only *Cine Mundial*, but *El Sol* and *La Pantalla* in Madrid, the Mexican periodical, *Excelsior*, the Chilean magazine, *Mercurio* as well as the American publication, *World Cinema*. It was in this capacity he met and befriended Rudolph Valentino in the spring of 1926.

Cué appeared in Valentino's entourage during a tumultuous time in the star's life. Although Valentino was enjoying an undisputed international popularity and an extravagant lifestyle, he was coping emotionally with the dissolution of his second marriage. His household records[3] at the time reveal his distress with their drastic itemization as proof of his increase in spending. His manager George Ullman struggled to pay those bills which were pouring in from Valentino's unrestrained and indulgent spending sprees.

Valentino returned from a successful European promotional tour in January of that year, where he attended the openings of his movie *The Eagle*; a trip he made with Manuel Reachi acting as his attaché. That same month his divorce from his second wife, Natacha Rambova was finalized in Paris.

---

3 "The Gray Book Ledgers" as submitted to the California Supreme Court by George Ullman, case filed as "S. George Ullman v. Alberto Guglielmi, Maria Strada, Bank of America National Trust, Teresa Werner and Ray Riley, State Controller", also ledger extracts filed as "Exhibit No. 9, 1926 'Gray Book', Household Expense" which are excerpted from the Baskerville Audit accounts, p.267.

Despite their rush to divorce, by all accounts both Valentino and Rambova were bitterly wounded and miserable in each other's absence.

In a move to assuage his loneliness, Valentino returned to Los Angeles that January, accompanied by his brother Alberto, his wife and "son". With construction ongoing on Falcon Lair and the surrounding property, the noise and disruption soon caused tensions to flare among the Guglielmi family with Alberto's wife suffering a nervous condition necessitating she move into a hotel.

It was also during this time, Valentino became involved in a relationship with actress Pola Negri. She was a fiery, determined woman and their relationship would be volatile and passionate. Her home in Beverly Hills would serve as a retreat for Valentino, providing him with a safe port from the familial storms taking place in Falcon Lair.

The emotional tension in Valentino's life at the time exacerbated when his work on *The Son of the Sheik* was completed. This left him without a contract and his mighty paychecks from his employer, United Artists ceased. As he was supporting a staggering financial overhead and with his debt mounting by the day, it was imperative his manager George Ullman secure a new contract for him immediately. Ullman would negotiate a second contract with United Artists with the first film under the new contract scheduled to be the story of the Italian sculptor, Benvenuto Cellini and titled, *The Firebrand*.

As a stop-gap measure until filming began on *The Firebrand* and Valentino's paychecks resumed, Ullman negotiated a loan to raise desperately needed cash. Under the terms of the $150,000 one-year loan secured with the Cinema Finance Corporation, Valentino's payments on the loan totaled $13,375 a month. [4]

If these numbers are calculated by today's currency rates, the high stakes machinations in Valentino's personal and professional life can be realized. These substantial amounts of money instigated efforts to gain control over Valentino, his lucrative career and his cash. This represented another insidious element in the Falcon Lair household during the spring of 1926.

Manuel Reachi was one of the power players with designs on Valentino's wealth and his presence in this book presents a timely insight. Reachi was reportedly attempting to convince Valentino that Ullman was a poor manager by alleging he could do a far better job. Ullman would survive the attempted coup as Valentino was secure in Ullman's prowess as a business manager and held faith in his loyalty and honesty.

---

4   George Ullman Appeals Case as cited – From the "Objection to Executor's First Account", p.153, also cited from George Ullman's testimony recorded in the "Supplement to the First Current Executor Account", p. 6 and records in the case file reporting premiums paid on the loan, p. 157. Also *Affairs Valentino* pp.312, 414.

Throughout this time of dramatic events and activity, subterfuge within Valentino's inner circle and subsequent tensions, Baltasar Cué was paying very close attention; recording it all as the fly on the wall.

❧ ❧

Cué's second time frame for research was the immediate aftermath of Valentino's death. He interviews those grieving their loss and writes about Valentino's funerals in New York and in Los Angeles. He also contacts Alberto Guglielmi, who arrives after his brother's death to make a bid to take his place on screen. Cué conducts interviews with Alberto Guglielmi and Pola Negri and witnesses the earliest days of the problematic settlement of Valentino's estate. By January of 1927, five months after Valentino's death, Valentino's story ends for Cué as his biography begins its monthly serialization. But a great deal was going on behind-the-scenes then, which was not reported by Cué.

For example, he wrote about the Guglielmi family unrest in Falcon Lair but did not report that the tension between the brothers Valentino involved money. According to Ullman, the fighting between them, "...definitely ruined Rudy's last few weeks at Falcon Lair."[5] Valentino's probate court records reveal he supported his brother's stay in Los Angeles with exorbitant weekly payments.[6] The brother's would part angrily just shortly before Valentino's death.

Cué also does not address a subterfuge underway in Valentino's posthumous world. He made no mention of and perhaps was unaware that a critical page of Valentino's *Last Will and Testament* was missing. He also did not report Alberto Guglielmi's petitioning Ullman, as the legal executor of Valentino's heavily-indebted estate, for advances against his future inheritance. And in the month in which Cué completed this book, January 1927, Valentino's sister Maria Strada arrived in Los Angeles to join her brother in a drive to oust Ullman and seize control of Valentino's estate.

As Cué's monthly installments of *The True Rudolph Valentino* were published, other events transpired concerning his subject which were not included in his narrative; such as Alberto Guglielmi undergoing several surgeries on his nose to resemble his deceased brother and efforts around the world to immortalize Valentino. This leads one to the conclusion that Cué most probably completed the writing of his entire book before the first installment was published.

---

5 *The S. George Ullman Memoir, The Real Rudolph Valentino by the Man Who Knew Him Best*, Viale Industria Pubblicazioni, 2014, p. 69.
6 George Ullman Appeals Case as cited, Baskerville Audit, Exhibit No. 9, "Household Expenses."

⚜

Although Rudolph Valentino's original intention was to write his honest and truthful story, certain aspects of this book were sourced to the studio-generated versions of events as this was the material available to Cué at the time. It merits mentioning, he was then an aspiring writer in Hollywood and eager to impress the American motion picture industry. His coverage of his personal access to Valentino at the height of his fame and published account thereof, immediately after the star's death, was without a doubt a golden professional opportunity for Cué. Just as the last installment of this book appeared in the February, 1928 issue of *Cine-Mundial*, he was rewarded by RKO Pictures and hired to be in charge of all of the studio's foreign advertising. [7]

With his own career goals in mind, Cué was not about to cast a single disparity towards Valentino's memory nor stray far from the carefully constructed studio versions of his life. He would do so out of respect and loyalty to his friend but to do otherwise would also risk his alienation from the motion picture industry. He was also well aware of George Ullman's efforts marketing Valentino's movies in order to raise funds to clear the star's heavily-indebted estate. Consequently, every word issued, whether by Cué or the general press, served to contribute to Rudolph's luminous legacy.

In this respect, Cué avoids several revelations. He does not mention that wealthy Italian importer Francesco "Frank" Mennillo was Valentino's Italian godfather.[8] Valentino would die in his godfather's arms but Cué identifies Mennillo only as "a great friend". He repeats the studio-generated myth alleging Valentino was homeless, starving and poor in his first days in New York City. This Horatio Alger version of events worked well to wrest every drop of sympathy for Valentino from his public and generate box office receipts, but it was not fact.

Valentino enjoyed the sponsorship of his godfather, Frank Mennillo from his day one in America as well as that of his sister-in-law's uncle and book merchant, Ernesto Filomarino.[9] Both men acted as his guardians. At the time, America was embroiled in xenophobia with Italians being the most persecuted ethnicity. Consequently, the earliest studio-generated versions of Valentino's life story expunged Mennillo and Filomarino's true roles.

Cué also constructed his narrative within the, then current, marketing parameters of Valentino's image in regards to his second wife, Natacha

---

7 Fundación Pablo Iglesias, Inicio Archivo Biblioteca Diccionario Biografica, Fernández Cué, Baltasar.

8 Interviews with the Frank Mennillo family, *Affairs Valentino*, pp. 25-26.

9 Manifest of Passengers for the *S.S. Cleveland*, Port of Arrival, December 22, 1913, Column 18, "Name of friend or relative and address in US", cited as Ernesto Filomarino, 215 Spring Street, New York, New York. Also *Affairs Valentino*, p. 442.

Rambova. The same month Cué completed his manuscript for this book, Rambova was publishing a book about her life as Valentino's wife, which included transcripts of her séance communications with her deceased ex-husband, "Rudy". In response to her séance revelations, Rambova became the recipient of widespread scorn and mockery by the press with some even blaming her for Valentino's death.

With divorce relatively rare at the time and still socially suspect, it was critical Valentino be portrayed as the victim in the story of the Valentino/Rambova break-up. All sympathy was bestowed upon him and Rambova was blamed mercilessly and reviled as a selfish, controlling woman who put her career above her husband's interests. I present documentation in my work on Natacha Rambova, both in *Beyond Valentino* and *Astral Affairs Rambova*, alleging this was not fact. Cué did not interview Rambova, yet he joined his fellow press in savaging her; marginalizing her, mocking her goals, her artistic abilities and belittling her presence in Valentino's life.

His rhetoric towards her, including homophobic stereotypes, stands as a less fortunate element of this time capsule. This was a time when slurs issued implying lesbianism were an effective way to impugn a woman's reputation. When this book was written, a misogynistic and homophobic press campaign was destroying the little that was left of Natacha Rambova's remarkably successful Hollywood career.

Despite Cué's unabashed antagonism towards Rambova, his treatment of Pola Negri was stridently opposite. Cué was able to interview Pola Negri and she seemed to exploit the opportunity after her lover's death to garner press via Cué's *Cine-Mundial* biography. Although others in Valentino's inner circle would down-play the seriousness of his relationship with Pola Negri, Cué appears to almost idolize the actress. He was criticized for this stance, at the time, by his Spanish-speaking audience and even accused of accepting money from Pola Negri in exchange for her extensive coverage.

In response to this accusation, Cué includes in this book, a letter from a Rudolph Valentino fan who scolds him for pandering to Pola Negri so soon after her idol's death. Although Cué was cautious in presenting studio-approved content in most other critical aspects of his narrative, in regards to Pola Negri he was not. She appears to have wooed the Spaniard, Baltasar Cué as well as Valentino's brother, Alberto Guglielmi.

Despite, it would be in Cué's accounts of personally witnessed and detailed scenarios that this biography becomes his unique story of Rudolph Valentino's life as well as a revelatory document of how the star's legacy formed in the weeks and first few months after his death.

Translator Renato Floris would open Cué's time capsule and in doing so face many challenges. The ten installments in Spanish, which can be found in the online archive, archive.org, were missing several pages. The search for these lost pages would not be soon rewarded. The pages #25 – 26, as published in the ninth installment and pages #121 -124 in the tenth installment, were found almost by chance. Floris spotted a photograph online of the cover of one of these issues containing the missing pages with the caption reading, "Property of Professor Fernando Purcell - Santiago, Chile".

Floris contacted the Professor who graciously sent photos of the missing pages. I want to thank Professor Purcell, "Full Professor of the History Institute and Researcher at the Global Change Center of the Pontifical Catholic University of Chile", for his valuable contribution.

With Cué's entire biography at last in hand, Floris began the translation of this book; a tedious, yet exciting process. Cué often wrote in the Spanish vernacular of the day and these phrases required research for an accurate translation. For example, it would have been absurd to literally translate a passage such as, "to be at the fourth question" when the accurate meaning of this phrase was "to be poor". Another example of Cue's vernacular phrases was, "plucking the turkey" which meant "to engage in amorous conversation". Floris' translator's notes, (t.n.) are included as reference to these interpretations.

The two articles included in this publication by Baltasar Cué, provide further context for this book's narrative and both have also been translated by Renato Floris. "The Consolation of Pola Negri" was published in *Cine-Mundial* in January of 1927, as an account of Cué's interview conducted in Pola Negri's home with Alberto Guglielmi present. "My Last Visit with Valentino" was published in *Cine-Mundial* in November 1926, as the account of Cué's last visit with Rudolph Valentino just a few days before his last trip to New York.

The True Story of Rudolph Valentino or in Spanish, *El Verdadero Rodolfo Valentino* should not be confused with *La Verdad Sobre Rodolfo Valentino* by Carlos Fernandez Cuenca; a thirty-page book published in Spain in 1927 and sold in street kiosks for 1.5 pesetas. Although the author alleges to have known Baltasar Cué, this pocket-sized book is full of inaccuracies.

This translation of Baltasar Cué's biography of Rudolph Valentino became a reality only as the result of one generous individual's belief in this project's importance. An immense gratitude is extended to the London Archivist who first discovered the original archive of the ten *Cine-Mundial* installments and then brought them to our attention. Their continued contributions to our work have not only immeasurably broadened this story but contributed substantially to the history of Rudolph Valentino as well.

A "Muchísimas Gracias" is extended to Señor Enrique Rabaudi of Buenos Aires for his tireless research and consultation regarding the meaning of Cué's quizzical phrases. I also thank Enrique for his efforts in searching for the missing pages of this book in Argentine archives and libraries.

Baltasar Cué's work on Valentino has never been published in English and has only been available to Spanish-speaking fan magazine readers. It is with profound gratitude and respect for his outstanding linguistic abilities, that I thank Renato Floris for his endless hours of painstaking labor in completing these translations. I believe those who study and appreciate the life of Valentino as well as the broader subject of Hollywood history, owe a tremendous debt to Renato Floris for making this book available to an English-speaking audience and for contributing in no small measure to the Rudolph Valentino body of accurate historical knowledge.

In completing the book which Valentino himself began working on in the spring of 1926, Cué presents a rarefied insider's vantage point and in this his friend Rudolph is kindly remembered. Valentino's wish, shared so long ago with reporter Alma Whitaker, has certainly been fulfilled.

Respectfully,

Evelyn Zumaya
Turin
April 2019

Table of Contents

The *Cine-Mundial* Installments

LA BIOGRAFIA INTIMA DE VALENTINO

Su Infancia

Su Adolescencia

Su Vida en Nueva York

Su Desprestigio Ahí.

La Mujer que más Amó
(Detalle inédito hasta hoy)

Mal Recibimiento que se le hizo en Hollywood.

Sus Matrimonios.

Sus Luchas.

Sus Divorcios.

Las Verdaderas Causas de Estos.

Sus Amantes Desconocidas.

Su Vida Profesional.

Sus Viajes a Europa.

Su Muerte.

La Subasta de sus Bienes y Mil Otras Cosas relativas a su Azarosa e interesante existencia.

"El Verdadero Rodolfo Valentino"

POR BALTASAR FERNANDEZ CUÉ

con la cooperación moral de Alberto Guglielmi Valentino y algunos de los mejores amigos del artista

Comenzará en el número de Mayo de Cine-Mundial

y aparecerá EXCLUSIVAMENTE en esta Revista en lo sucesivo.

Full-page advertisement with Alberto Guglielmi Valentino's letter of endorsement. *Cine-Mundial*, April, 1927.

CINE-MUNDIAL'S

The True Rodolfo Valentino

By

Baltasar Fernández Cué

The author dedicates this work to his friends,
Alberto Guglielmi Valentino, Manuel Reachi and Douglas Gerrard,
brother and friends of the "Sheik" respectively.

Installment

I

A Popular Man, Unknown

One day, after one of those gracious lunches which were improvised daily in the little dining room Valentino maintained next to his United Artists' dressing room, and finding myself alone with Rudolph and Manuel Reachi, I thought it an appropriate time to speak to the actor of a curious promotional project which occurred to me.

As Rudolph Valentino was constantly annoyed by the strangest propositions, sometimes by friends and some even by mere acquaintances, it was hard for me to decide when to explain my idea; this despite my not having the slightest doubt about the advantages it offered without a demand for expenses or any other inconvenience worthy of consideration. That day, however, I was able to speak with him directly about my idea and with all spontaneity, because I found the "Sheik" to be in a good mood during the course of our happy lunch which was extraordinarily delicious.

I suggested, then, that he relate to me during his leisure time, the true adventures which his hectic life was full of, and that he would authorize me to publish this with a suggestive title, which could be for example, "Valentino Rodolfo, The Ace of the Screen". Seeing the positive response with which he welcomed the presentation of my idea, I continued to explain to him the manner by which I could generate the maximum publicity and interest without causing any damage to his good reputation.

My plan included a probable legal involvement which might lead me to sleep a few nights imprisoned because of the fierce protest against my "defamatory" book which could be submitted to the authorities by the protective representative of the actor I allegedly defamed.

This unlucky occurrence would grant Rudolph the fortuitous opportunity to express once again his well-known respect for the freedom of the press, ordering his agent to withdraw any lawsuit; since the work did not refer expressly to Rudolph Valentino, but rather to an imaginary being whose name is Valentín Rodolfi. My book would be publicized everywhere and the "Sheik" would consequently stand before the general opinion as a liberal and magnanimous gentleman.

The Puritans - bugaboo of every person with any notoriety in the United States - they would have no right to charge Valentino, since it would be a frivolous allegation made that my work referred to him. But there would not be a reader who in his heart would question it. And the responsibility of this very clear insinuation would fall completely on my shoulders. My profitable mischief would be far from being rejected and for this I would deserve applause in a country where the cult of advertisement - in commerce as well as in politics, art, society and even religion – justifies itself by the insinuation of the superiority of the Anglo-Saxon race.

Living witness to this proposal is Manuel Reachi. As soon as the explanation of my project was finished, Rudolph Valentino; the cinema star and serious lover of marketing to whose magic created his fame on screen, jumped up, clenched his fists to give even more energy to his words and exclaimed joyfully,

"Caramba! I really like this idea!"

We agreed the idea of creating such a book should not be revealed by us three until it was time for it to be published. This was essential for the realization of the project, because Rudolph's will was like a weather-vane and always pointed in the direction of the last suggestion's wind.

He promised me seriously on that same occasion, that he would relate to me his most interesting adventures. But he was then very busy with the film, *The Son of Sheik*, whose completion was of great importance to him in order to strengthen his feeble financial situation which was so compromised by the rash expenditures of his last trip to Europe. As most of his leisure time then belonged to the lucky Pola Negri, we agreed that upon his finishing the film, he would devote all the time necessary to telling me everything; especially about his love affairs.

"And what I forget to mention will be told by Manuel and Douglas," added Rudolph, referring to his two favorite comrades: the Mexican Manuel Reachi and the Irishman Douglas Gerrard. They, like many other musketeers, shared with him the enjoyment of many adventures in New York and in Hollywood, although with more luck.

After that day, every time a propitious occasion presented itself, I brought up the subject of this book. We saw each other frequently during the final weeks of his last work and whether after lunch, when the three of us were alone, after dinner, while sitting in his office, while he was retouching his make up or changing the Arab dress in front of the glowing dressing table, we used to discuss various phases of the project. Sometimes, Rudolph related a few interesting stories of his life. Other times, Reachi played tricks to correct an error or to tell a forgotten and delicious detail. To share the stories of others, Rudolph opened a drawer in his desk and handed me some useful documents including a letter, a portrait, a newspaper clipping and a copy of an otherworldly message.

One day he called his secretary and told her to give me the only copy he had of the story of his life, published years before in one of the most important film magazines in the United States. Miss Margaret Neff gave it to me accompanied by other similar documents; this while Rudolph recommended them to me as if they were precious jewels or some ancient parchments which could not be replaced in any way. He made a huge qualification about the quality of the content of one of these documents; he wanted to be sure to emphasize to me that this was a story reputed to be his autobiography titled, "My Life Story."[10]

How That Story Was Written

Anyone who is not familiar with the usual procedures followed in Hollywood studios, will find it hard to believe that Rudolph Valentino declared, even in a private chat, that his "autobiography" was not reliable. In reality, as a biographical document, no writing produced by the motion picture studios about the private lives of their artists can be considered reliable.

The mission of the aforementioned marketing offices, which form one of the main aspects of the film industry, is to ensure what the public thinks about the companies, the artists and their films and hope their thinking will push them favorably towards them. It is therefore necessary to share with them all they can to make the public sympathetic to popular feelings such as virtue, intelligence, amenity, generosity, ingenuity, culture, etc.

The truth does not mix with such important commercial activity. Profit is the only objective. And just as it would be naive to believe that all

10 "My Life Story", *Photoplay* Magazine, January – June, 1923.

the medicine we see advertised in the newspapers has all the wonderful virtues attributed to it in the corresponding advertisements, so it is also proof of great innocence to believe as much when the press tells us about the cinematographic companies, its artists and its films.

In the United States at least, the Hollywood marketing agencies send not only the propaganda to be shown before a film's first exhibition to the movie theaters, but they also send the reviews which the local press should publish after the premiere. What the readers of the newspaper of this or that town located thousands of miles away from Cinelandia do not know, is that the reviews they read after having seen the film the previous night were written many months before by some employee of the film producer and which have already been published in all the towns where the same film was shown.

In the same way, those wise opinions which are often published as if they had been expressed by movie stars were generated in many cases by the brains of marketing agents. This is how one often finds the wit which the stars themselves do not always possess. If one has little experience in the ways of Cinelandia, they must be careful about praising a star for an opinion read in the press alleging to have been written by the star. In most cases, the opinion did not come from anything which was actually said. Of course, Rudolph Valentino was not one of these cases. But he also did not write the "autobiography" which circulates around the world allegedly as it came from his pen.

His absorbing professional and social occupations and his varied hobbies, left him little time to write such articles for journals. On the other hand, he lacked the special technical knowledge to do so. In Hollywood studios, even to write the most simple nonsense it is necessary to follow the corresponding technique. The emphasis is always the completion of the marketing agent's mission.

Each paragraph film companies publish as advertising, whether it refers to themselves, their staff or their products, must be written according to longstanding rules which dictate the most convenient way to produce a desired effect. These rules determine precisely what needs to be said, how to say it and when to propagate it. If what is convenient to disclose is not within the field of truthfulness, it is created within the field of invention. If the truth is inconvenient, it is best to say nothing.

What Rudolph did was to tell an advertising agent some of the great guidelines of his life as his memory recalled them, as his criteria and taste formulated them and as his professional conveniences allowed. And since he was very human in doing so, vanity did not stop him from introducing his quota of fables. The advertising agent, in turn, took this data and through his own ingenuity and fantasy wrote what seemed appropriate. And since, far from hurting Rudolph, this presented him in a flattering way, the actor, instead of amending the mistakes he noticed, was happy and grateful.

Only in this way can it be explained that the "autobiography" of Rudolph Valentino called "My Life Story" relates events which the actor knew very well never happened. It is also understood that the actor appeared to be known within the unique understanding of an American audience and which is unfamiliar in Europe. For the habits and traits of an Italian, for the "Sheik", were respectable habits until the last day of his life.

He shared his concerns with me as to just how defective "My Life Story" was. It was truthful only in regard to the family in which he was born, as to the constitution of his family, to some dates, to the films in which he took part and to some of the personal relationships in which he found himself in life. He was clearly not satisfied with either the errors nor the irreverence.

However, in that "autobiography" which Rudolph himself deemed inaccurate and incomplete, are included all the versions of the actor's life which have circulated and are circulating throughout the universal press, and which have been published in the form of books. For one reason or another, some more well-informed, had the honesty to publish some truth.

The last time I spoke with Rudolph Valentino about our projected book was in his beautiful home in Beverly Hills and two days before his trip to New York.[11] He calculated it would take him about three weeks to return. And then, before beginning his next film, *Benvenuto Cellini*, he would devote an entire week to telling me about his never-told adventures, or rather, the ones which remained to be told which would be the major part of the book's narrative. Manuel Reachi would act as a living witness to the interviews.

What we could least imagine in those moments of happiness and good humor was that our next meeting would be in the church of San Vicente, partaking in the solemn funeral honors with which his mortal remains were dismissed from the world of the living. We could never have then imagined that the data, documents and indications he himself gave me to write this book of his life, would also be used at the same time as the data relating to his death.

11 Refer to "My Last Visit with Rudolph Valentino" in this publication.

The Idol

It was with great difficulty I organized the reports, those Rudolph himself gave me and those I picked up in conversations with Manuel Reachi, with Douglas Gerrard and with other friends of the deceased who were related in one way or another to the subject of my research. My research gradually began to sketch a personality which did not coincide with the one the public knew as authentic or as the one we knew closely and personally during his last dazzling stage.

It is true that whoever knew him personally, even in those splendid moments realized how different he was from what was publicly believed about him. Having witnessed his private life, it is also true that one could notice a trace of sadness or misery in him which seemed at odds with the series of triumphs permitting him to achieve one of the highest heights of popularity in history. The observer, however, was inclined to attribute such a mood in him to some excess which was diligently deepening dark circles under his eyes and undermining the resistance of his body which was so apparently healthy and vigorous.

Even those of us who were close to him, without knowing the depth of the mystery of his past life, felt inclined to accept with some amendment, the popular versions of his character and adventures. Rudolph was also for us, essentially a young man who, because of his beauty and magnetism, made feminine hearts beat lovingly everywhere. He was solicited by beautiful women of all races of the earth and found a conquest wherever he set his hypnotizing eyes; to then revel in the opulence as one of the happiest men in history.

For us, Rudolph Valentino was a Don Juan raised to the umpteenth degree. Much more still, he was a Don Juan, a Beau Brummel, a Petronius, a Croesus, a Bluebeard. . . all in one human form. There was so much evidence which imposed this belief on us!

There were not only the packages of love letters arriving daily from unknown admirers scattered all over the world, but also those he received from well-known women. Artists, aristocrats and millionaires were among his most enthusiastic correspondents. One day, while in his company, I saw the letter of a princess arrive to his hands with a request for his portrait and a dedication and perhaps some correspondence. Once again, at a party where all the beauty the world so admires on-screen revolved like a dreamed vision, I walked through a provocative crowd with Rudolph and I can not forget the expression with which certain eyes of universal fame were shamelessly calling him.

Other times, in the most elegant centers of Los Angeles, I saw how conversations were suspended and all feminine eyes were fixed anxiously on those of the "Sheik". Others, as he traveled through towns where he was not seen so often, ripped the buttons from his clothes to keep them as a reminder of his unforgettable visit. We knew, as fact, that other women paid more than a few mysterious visits to his dressing room or his elegant residence in Beverly Hills, significantly called "The Falcon's Lair".

Even after Rudolph Valentino died, what a thrilling manifestation of love the beautiful sex gave him everywhere! In New York, disorder became desecration, motivated by the enthusiasm with which the multitude of admirers struggled to approach the coffin and pluck even the most insignificant relic from the beloved. From New York to Hollywood the mortal remains of the actor traveled accompanied by a demonstration of national mourning as never had been experienced by the most popular heroes of this great republic.

Later, Alberto Guglielmi Valentino and the executor of Rudolph's will, George Ullman, received many letters from countless platonic brides who sobbed inconsolably everywhere. Many of them, in all languages, asked for a memory; any object, however insignificant which had been touched by the actor. Sometimes, a high price was offered for an object of lower value. During the days when the furniture, books, paintings and other art objects belonging to Rudolph were displayed for the public as a prelude to the auction, a thousand cars on a devout pilgrimage, climbed along the road which leads to the actor's last mansion over the hillsides and ravines of Beverly Hills.

It was worth seeing, this exciting show in which an elegant crowd with sad faces, paraded religiously before the objects which had surrounded the "Sheik" in the last phase of his life. Such was the desire to preserve some memory of him, that notwithstanding the general quality of the visitors, the detectives scattered secretly among the crowd and had to empty not a few hands which had stealthily seized small objects. The frustrated thieves could well pay the high price, but they did not have the patience to wait until the next auction.

In this sad liquidation in which many of Rudolph Valentino's goods were sold to the highest bidder, there was one woman who paid twenty-five dollars for a simple handkerchief used by the actor. There were also many women who cried. And noting one curious psychological case; it was when the actor's dogs were put on sale when the most tears were shed by the women present.

As a curious mention, few can surpass the following in psychological detail. Among the letters Alberto Guglielmi Valentino received from all parts of the world after the loss of his brother, a letter arrived one day to Rudolph himself and this was some two months after his death. He died on August 23. On October 22, a simple American from a town called Conway, Arkansas, wrote the following brief but amazing epistle.

"Dear Rodolfo,
I have seen many of your films and I like to see you performing and the last one I've seen was "Rodolfo Valentino in The Son of the Sheik". I send this letter entrusted to your secretary. I want to see all the movies of you that I can. I was very sorry to know about your death and I need you to do me the favor of sending me one of your best and most recent portraits. My friend received the best picture of you the other day. I hope to receive one like hers."

It was as if the dead man were still living the life of his worldly business. As if in his metaphorical immortal life, he could follow the hustle and bustle of perishable life. But despite all these manifestations or perhaps because of themselves, when *Cine-Mundial* choose me to complete the mission of writing a biography of the ill-fated artist, there was such a disparity between the Rudolph Valentino of public opinion and the Rudolph of reality, that I was afraid to present readers with a portrait so little resembling the actor they knew. My portrait of him was faithfully created from his natural self, while the "original" version of his personality as popularized around the world is but a product of fantasy.

The Pessimistic Star

Coincidentally, a phrase and a smile at last came to help me from my deceased friend's brother. We were alone, Alberto Guglielmi Valentino and I in the bungalow he occupied in the spacious gardens of the Ambassador Hotel in Los Angeles. He was in bed due to a slight illness. In addition to his physical condition, he was tormented in those days by a sentimental crisis provoked by his being restless in a situation which he could not control.

He longed for the company of people of his own culture who would be capable of understanding him. And I was one of the friends who was in a more favorable condition to visit him often. That day, like so many others, Alberto and I talked about his worries. As in other times, Kabar, Rudolph's dog who shakes hands with visitors and from time to time approaches them to be caressed, seemed to listen philosophically to our conversation. In his sad eyes there was always a longing for his disappeared owner. But on that occasion it could be said that the dog's tears of pity where for Rudolph's brother, who complained about his fate with his sad accent .

Alberto was at the time consumed by absolute pessimism and in such a way as to darken his state of mind and his thoughts. He did not find a hint of joy in his present life, nor in his past years, nor in those he thought he would still be living. With macaronic sentences, he painted his life in the darkest colors; this because he always insisted on speaking to me in Spanish and without completely leaving his Italian altogether. He had lost his father at the age of fourteen which left him, at an early age, as the only manly head in the family. He was the only help his mother could count on to solve the serious problems of her widowhood.

He acted as an advisor in his home and as a father for his siblings Rodolfo and Maria, who were still children. At the time, when boys of his age were enjoying appropriate games, he had to perform his fatherly duties as an elder brother without a father. Then, he married far too young. His wife contracted a nervous illness which required him to take care of her as a loving husband. Because of this illness, which was aggravated by the climate of California, he had to deprive himself of time with his brother. His brother who was anxious to create a home life and who brought Alberto, with wife and son, to warm his elegant mansion which at that time was so devoid of affection and love.

When the two brothers separated, after failing in their desire to create a common home, Alberto left his brother at the pinnacle of his glory. Just as an awareness of a fraternal triumph inspired hopes for happiness, the death of Rudolph came to give Alberto the least expected blow of his life. In those moments, he told me of his endless misery, his separation from his wife and son, his nostalgia over his home and country, his worrying about his wife's illness and his own sicknesses. Job's lamentations could not surpass in sadness, Alberto Guglielmi Valentino's attempts to convince me that he was the most unfortunate man on earth.

In vain I strained my imagination to find some phrase which could comfort him. Every attempt I made was rejected by a new, almost aggressive, volley of grim arguments. However, I insisted in my comforting efforts. With less conviction than good will, I reminded him of his brother, suggesting him as an example of optimism.

"You have to be like Rudolph. Face life with courage and with a firm belief in triumph. Just as he smiled confidently and happily with women and as a conqueror; that's how you should smile at life. Strive to be happy, and you will be as happy as he was."

"As happy as Rodolfo! Ha, ha!" Alberto Guglielmi Valentino laughed sardonically. "He suffered too, even because of the women. If you saw the worries they caused him and how pessimistic he was because of them."

According to Alberto Guglielmi Valentino, a grim state of mind seemed to be the most common trait shared by the two brothers. I was not then surprised to discover in my research, a Rudolph Valentino so different from the one known to the world. I was motivated by the honest purpose which should guide all researchers seeking the truth; the impartial willingness to go wherever the truth is and to show it as it wants it to be. But I hesitated when finding it so naked of all the ornaments which the popular fantasy attributed to it. It was my great luck that the actor's own brother gave me, albeit unconsciously, a confirmation of my conclusions and which inspired me to declare them.

I then believed myself authorized to copy the formidable title with which the Yankee writer Bruce Barton has just published his most original version of the life of Christ as, *The Man Who Nobody Knows*. But Rudolph Valentino has been known by a few close intimate friends. I had, then, to limit myself to head these biographical chapters with a slightly more modest title, *The True Rudolph Valentino*.

I can assure readers of *Cine-Mundial* that if they were not close friends of Rudolph Valentino, they do not know the real personality of the great Italian actor. Even if they have seen all his films, even if they have read all the interviews with him held both real or supposedly, and even after having read all the biographies and autobiographies which continue to pretend to describe faithfully the life of the "Sheik", they still do not know the man who is well hidden under his own popularity.

The following pages tell frankly and truthfully of that man.

Installment

II

A Migrant of So Many

Rodolfo Guglielmi was born in Castellaneta, Italy on May 6, 1895. His father, Giovanni Guglielmi was a veterinarian who was then the inspector of the municipal slaughterhouse. His mother, Gabrielle Barbin was French. He was the third child of the Guglielmi couple. Before him, his sister Beatrice who died in infancy and his brother Alberto, were born in Rome. After Rodolfo, there would be only one other offspring in the home; Maria. Rodolfo spent his childhood in Castellaneta.

Even in those early days, the two salient features of his personality were beauty and a mischievous spirit. He was a beautiful little devil with a dark face and long black curls. Before reaching the age at which children usually enter school, it became necessary to entrust him to a female teacher; not only for the purpose of receiving instruction but to prevent him from fighting with his mother.

Alberto learned his early lessons and began to receive private instruction from one of his mother's friends. But as Rodolfo was unbearable in the house, his mother sent him to attend the same classes as his older brother. Rodolfo was not obliged to study, but merely to sit still and this proved more difficult. More difficult for two reasons; because his character was restless and because his natural retentive faculty caused him to absorb knowledge with little effort.

From those early years of his life, Rodolfo demonstrated the ease with which he learned by just listening; a characteristic which always served as compensation for another no less dominant aspect of his character which was his lack of fondness for study. Because Rodolfo never applied himself as a student, it could be said he detested books. However, he retained everything he heard and this made him seem a better student than his many companions whose eyes tired trying to study a lesson. His brother Alberto told me, with plausible modesty, that by the time he completed those first childhood classes, Rodolfo had learned, with no studying at all, much more than he had.

One of Rodolfo's most innocent childish pranks left more of a physical imprint than those he received from more serious misbehaviors. One day when he was barely five years old, he found his father's straight razor on a dresser. Already believing himself to be a little man with hair on his face by an incipient beard, he took the knife, placed himself before the mirror and without wasting his time in applying soap, he began to shave. His mother, who like so many others to whom Providence entrusts the upbringing of a rogue, passed most of her days in two great and absorbing worries; one, scolding Rodolfo for his pranks and the other, watching him in order to discover those pranks before they occurred. When Rodolfo, the little devil was too silent for a long time, his mother would run from room to room in a hurry fearing something serious had or would happen.

Rodolfo's initiation into the manly habit of shaving had to be done in solemn silence and this immediately attracted his mother's attention. When she discovered her son standing before the mirror, she could not contain her cry of horror. Several streams of blood ran down the boy's right cheek where the fine edge of the razor, so clumsily wielded, penetrated without mercy. The little boy who thought himself a man, turned smiling towards his alarmed mother and with all calm asked,

"But what's wrong, mother? Can't you see I'm shaving just like father? "

Those who have seen Valentino's face have noticed a straight scar on his right cheek. This was the indelible memory of his first claim to manhood.

Maria was the accomplice in Rodolfo's domestic antics since the time she began to walk[12]. Alberto, in his capacity as elder brother, had the tendency to consider himself a man. He looked over his shoulder at his little brother whose actions he felt were far too childish. Of course, at times, friends of Rodolfo and Maria joined them in their antics. And it was thus Rodolfo began from his childhood days to be closely linked to the beautiful sex, which would would bring him so much joy as well as misery.

From very early in his life, those gatherings of young friends instigated love affairs. And it is obvious from the first adventures of the future "Sheik" that he was not so lucky; as he preferred girls who were much older than him. He was about six years old when he fell madly in love with a nine-year-old girl named Teodolinda. He found it difficult to approach her because he still lacked the courage which experience brings and because she

12 t-n: *"despegar las manos del suelo"*- (to raise the hands from the ground) - to begin to walk.

was coy and elusive. As if that were not enough of an obstacle, little Teodolinda was usually in the company of an older sister who was ugly and irascible. She was for young Rodolfo, a frightful scarecrow; both animated and aggressive.

After a long period of silent, platonic contemplation and at a sufficient distance from the threatening fury of the sister, at last came the favorable night. It seemed to the future "Sheik" to be especially so as the sky seemed to be inviting him to whisper into the ear of his beloved the most tender phrases his passion could inspire. Teodolinda had gone alone to the rosary. He waited for her crouched in the shadows of the neighborhood where he felt capable of tremendous feats.

He rehearsed his beautiful phrases of love under the inspiration of the stars twinkling above. After a long time of great restlessness, the little girl returned from the church. Rodolfo hesitated as the quick steps of his beloved walked towards him. Remembering the phrases inspired by the twinkling stars, he whispered in a tremulous voice;

"Teodolindita, I love you!"

When the girl heard this, she ran up the stairs to her home and followed closely by her beau. The resonant hollowness of the wooden steps produced such a loud noise, that Teodolinda's sister became alarmed. With a tirade of unusually bad words, she began to slap Rudofo on a certain innocent part of his body which had as much to do with his heart at that moment as with the days of penance.[13] Rodolfo left that adventure with no desire to return to the house where he received his first and unforgettable experience in love.

He engaged in his next important amorous adventure when he was ten years old and more confident in his love experience. During this time he lived in Taranto, where his family moved when his father was promoted to the position of inspector of the city slaughterhouse. The home in which they lived was divided into two houses. In one resided the Guglielmi family and in the other, a friendly family comprised of a father, mother and a beautiful daughter of fifteen years[14], recently graduated from a school run by nuns.

There was not a single day in which the two families did not visit with each other. And for Rodolfo, he became so sociable upon the neighbor's daughter's return from school, he not only visited her home in the company of his family members, but, at times, visited her on his own. Of course he fell in love with the beautiful maiden and boasted about his love

13 t.n.: *Las cuatro témporas*- (the four seasons' days of religious penance or days of penance).

14 t.n.: *De quince abriles* - (of fifteen Aprils) - fifteen years old or related to a teenager.

even more than ordinarily so. Now Rodolfo was always dressed impeccably even though the family maid did not have time to devote herself especially to the care of his clothing. She considered him somewhat of a brat, so he ironed his own clothes if he wanted to wear them without wrinkles. His outfits for the day would correspond to whomever he aspired to be, as he often acted as if he were the Beau Brummel of Taranto.

One hot summer afternoon, Rodolfo stood in his underwear, very engaged in ironing his breeches. The street, seen through the balcony balusters, appeared abandoned. Taranto was napping. From the neighboring fields and gardens came the monotonous lullaby of the crickets and the cicadas songs. But in the passionate brain of the little Don Giovanni[15], who was dragging the iron from one end of his pants to the other on the table, the noise was far from numbing his burning ideas. This being the image of the neighbor girl napping on her bed.

Little by little, as the iron slid lazily to and fro, he imagined the tempting scene which gave him a vague, but powerfully attractive delight. Rodolfo put the heavy iron aside. He looked towards the door. He looked out through the balcony. Not a soul was passing through the street. He mounted the window sill, secured his feet on the cornice of the façade and walking slowly and cautiously, exposing himself to a sure death if he fell, he inched along until he reached the balcony of his beloved's bedroom. The window was half open and he entered with his heart beating full of emotion.

He stood for a long time hidden among the curtains while staring at the beautiful girl, who was wearing little but her shirt as she lay stretched out on her bed. The young intruder hesitated, torn between his eager desire to go kneel by the bed and his fear of receiving another whip lashing as he was given on many unforgettable occasions. The girl startled and moved unexpectedly. He turned to flee and she, seeing him but as a figure through the curtains, began to shout and loudly. This woke everyone in both houses with both families alarmed. The "thief" was sought in every corner.

Explanations of the mystery were devised. Could it have been the girl's dream? Or was it indeed Rodolfo, the mischievous, incorrigible little boy? When the door of the room in which Rodolfo was standing was finally opened, there he stood calmly dragging the iron from one end of the pants to the other. He acted as if he knew nothing had happened. He did not waver in this and it was useless to try to extract any confession from him.

Rodolfo's father felt in his heart the pride parents feel when they discover in their sons the first fruits of manhood. But at the same time, he felt that incident was the final proof he needed to convince himself it was

---

15 t.n.: *Tenorio* - the family name of Don Juan the heartthrob of the Mozart opera.

time to do something with his younger son; something more effective than a scolding, beating or any other fatherly punishment.

Rodolfo was immediately imprisoned as a boarding student, in the Dante Alighieri School in the same town of Taranto where his family lived. There he continued to undergo a correctional process for one year (1906) when his father died. He was then sent to the Collegio della Sapienza in Perugia, where the orphans of the members of the Health Corps, to which Giovanni Guglielmi belonged, were educated. For three years he remained there preparing to pursue a technical career. It was in this same institution he began to dedicate himself to sports, becoming one of the first soccer players.

At this time, the poet Vittoria Aganoor Pompilj, who was a friend of the widow of Guglielmi and lived at that time in Perugia, effected a positive spiritual influence on the future actor. It was she who played the role of Rodolfo's mother while he stayed at the Collegio della Sapienza. The boy developed a deep affection for the poet and her husband, who treated him affectionately as they sowed in his spirit the first seeds of art.

In time, that loving marriage tragically ended its days. Vittoria died in an accident[16] and her husband committed suicide before his wife's corpse. But the memories Rodolfo kept from them were unforgettable. When he returned to Italy for the first time after having triumphed in art and achieved extraordinary popularity, he one day ignored the flattery being lavished on him, and made a special trip to Perugia to place a wreath of flowers on the grave of those great friends of his adolescence. Those he considered to be the first sowers of the artistic harvest he was gathering at the time.

But even the affection and advice from that second mother could not force the young man to adapt to the discipline of the Collegio della Sapienza. His free nature clashed with the strict regulations of that institution to the point of his being expelled. The director, in consideration of the widowed mother, sought a gentle way of advising her to take her son to another, less severe school, where he would be able to develop his personality more freely.

Rodolfo then attempted to enter the Naval Academy, traveling to Venice for preparatory studies. These would be the only lessons of his life which he accomplished with the proper application. How great his disappointment would be when he learned he was rejected because he did not reach the required physical dimensions!

As a last resort, he joined the Agriculture Academy of Nervi, where in addition to formally dedicating himself to the institution's special studies,

16 She died of cancer in Rome on April 9, 1910.

he began to learn English and Spanish. These were languages which, due to his later relationships, he came to speak with great expertise. He did not need to include French in his study of languages because as a child he learned it at home from his mother's lips.

In this school of agriculture he also discovered an opportunity to apply his already vast amatory experience. It is true there was a girl there; the cook's daughter. How many idylls and comedies and even tragedies can a single woman inspire if there is a man in her vicinity who can be used to create the corresponding intrigue!

The daughter of the cook of the Academy of Agriculture was not exactly a Venus; but since there was no other, she was at least an inviting Eve. The boys at the school, at the age when they begin to do rash things for a notorious woman, were all crazy for her. To engage in such activities you need less years of study than those required to study agriculture. This Dulcinea of the school lived no less than on the top floor of the barn. There was not, then, a schoolboy who did not sigh with relief when it was his turn to tend to the cows. Rodolfo was one of those who dreamed most of such interesting bovine exercises.

At last, it was his turn. Even before this occasion the cook's daughter started to pay attention to him as he was the most good looking and handsome in the school. It seemed guaranteed they would understand each other and easily. She was already waiting for him on the balcony. He, glowering at the cows which seemed so interesting to him until that moment, watched her ecstatically from the fragrant entrance of the stable. But at that moment, a professor arrived who was little inclined to romanticism and he pushed the young man out of the barn and put an end to the idyll.

Rodolfo, however, could not resign himself to squandering the opportunity he saw glistening in the cook's daughter's eyes. That night when all the lights of the school were out, he let himself down through the window to furtively stand under his Dulcinea's window. He whistled softly and harmoniously. Nothing. He whistled with no less softness and harmony. In anxious expectation in which his youthful heart beat fast, his black eyes strained to see in the darkness of the balcony some indication that the sunrise was approaching. This would signal the appearance of the cook's daughter.

Another soft whistle fluttered in the silent night as he climbed the balcony. This time he received an answer. At first it was a shrill whimper which shocked him and then there was quiet in his poetic corner. The noises turned out to be nothing more than the maternal moanings of a cow in labor about to bear an untimely calf. The birth of the calf drove away all hope of a conquest for Rodolfo and he returned to bed.

After successfully completing his studies of agriculture without any further extraordinary events, he returned to his home in Taranto to see how he could use his knowledge to fend for a living. He was then seventeen years old. While there was some opportunity for him to begin working, he instead devoted himself to savoring the delights of a playful life in the company of military officers of the cavalry and the navy and dancers.

With only the scarce resources his mother could provide for him, he relied on his own beauty and character to be accepted into those orgies, where he could have intimate relationships with beautiful actresses, including one famous *prima donna* with whom he had a lasting love relationship. However, the day arrived when he became convinced he needed more money to play a respectable role among his carousing companions. He needed to be able to afford expensive gifts to give to his beautiful lady loves and to be able to dress well. How would he acquire the resources to do so with dignity without leaving the bohemian environment which offered him so many delights?

The only idea occurring to him was to establish an advertising company in partnership with another boy named Guglielmo Aliotta. They rented the curtain of a local theater upon which could be announced advertisements of the businesses of Taranto. Rodolfo's mother, of course, recognized the benefit of her son thinking about working and helped him financially. But the incipient young businessman managed his company according to a peculiar system. All expenses were to be paid by his mother; all the proceeds were for him and his partner to have fun.

Of course the day arrived when Rodolfo's mother was forced to disapprove both of the system of the advertising company and the life her son was leading. This resulted in a discontent which became a form of weariness for the young man. He was already tired of life in Taranto. Taranto, for him, was much the same as the rest of the country. He began to tell family and friends that Italy was not for him as he dreamed of broader horizons.

Without his mother's approval, he decided to flee to America and this without pausing to think how to raise the money necessary to finance the journey. When first requesting a passport, he was denied because he was too young. But when he turned 18, in May of 1913, he decided to embark at all costs. His mother consulted with Alberto, who lived as a married man in Reggio (Calabria), and with other elderly members of the family. Everyone felt Rodolfo did not possess a very flattering attitude about his homeland and that, therefore his emigration to America was approved. There, at least there would always be some hope even for the inept, the unsuccessful or the misfits of old Europe.

The Guglielmi widow offered good advice to her son Rodolfo, gave him clothing, paid his second class ticket and sent him to New York with funds so that when he disembarked in that strange land he would not be without money. And so off went the young madcap like so many other emigrants. He would leave his mother sad, and unbeknownst to him, from that painful moment of their farewell they would never see each other again.

To Alberto, Rodolfo said goodbye telegraphically. He had promised to go to Reggio to give him a farewell hug; but, at the last minute, he excused himself on the pretext that an urgent matter forced him to go to Turin. There lived the *prima donna* whom Rodolfo loved so much at the time.

A few days later, on December 9, 1913, the young man embarked in Genoa on board the transatlantic liner, the S.S. Cleveland of the American Hamburger Company. Between Genoa and Naples he met a French lady who would comfort him in the absence of the *prima donna*. But this tempting new woman traveled in first class. [17]In Naples, he then renegotiated his fare to New York, moving to the same first class as that beautiful woman whom he was already beginning to love. With her, he immediately established an affair that served not only to liven up his first transatlantic journey but also to afford him the opportunity to spend almost all the money which his mother gave him for his use when he disembarked.

He arrived in New York on December 23, 1913 with his pocket almost empty but with the soul still full of illusions. Italy, with its beautiful open horizons and brimming with light, had seemed too small. But oh, now he was in New York! And that immense city, despite its asphyxiating dark streets and its petty ribbons of sky above where one's sight seldom rises, would soon seem for him, too overwhelming.

---

17 Among the thirteen passengers traveling in First Class aboard the *S.S.Cleveland*, there was only one French lady, Ms. Elly Roberts, thirty-five years old from Saint-Raphaël Var of the PACA Region of France. She was traveling with her husband Albert, thirty-five years old and their twin children, Ursula and Herbert, aged nine years old.

Installment

III

Rodolfo the Dancer

On the recommendation of a traveling companion, the newcomer Rodolfo was installed in a modest guest house on West 49th Street. His compatriots seemed much more eager to question him about news from Italy and about his own personality, which would guide him in the mysteries of a strange, new country. As Rodolfo brought his diploma from the Nervi School of Agriculture with him, he felt he needed help from no one. This would surely help open the doors of prosperity in a country where agricultural wealth is one of the fundamental pillars. Besides, what difficulties could he possibly find when so many ignorant and clumsy Italians found it relatively easy to make their fortunes? He also knew how to dress and present himself correctly.

Despite these confident considerations, upon arriving in New York, Rodolfo was not nurturing the same illusions he had while rocking on the waves as a passenger on the "Cleveland" and trying to distinguish the Yankee coastline as seen through the winter mists of the horizon. The indifference which greeted him in New York left him disconsolate.

In Taranto, it was almost impossible for him to walk a hundred paces without finding a smile, a friendly word, a flattering look. In New York, there was not a friend, not an acquaintance, not a greeting … nothing. He felt as if he were a despicable intruder. In Taranto, who dressed better than he did? Who was better than he?

In New York on the other hand, everyone was as well dressed. Even the most vulgar people there were young handsome men who dressed relatively well. It seemed in New York there were no country people, properly speaking! It seemed those thousands and thousands of people who paraded day and night through the mighty human channels, which are the streets of New York, belonged either to the upper class or the middle class! Rudolfo felt himself reduced to an insignificant atom. When he lived at home in Taranto, Italy looked very small to him. Here, in exile in New York, he was the little one.

In his first, lengthy letter he wrote to his mother from New York, he exuded disillusionment in every paragraph. Despite this, the young emigrant hoped to disguise his mood with some irony as he wrote about the general custom of chewing gum and other notable aspects of American life.

The day after his arrival was Christmas Eve[18] and the next day Christmas. This was a time for house parties even for mischievous boys like himself. Oh the carols, the Chrismas decorations, the manger scenes; all which so delighted him in childhood and even in the last few years when he'd observed it all with the confidence of one who begins to believe himself man!

Undoubtedly, New Yorkers were going to celebrate those Christian days and madly so and he was ready to celebrate with them. Everything in the streets and in the shops was resplendent with the feast of the Nativity of the Lord. Rodolfo, however, would spend those days alone, experiencing an icy cold not only from the weather but from society; Christian days and not a hand extending sympathy in his solitude! It was as if he were in the Sahara. Yes, in the Sahara. It was for him, so lost in his feelings and nostalgia, just an avalanche of pedestrians appearing as grains of human sand. Decidedly New York, with all its millions of inhabitants, was a desert and the most populous desert on earth.

This desolation inspired him to long for home. But he could only go there in spirit. Despite the scarcity of his resources, he did not hesitate to use those resources to send a cable to his mother in order to be with her in those holiest of moments. He had so many memories of her irreplaceable motherly affection and began to appreciate her as he never had in his native land.

Inevitably, through such longing his finest resolutions were made. It was necessary for him to find work in order to enjoy being that ineffable gleeful spirit which he had been on the other side of the sea. He had to fight on. In the first letter he wrote to his mother he pronounced, "Life is a struggle, I am going to fight and I have to win!"

The struggle would involve his just picking up a hoe or some other such weapon and surrendering to manual work. This was not so easy to find and he would have been on a better battlefield had he been more fluent in the language of the country. He began, then, to learn it. Meanwhile, he walked the New York streets to familiarize and found some corners where young people in his situation happened to meet. He also made friends, especially at the Bustanoby café where he could speak French with the waiters.

---

18 t.n.: *Nochebuena*- (the good night) - Christmas Eve.

He must have exuded a sense unhappiness on his face while in that café, for some cheerful young people who also spoke the Gallic language, felt sorry for him. They invited him to join their group as a distraction. Two members of this group were Austrian counts. Rodolfo then had more reasons to frequent the establishment and there, little by little, he came to know the friends of those new friends. It was also there where he perfected his dancing and learned the tango and the one-step, which were previously unknown to him. In Taranto, he only practiced the waltz, the mazurka and a few other more antediluvian dances.

He noticed, however, that he was learning little English. This was because in the café as in the guest house, everyone spoke French or Italian. He then moved to another house where nothing was spoken but English and it did not take long for him to make himself understood.

He was convinced he could not wait any longer to find work to his liking and in need of money, he was forced to work as hard as he could. His famous diploma did help him secure a position as a gardener, which was not worth much, but at least served to show him how little that diploma really meant. He found another job earning fifteen dollars a month where they also provided him with food and lodging. Despite his diploma from the Nervi School of Agriculture, he accepted work as an apprentice gardener in Central Park and soon left this occupation because it did not solve even a single problem of his life.

Rodolfo dedicated himself to walking from here to there and everywhere[19] in search of any occupation which would provide him with food. He was left without a penny and without a friend to offer a hand in such a depressing situation. He even experienced the shame of being thrown out of several guest houses. One day, after walking miles and miles in search of employment, he arrived with bloody feet to one of those guest houses where he had left all his luggage as hostages. He asked the owner to allow him to open a trunk to take out some shoes and put them on. His request was denied. His friends from the Bustanoby café helped him out at times; but they faced their own problems. Even the title of count seemed less productive than the title granted to him by the Nervi School of Agriculture.

At times, Rodolfo slept in a nightly boarding house where a bed cost twelve cents. On the days he did not even have that miserable sum he slept in Central Park. There, in the midst of those nocturnal shadows, all of the illusions he brought from Italy vanished. In New York, Rodolfo began to live according to very different rules from those he had obeyed in his distant

---

19 t.n.: *Andar de la Ceca a la Meca* - (to go from the mint to the Mecca) - from here to there and everywhere.

41

homeland. He searched for work every day and at all hours. No occupation seemed too low if it gave him pennies to eat. He cleaned the nickel-plated parts of cars to earn a tip. He swept. He did everything he was allowed to do. Sometimes, he went to those canteens where free lunch is served for those who bought a drink. He used to eat his lunch and then run away just before being asked what he was going to drink. This because he lacked the five cents for a glass of beer.

Some say he washed dishes at that time of his sad New York life. The truth is there were days when washing dishes would have seemed like a luxury. He would have cleaned them with his tongue and for free.[20]

It was then he came to think seriously about suicide but a casual encounter would save him. He had not had any place to go for three days when he met another Italian who was not faring much better, but who at least had a room to sleep in. He took him there to share that room. Afterwards, the Italian friend gave him advice. He said Rodolfo had to humble himself and act as an inferior and ask favors from even the people whom he despised. He had to be willing to do whatever was necessary to make a living. He reminded him that he was not in Taranto but in New York. Consequently, Italy's scruples had to be left behind. Rodolfo left that hospitable and comforting garret, determined to take more care in that society which had yet done nothing to satisfy his hunger.

In the club Maxim's, the piano player was a young man belonging to a distinguished family of Taranto. He had already suffered the low times similar to those his fellow countryman was suffering. Rodolfo humbly asked him to help him look for any kind of work. The pianist recommended he speak with the head waiter, whom he had already met at the Bustanoby café.

There, the head waiter received him as a friend and remembered Rodolfo as being a good dancer. He proposed he join the Bustanoby café because there was always a need for dancers for women who lacked a partner or because their companion could not dance. Rodolfo would not receive a salary for that position but he would receive food and be able to receive tips from the women who danced with him as gratification for his instruction. In addition to this, they could lend him a room where he could give private lessons if the case arose. In this way, the young graduate in the School of Agriculture of Nervi, became Rodolfo the Dancer.

He lived like this for a season while increasing his circle of acquaintants. At times, instead of dancing in the Bustanoby café, his clients took him to other dance halls, incurring the expenses and the salary

20 t.n.: *De balde* - (from the bucket) - for free.

on their behalf. There were several women who boasted of having given him money at that time.

Among the lady friends he met while living in these conditions, there was one who gave him good advice and helped him to effectively take advantage of his talent. She suggested the idea of looking for a partner to dance in theaters.

"Surely, you can not be satisfied with this kind of life,"added Rodolfo the Dancer's interested female advisor.

She then introduced him to the famous dancer Bonnie Glass, who after having danced a few steps with Rodolfo, hired him for fifty dollars a week. They danced with great success in Delmonico, in Rector and caused a sensation in the Winter Garden by resurrecting a dance called the "Cake Walk". They performed in countless theaters. Then, Bonnie Glass opened her club Montmartre, in the basement of the old café Boulevard, and raised Rodolfo's salary to one hundred dollars a week.

From time to time they returned to the theaters of New York and other cities. In Washington, in the presence of President Wilson, they were called to perform sixteen times due to the enthusiasm aroused by their pantomime waltz. Around this time Rodolfo also devoted himself to learning aviation. Bonnie Glass then opened her "Chez Fisher" on 55th Street and Rodolfo danced with her there until she married Ben Ali Haggin and retired.

Rodolfo the Dancer, by then already famous, became a partner of the dancer Joan Sawyer with whom he made a tour of variety theaters including the Woodmansten Inn. Joan Sawyer paid him one hundred dollars a week. This would mark the beginning of a relationship which would have its outcome in one of the most famous tragedies in New York.

Among Joan Sawyer's closest friends was a young sportsman named Jack who was elegant, aristocratic and good natured. He was not only known for his personal qualities but for his family and social relationships as well. Jack was married to an aristocratic and beautiful South American woman named Blanca. She was educated as a princess in the best schools in France and England. Elegant, refined and haughty, she belonged to one of the most prominent families in South America, where her surname suggested ancestry, prestige, power, wealth, distinction and respectability.

Jack, although he loved Blanca, never appreciated her worth or how much her love meant to him. Despite her being raised as a true South American princess, Jack lived as if he were single and abandoned his extraordinary and fortuitous home life, preferring the company of rascals[21]. Through Joan Sawyer, Rodolfo met Jack and they became friends. Through Jack, Rodolfo met Blanca.

Blanca began treating Rodolfo as the proper dance partner of a lady of her lineage. They saw each other frequently at parties in Jack's residence and in the public places where she used to go with her friends or with her husband. Rodolfo the dancer entertained the ladies thanks to his ability to dance.

Little by little, Blanca and Rodolfo became closer friends. She found in him, perhaps, the respect instinctively desired by a wife who does not find it at home. He found something else; an inspiration which elevated him above all the social sorrow he had endured since arriving in New York. Both Blanca and Rodolfo found themselves enjoying an exquisite consolation to their common nostalgia.

Rodolfo fell in love with that extraordinary woman. He fell in love with the purest love of his life. And Blanca? ...or "Bianca" as Rodolfo always called her, no matter how haughty and refined she might have been, she could not cease being a woman even for a moment. Rather, she has always represented the very essence of femininity for Rodolfo.

Loved or not by the friend who adored her so much, it is more than likely she took advantage of her relationship with Rodolfo the Dancer, perhaps to inspire jealousy in her husband. In the least, she conquered the Italian's heart and used it in a troubling situation in her home. It so happened Blanca and Rodolfo met together quite often and in this way managed to garner the attention of her husband as well as many others.

The beautiful South American aristocratic woman grew tired of enduring the disloyal behavior of her husband whom she wished to divorce. But she lacked any evidence of his infidelity. She begged Rudolph to act as a witness, he who was so well acquainted with Jack's relationships with various women. But Rodolfo took the high road for his friend and refused at first to testify.

Jack grew jealous of Rodolfo and his anger was about to explode. One night, as Jack was having dinner with friends at the Café des Artistes, Rodolfo arrived to join the group as he had so many previous times. It did not take long for Jack to provoke a dispute with the dancer by asking him who he thought he was to go around dancing with his wife. To which Rodolfo replied,

"I respect her as a lady."

21 t.n.: *Gente de trueno* - (people of the thunder) - rascals, astute, mischievous and brutish people.

"Well, then, we do not want any pimp here," Jack added and he then threw the contents of a glass of liquor at Rodolfo. Rodolfo did not make the slightest movement to react and told him,

"Jack, your wife has insistently asked me to testify against you in the divorce trial and I have not accepted until now because I believed you were my friend. Tomorrow I will go to tell her that I am willing to declare how much I know about you. "

He did just so and as a result of his testimony, the South American noble lady Blanca was able to divorce Jack. But this was only the first consequence of the dancer's statement.

Jack, being astute, knew Rodolfo lived in a house with a somewhat shady reputation. Jack reported the house to the police and one night, by surprise, the authorities arrived and arrested Rodolfo, accusing him of engaging in white slave trafficking. For several days he remained in jail until he came to the aid of a Jewish lawyer.

From that moment on, Rodolfo the Dancer was despised by all those who knew him; especially by those who praised Jack for taking action against the offense which Rodolfo seemingly inflicted on him. Not only did they give Rodolfo no further work, they did not greet him when they saw him pass by. For them, Rodolfo the Dancer was no longer a lord or a Count but someone dedicated to the slave trade. He was banned from the café Montmartre and the Sixty Club, which he used to frequent.

It was therefore necessary for him to leave New York and go somewhere, where no one knew him. Hollywood then began to be the land of promising artists and it was there Rodolfo wanted to flee; but he did not know how.

After many jobs and further humiliations, he was cast in a medium operetta company traveling west performing, "The Masked Model". And through this, the discredited Rodolfo the Dancer sought better luck in the land where the sun sets. His escape from New York, however, did not end the repercussions of his testimony against his former friend Jack. The worst was still to come.

According to the decree of divorce which dissolved the civil union of Blanca and Jack, the only young son of the marriage was required to stay with the mother six months of each year and with the father the other six. Both parents adored the little boy. Jack also claimed he still loved Blanca and said he hoped to win her back by using his son. But Jack did not amend his way of life. To the contrary; he attended wild parties without caring for his small son who witnessed his bad example.

The boy used to innocently tell his mother about the extraordinary things which happened in that father's home where he lived half of the year. The child described nakedness, drunkenness, abominable incidents and these stories affected the maternal heart with the cruelty of a dagger. Naturally outraged, Blanca did what she could to tear the fruit of her womb from that immoral environment. Under the pretext she was going to take a trip to South America, she recalled custody of her son. Jack did not budge. Blanca pleaded, demanded, resorted to all peaceful means she could think of to have her son live with her where he would grow in an exemplary environment. Jack left her without a hope of a solution.

One winter day Blanca, determined to have her son back, got into a car with the boy's nurse and went to Long Island where Jack lived. When she entered the mansion, Jack believed she was coming to join him again and walked towards her with open arms and a smile,

"Blanca! Finally!" he exclaimed.

The little boy had already run into his mother's arms.[22] She wanted to take him away, but his father stopped her.

Blanca then pulled a revolver out of her sleeve and with admirable serenity, said,

"You have ruined my life and you want to steal my son to ruin him too, eh? Well, take. . . take this. . ."

She fired several bullets into the athlete; the man whom years before she loved. When he turned to flee, she continued firing until seeing him fall into a pool of blood. She then realized he could no longer keep his son from her.

Blanca sat mute and stoic on the threshold of the front door. There she waited for the police to arrive to take her to a jail cell. Jack did not die immediately. Still, while struggling between life and death, he gave Blanca more torment. He told her he could still leave her without her son for whom she had made such a great sacrifice. Once in the jail cell where she felt so defeated momentarily, Blanca hoped for Jack's death, praying he would die so she would not have to go through trying to kill him again. It did not take long for him to die.

22 The DeSaulles murder took place in August and the child did not witness the murder: *New York Times,* 8/10/1917, "DeSaulles Killing Re-enacted by Maid", *New York Times*, 8/6/1917, "Mrs. DeSaulles Tells Her Story of the Tragedy" and *New York Herald,* 8/6/1917, "Mrs. DeSaulles Arm Nerved to Kill Husband".

It was not a great effort for Blanca to dominate the jury with her beauty and elegance, her haughtiness, her refined aristocracy, her unheardof serenity and her patent character of a dignified wife and loving mother. This all contributed to her subjugating the hundreds of souls who, as judges, jury or as spectators, watched her in a dreadful collective look which should have been an overwhelming accusation but instead became a silent tribute to a most regal prisoner.

During her legal process, the behavior with which Jack tormented and humiliated his wife was made public and at the same time it was revealed he was a bad example to his young son. Blanca was acquitted. With her head raised high, she left that cell where she was lost for some time in the events of the proceedings which she wanted to forget and be forgotten.

In the same jail cell where Blanca, the South American noblewoman was imprisioned, a beautiful Yankee lady whose name was linked to another great New York tragedy had also been incarcerated. Blanca, in telling her story to an intimate friend with whom she met in her subsequent wanderings, recalled the coincidence and ended her story with these words which beautifully and masterfully differentiate the effects of those two captives in that same cell,

"She made it famous. I made it *chic*."

Blanca remains a fine unwritten drama, perhaps because Oscar Wilde died before she was born. Perhaps it was the spirit of the author of "Salomé" who suggested this idea to me. But those gemlike words seem to compensate for the death of a husband unable to appreciate the woman who uttered them.

Some years later, when Rodolfo the Dancer was already living in Hollywood and working as an actor, he used to tell some of his friends about what happened in New York. Among all the shadows of that scenario so full of misery and pessimism, there was only one ray of sun which put a smile on his face. He remembered "Bianca" without equal, of whom he said, in romantic moments,

"She was the purest love of my life."

Some years later and only a few months before he died, Rodolfo learned a friend of his was going to South America.

"Do you know of "Blanca"? he asked.

"Much."

47

"Will you see her? Could you give her a message?"

"With pleasure."

"Well, tell her, just in case she has not seen my films, that Rudolph Valentino is the same Rodolfo Guglielmi who used to dance with her in New York. Tell her that I have never forgotten her and that I would be very happy if I could correspond with her. And if she agrees to that, then send a cable to this address in Paris so I can write to her right away."

According to some of Rudolph's companions during his last stay in Europe, as he arrived in Paris, the South American lady Blanca was also in that city. At Rudolph's urging, a lady friend of both called Blanca on the phone and told her about the arrival of her old friend. She also told her that he was there and wanted to speak with her.

"But I am married," replied the noble lady with an unequivocal tone of rebuke.

"It does not matter! Look, he's going to explain to you now," said the intermediary .

"Bianca!"exclaimed Rodolfo with a trembling voice as he took the phone. And he repeated the beautiful name again and again. He would never receive an answer because Blanca hung up the moment she heard his voice.

Some time later, the person to whom Rodolfo had given the message in Hollywood, arrived in South America. He found Blanca had not only married a man who was very worthy of such a refined personality, but that both were in love with each other and living in a model home. Appreciating these fortunate circumstances, the person carrying the message of love from Rudolph, walked away without saying a word about his delicate mission.

When he returned to Hollywood he did not inform Rudolph of his noble diplomatic failure. This because many bouquets of flowers had by then dried next to the tomb of that conqueror who, despite having thousands of female hearts ready to serve him, knew the bitterness of not reaching the one woman who interested him most; the one supreme woman he loved with his purest love.

Installment

IV

Against The Wind and The Tide

The operetta company which hired Rudolph in New York as a dancer would fail as it wended its way across the country. However, he was lucky enough to arrive in San Francisco where he lived for a while, often due to his dancing, sometimes only due to a miracle.

There, as in New York, his poise and dancing skills earned him profitable social relations. Most notably was the distinguished wife of Jack Spreckels, who was his best friend in that happy port and who helped Rudolph by having her husband introduce him to people of importance in the region.

Thus Rudolph was engaged, for a while, in the purchase and sale of securities while working as a broker and it was in this occupation he nurtured his dreams. One fine day he ran into Norman Kaiser, whom he first met in New York. At the time Rudolph met him in New York, Norman worked as a salesman for a factory manufacturing trunks. This factory belonged to his father, a wealthy German industrialist. Norman and his family were fond of Rudolph during his ill-fated days in New York. So when he reconnected with his kind friend in this distant land, he rejoiced as if he were a member of his own family.

"Hello, Norman! How are those trunks selling?"

"Now I laugh at those trunks. I am nothing less than a silent actor! Have you yet to admire me on the screen?"

Rudolph's friend now called himself Norman Kerry, as Germanophobia was rampant in the United States at the time. For this he thought it prudent to remove all dangerous traces from his name.

Norman was more a lover of art and bohemian life than of industry and parental authority. He had abandoned the secure future he had with his wealthy family to enjoy the adventure of looking for a less easy future in the challenging world of Cinelandia. There he prospered sufficiently to feel proud and optimistic. At the time he met Rudolph, he was in San Francisco with Mary Pickford's company, filming scenes for the movie, *The Little Princess* whose young gallant was played by Norman.

He was of mixed Irish and German background and one of the most handsome actors on screen; proud to demonstrate in his character the wit of the race of Shaw and the spirit of a Prussian soldier. All of this earned him as many hundreds of dollars a week as he made selling trunks in one month. Rudolph was amazed to hear the fantastic stories about Hollywood which his friend, the ex-seller of trunks from the Kaiser factory, shared with him. He was about to be carried away by the ensuing temptations.

"Leave the life you're living now, man. Judging from your clothes, it's not going very well for you, just to say. On the other hand, if you come to Los Angeles, I will help you get into the studios. Do not worry about money issues. I have enough for both of us."

However, Rudolph made no such decision at the time. There was surely something keeping him in San Francisco. Some lady, perhaps? He preferred to say he hoped to earn a great deal of money in San Francisco buying and selling stock shares. He once earned fifty dollars in a single day which was as much salary as Norman was earning at the time. However, in this profession Rudolph was only a beginner. With a little more experience and by increasing his contacts, he was sure he could earn much more. To succeed in that occupation, he believed he just needed to find out who would be the buyers and what Mr. So-and-So[23] wanted to sell!

"In a year I could make a fortune, Norman, and in two, another much higher, and in three. . ."

But as the sale of U.S. Government Liberty Bonds began, he did not sell another single share. It was then Rudolph agreed to accept the offer made by Norman Kerry and travel to Los Angeles. There, his friend welcomed him with open arms, accommodated him on his own account in the Hotel Alexandria, which was the best in the city and introduced him to all his friends in Cinelandia.

---

23 t.n.: Fulano is a person whose name is unknown. The word has its origin in the mozarabic word *"fulán"* which means "this man".

Rudolph, like so many other aspirants who arrived intent on conquering the screen, discovered a new world on this remote shore of the New World. This world was very new in its art, its industry, its mixture of races, its customs, its methods and its ideals. There was no social value there that he had known anywhere else, even in the over politeness or the lack of politeness.

In this strange environment, Rudolph was surprised to find no work despite all of his magnificent recommendations. There were thousands of people like him who relied upon their door knocking abilities to get by. There were even those who had more experience at that than he did and those prepared to make more sacrifices. There were those who were willing to suffer as many humiliations necessary to achieve what he was looking for by relying on his having been a dancer in New York and his friendship with Norman Kerry and his friends.

Nevertheless, many of those people aspiring to the glory of the screen used to go hungry. To rid themselves of such privations, they were forced, not infrequently to take refuge in some hotel or restaurant. There, adorned with their beauty and illusions, they accepted happily a humble task of washing dishes when they did not have to turn to a less honorable means.

But Rudolph, at last, found work as an "extra" earning $5 a day; less than what he earned as "Rudolph the Dancer". It was Emmett Flynn, the director of *Monte Cristo,* who gave him his first role in the movie *Alimony* (with Universal) in which the lead actors were Norman Kerry and Wanda Hawley. One amusing detail of that modest debut; while working in that movie, Rudolph met another "extra" named Alice Taffe, who became Alice Terry and would be famous in the same movie which made Rudolph Valentino famous, *The Four Horsemen of the Apocalypse.*

After that long-awaited initiation into the movies, he was again without work and forced to repeat the same daily ordeal. He walked from studio to studio, from friend to friend and in search of another opportunity however small the part. Meanwhile, he still lived at the expense of Norman Kerry; no longer in the elegant Alexandria Hotel but in a modest "apartment building."

Rudolph managed, barely, to find work and always as an "extra" in occasional movies. He grew disillusioned as he faced the bitter reality of the studios which was so different from what one imagines before knowing about them. He took refuge again in his old profession, the one he was eager to forget.

Rudolph was again the dancer of New York; this time dancing in cabarets around Los Angeles and for the modest sum of $35 a week. This was the same that a miserable "extra" in Hollywood was earning, but there he had sure food without having to endure the humiliation of someone supporting him. Additionally, he hoped he would be discovered by some of the film directors who frequented the cabarets.

With no one discovering him, he began dancing in the Hotel Maryland in Pasadena as the dancer, Kitty Phelps' partner. She was the first woman he fell in love with in California; despite his having many affairs with more than one Eve before meeting her.

Thanks to a well-timed contact from Emmett Flynn, Rudolph returned to work in the studios; this time in a lead role in *The Married Virgin*. In this movie he would at last be recognized instead of being lost in a heap of anonymous "extras". It made no difference to Rudolph that he was only paid fifty dollars a week. He played his part as best as he could and confidently waited for the Hollywood moguls viewing the film to offer him a fabulous contract.

He waited in vain. Just when filming ended, a lawsuit was filed which delayed the film's showing until Rudolph had already become famous. When the film was finally released, it was not he who profited from his first important role; it was the producers who took advantage of Valentino's fame.

Rudolph's ascent in movies was not immediate, even after he appeared as one of the lead actors in that film. Finding himself again in trouble, he accepted another position of "extra" offered by Emmett Flynn. On this occasion, he was paid $7.50 a day during the duration of filming. This was instead of receiving pay for a set period of work which was the then usual practice in Cinelandia.

Soon after, Robert Leonard and his wife Mae Murray, who previously knew Rudolph in New York, cast him the role of lead actor in *The Delicious Little Devil,* being paid one hundred dollars a week. Then, in his next film, *The Big Little Person* also with Mae Murray, he was cast in a lead role. But in another film role in *Nobody Home*, there was no suitable role for him and Ralph Graves, who had just won a beauty contest, was cast.

Rudolph then worked under the direction of Paul Powell, James Young, D. W. Griffith and Sid Grauman, sometimes as an actor and sometimes as a dancer in film prologues. And in this way he was permanently establishing himself in the film industry.

In his autobiography, Rudolph recounts this first stage of his career in Cinelandia, yet the reader who is familiar with his actual life can not help but think he commits a great injustice in that story by omitting the name of someone who, without any doubt, was his best friend at the time.

An explanation of such injustice comes to mind. The famous autobiography was written under the influence of Natacha Rambova, who convinced Rudolph to distance himself from his friend. Fortunately, while continuing to read the story attributed to Rudolph, we see this corrrected in some brief lines which by themselves are exceedingly significant.

"Working at Universal, I met Douglas Gerrard, who became my best friend. He was one of the directors there and tried repeatedly to get me into his films but it always happened that I was busy somewhere else when he needed me. However, our friendship was constantly increasing and for some reason I never got to know, nobody loved me very much in Hollywood... Douglas was the only one who invited me to go out with him and every time he gave a party he wanted to be sure to have me invited. The parties were often given at the Hollywood Athletic Club."

Perhaps Rudolph was not so loved in Hollywood and on many occasions he said he thought he knew the reason why. Across America, he was referred to as a "pimp"; a name first whispered about him in the artistic centers of New York. For that reason he was rejected in many Hollywood homes. It was Douglas Gerrard who, despite the warnings made to him more than once, decided to help that poor boy remove the heavy burden of such a discredit from his shoulders.

Douglas met Rudolph at Universal studios. Rudolph had just debuted as an "extra" in the movie *Alimony*. Douglas was a director who had already discovered several artists who became famous; Patsy Ruth Miller, Ruth Clifford and Monroe Salisbury. The actor Charles Gerrard, introduced Rudolph to his brother Douglas by encouraging him to cast him in his next film. Then, Norman Kerry introduced Rudolph to Douglas on another occasion in a restaurant. It seems Norman and Charles wanted to expel the burden Rudolph represented.

Some time later, Douglas directed a film titled, *The Hand of Velvet* and a discussion arose as to some Italian customs relating to the film. Douglas, who visited Italy, maintained his arguments while other members of the company argued in the opposite direction. Rudolph, who was present as a curious by-stander, approached Douglas to say,

"Mr. Gerrard, you are right. I'm Italian, and I know it's like that, it is just as you say."

This served to remind Douglas that this Italian had already been introduced to him twice even though he could not remember his name. And since it was lunchtime, he invited Rudolph to join him. The first observation the Irishman Gerrard made of Rudolph Valentino was that he ate with extraordinary voracity. So much so, Douglas could not resist the temptation to express his admiration for his appetite.

"Mr. Gerrard, it's not appetite, it's hunger. If you knew..."

Douglas changed the direction of the conversation to prevent any further humiliating confessions by Rudolph. But his great Irish heart beat full of sympathy for that poor young man who found hunger where he hoped to find opulence. From that moment on, Douglas Gerrard was the unconditional friend of Rudolph Valentino.

Rudolph visited Douglas both in restaurants and on stage and his new friend gave him work in several of his films, recommended him to other directors and introduced him to his friends. As it turned out, Douglas' clothes, hats and shoes all fit Rudolph perfectly. From the moment this was discovered, Rudolph had at his disposal one of the best-equipped wardrobes in Hollywood. There he could resolve any need for clothing, both for work in the studios or to attend a social event.

In those instances, Rudolph used to change clothes in his friend's house, leaving his own suit there to change back into when he returned Douglas' clothing. On some occasions, he forgot to return his friend's clothes. And thanks to that carelessness, understandable between great friends, Douglas would witness a curious spectacle. During the auctions of the great dead actor's property, his admirers paid unusual interest in purchasing some relic of the fallen idol and unknowingly bought some of Douglas Gerrard's suits!

And there, still hanging in the Irishman's wardrobe, and often with certain patches to inspire pity, were the suits of Rudolph; the very ones he left there years before in exchange for those belonging to Douglas which were sold to the highest bidder.

It was also Douglas who explained to Rudolph the mysteries of makeup and who paid for him to take riding lessons. He also taught him to speak a decent English and to dress the English way. Since Rudolph was passionate about all things from England, his highest ideal was to look like an English gentleman. From this point of view, he sometimes appeared snobbish even during the height of his fame. He pretended to simulate some lord whom he admired, yet despite this, his Italian gesticulating dominated.

Douglas Gerrard relates amusing anecdotes about that aspect of the personality of Rudolph Valentino. When he still lacked the confidence to visit Douglas whenever he wanted, one night Rudolph unexpectedly showed up to give him a bottle of Italian chianti. Rudolph also brought a photograph of himself inscribed with an expressive dedication which he gave to Douglas. He asked his friend to install the photograph along with those covering the walls of the room. There, Douglas displayed photographs of the most outstanding personalities of Hollywood and a few notables of Europe such as Anna Pavlova and Sir Herbert Beerbohm Tree.

Douglas asked his friend where he wanted his portrait to be placed. Rudolph chose the most visible place in the room, between Tree and Pavlova, which were the favorites of Douglas Gerrard since he had acted with both as the young gallant. Rudolph the dancer, then an "extra" in search of work, was thrilled when he saw how the Irishman granted him his request. Rising to the circumstances, he said with much ceremony,

"Thank you very much, Monsieur Gerrard, in my name and in that of my compatriots for the importance you grant to the Italian nationality."

To which Douglas answered no less ceremoniously,

"I, too, *Signor* Valentino. Thank you for the honor you grant me by giving me your beautiful portrait and the bottle of chianti. I beg you to convey to your courageous compatriots my deepest gratitude for the help they are giving to my country in its glorious effort for Democracy."

And both actors bowed several times. That scene demonstrated the contrast between the two friend's characters which would make their friendship all the more enjoyable. One always tended to be solemn and was extraordinarily late in appreciating the good humor of others. The other, joking eternally.

One night when Douglas gathered together John Gilbert, Rudolph Valentino and Ralph Graves in the Hollywood Athletic Club, Charlie Chaplin arrived. Chaplin used to join the regular group of friends to share in the amusing banter which Douglas always inspired in those three inexperienced artists. On that occasion they were discussing a subject which was terribly serious; John Gilbert wanted to commit suicide.

Rudolph and Ralph Graves were on the one hand frightened but on the other they were admiring Gilbert because he dared to reveal his suicidal temperment. For the first time they looked at him as a being somewhat superior to them. Both advised him to have a little patience and added that there is no evil which lasts a hundred years, etc., etc.

Douglas, who was the eldest of the four and whom, therefore, they all looked upon as the appointed counselor, was inclined to agree with John Gilbert.

"Suicide is sometimes an irreplaceable remedy. Do not you think, Charlie?"

Gerrard thus invited Chaplin to join the conversation.

"No doubt," said Chaplin. "I know of no evil which suicide would not heal."

Given the opinions of these two important figures in Cinelandia, Gilbert boasted of seeing his suicide criteria authoritatively supported, while Rudolph and Graves began to also feel convinced. Ralph Graves, however, was a practitioner of "Christian Science" and it was for this reason he objected.

"But those evils exist only in our imagination."

"Does it seem so little to exist?" Douglas asked.

"Yes, it would diminish the world if we suppressed our imagination. Neither evil nor good would exist in that case," said Chaplin.

"But, gentlemen," interrupted Gilbert with more energy than ever, "This is not about evil or good. It's just that I want to end my life."

"So then the only thing to discuss," Douglas continued, "is whether the right moment has come."

"And the form of suicide is also important, Douglas," Chaplin whispered so that the others could clearly hear him.

"As for that," Valentino declared seriously, "I believe nothing is safer than firearms."

"Well, I insist," Graves the Christian Scientist said piously, "that even after resolving in favor of suicide, the right thing to do is raise your eyes to heaven and ask God to take your life, since he was the one who gave it to you."

Chaplin looked at him with great pity and said, "It would be much more practical to rely upon an automatic guillotine."

"But considering," Douglas summarized, "and bearing in mind that he is now an actor, it is logical that a more theatrical procedure be sought. For me, being the film director that I am, I would be much more pleased if John Gilbert took a trip to New York, descended down to the underground railway and threw himself under the wheels of a train running at full speed. The only drawback is that Gilbert lacks money. That is one of the reasons why he wants to commit suicide. But we could all make a contribution."

Gilbert, Rudolph and Graves by then had some clue as to what they were talking about. The first, forgetting his grim ideas, laughed. And only at that moment did Rudolph begin to suspect Douglas was joking. Turning to Chaplin, he whispered in his ear,

"I think Douglas is kidding."

"Oh no!" Chaplin whispered in Rudolph's ear, "I think he is speaking very seriously."

About that same time, Rudolph fell in love with several women. Some corresponded with him and with some he engaged in intimate affairs. Among these are women who today are happily married to notable characters on the screen and in society. Others paid little attention to him. But perhaps none had as much disdain for Rudolph as Gloria Swanson, whom he was madly in love with at the time. Once he borrowed money and spent it on flowers and chocolates to take to Gloria. The story goes that she threw the flowers and chocolate in his face and hit his nose while slamming the door.

The most interesting love affair Rudolph Valentino had at that point in his life, was the one with a woman who made his heart race; the star Mary Miles Minter. One night, Douglas invited Rudolph and Ralph Graves to dinner at the Hotel Alexandria. The restaurant was animated and many guests were dancing. As the couples passed by Douglas' table they greeted him warmly since he was famous as an actor, director and pransker. His two companions were still almost unknown.

Among the dancers was Gerrard's friend, Mary Miles Minter. Every time she passed by his table, she stared in such a way that it gave Douglas ideas. He saw, however, that the looks were not just for him, the well-known actor, but also for the two young unknown strangers. They begged to be introduced to her and Douglas generously complied with their wishes. They then began chatting with her about her next movie and Rudolph exclaimed,

"Oh, how much I would like to be playing the part of the young gallant next to you!"

"Well, look," Mary said confidently, "I think that in that movie you would be better cast playing the bad guy."

With that brazen retort, Mary Miles Minter opened the doors of friendship with the young Italian. Since that exchange occurred, Rudolph accompanied Douglas every time he went to the Hotel Alexandria where Mary Minter lived with her mother, Mrs. Shelby and her sister Margarita. Ralph Graves also used to accompany them. A competition began between Rudolph and Ralph to see who could first conquer Mary.

After a while, it seemed Graves had the advantage when Mrs. Shelby invited him to accompany them to Santa Barbara. After this invitation, Ralph Graves was almost always and everywhere with his beloved; this while Rudolph raged. In a gathering of friends, in which Graves was not in attendance, a rich young man named Harry Ham, invited everyone including Mary, to spend a few days at his mother, Lady Sharp of London's farm in San Bernardino (California). The invitation was for Holy Saturday and everyone was in attendance except for Ralph Graves.

Rudolph promised to cook them all a spaghetti dinner, which he did to everyone's delight; to everyone's delight except for himself. That evening Douglas said to him,

"Today you were not happy, eh? You have not had the pleasure of seeing Mary."

"I've seen more of my spaghetti than her, Gerry. But after all, it's not your fault. You have shown me once again that you are my best friend."

He was, yes, Rudolph's close friend. But he was also his own best friend. While Rudolph was in the kitchen busy preparing his Italian dinner, Douglas convinced Mary Miles Minter to walk with him around the garden. There, in the light of the moon, he recited a poem to her which he wrote titled, "The Princess of the Golden Veil". The poem, on that occasion was inspired by her, but on other previous occasions it was inspired by many other blondes. Whatever the occasion, the author altered the poem depending on the light provided, whether it be the moon or the sun or some electric light bulb.

In the early morning of that Easter Sunday, everyone went up to Mount Roubidoux, where every year on that date thousands of Christians gathered to celebrate the Resurrection of the Lord. They then went down to the Mission Inn for lunch where they visited that true Spanish museum which was rich with relics. Rudolph took advantage of the day's excursion.

He did so by dedicating himself to Mary Miles Minter as much as he possibly could. In the chapel, he knelt close to her before the altar as if to celebrate the coincidence of their both being Catholics. Now, Mary Miles Minter extolled, above all the hands of the Virgin as she pronounced the Hail Mary's, ticking away those innumerable precious sparkled stones of her rosary.

"Yes, Mary, the hands of the Virgin are very beautiful; but your white hands do not seem any less beautiful to me."

From that day on, Rudolph saw Mary often and it was Ralph Graves who now grew enraged. The most curious aspect of this situation was that Douglas, who from the beginning expressed the most interest in Mary, far more than her other two young suitors, seemed to forget their interest. He paid great attention to the glances and the kindness Mary expressed towards him. Douglas came to feel unusually attracted to her. So much so that when Rudolph told him one day, very passionately,

"Gerry, I would marry her and very willingly!" Douglas was about to answer him,

"That's a laugh! I would marry her too!"

But Douglas preferred to keep his true feelings to himself. A few days later, Mary Miles Minter and her family left for New York. Douglas went to the station to say farewell to them and had, in addition to the usual gifts for Mary and her sister, a book her mother Mrs. Shelby asked for.

"Gerry, let's see if you can find me that book, *The Four Horsemen of the Apocalypse* that is being talked about so much. I want to read it on the trip."

Until that day, Rudolph had never heard of Blasco Ibáñez or the book which would soon make him so famous around the world.

It is not known just how Mary Miles Minter would manage to accomplish what follows, but my lady readers will probably understand it better than the men and myself. The fact remains that until that last minute and without having communicated a word about it with each of her three admirers, each one of them believed he was her preferred beau.

In their conversations, they spoke of her as a common friend and they even sent her letters, telegrams and postcards signed by, "The Three Musketeers". But at the same time, secretly, each one of them wrote separately to her while she was in New York.

For Rudolph she was, "My beautiful Maria," for Ralph Graves, "Dear, sweet, little Maria," and for Douglas Gerrard, "Princess of the Golden Veil."

It was not long before Douglas nearly fainted upon receiving a letter from Mary Miles Minter which included these lines;

"While I write to you these sincere words, which spring from the depths of my heart, a beautiful incarnate rose, which has been swaying on top of a delicate vase, has, little by little, dropped on this paper a few fragrant petals. I tear off what is left of the flower and I send it to you, Gerry, as a fond memory of your princess of the golden veil."

Douglas kissed the flower very carefully as not to damage it.

After a while, he heard Rudolph knocking on the door, his knocking seemed full of enthusiasm. This because Rudolph always knocked three times on Douglas' door. If he was sad, which was usually the case, his knocks were slow. Whenever he was happy, his knocks sounded faster but on this occasion they rattled faster than ever.

"But what's going on, Rudy? Have you signed some great contract?"

"I'm happy, Gerry, I'm happy. Finally, she wrote to me!"

"Who?" Douglas asked fearfully wondering if she was the same woman who wrote to him.

"Her! Man, her, Mary! Who else would it be? Look, look what she says to me. 'While I have written these sincere words, that come from the bottom of my heart'."

"Yes," Douglas warned, not knowing whether to laugh or to be sad, "I know how it goes, and 'a beautiful red rose'."

"And how do you know?"

"Because I received a letter which was exactly the same."

While comparing the two letters, they discovered the only difference was that Rudolph's ended with, "I send it to you, Rudy, as a fond memory of your *beautiful Maria*."

"Gerry, I think she's kidding us."

"Decidedly, Rudy, you are very insightful."

Douglas and Rudolph understood, of course, that Ralph Graves would have received an identical letter and they went to confirm this. Ralph looked at them over his shoulder, like a victor over the losers. However, the only difference between his and his two visitor's letters was that his ended in this way; "...and I send it to you, Ralph, as a fond memory of your *dear, sweet, little Maria*." None of the three men had any further interest in Mary Miles Minter.

A few days later, Douglas Gerrard hosted a great dinner at the Athletic Club in honor of Pauline Frederick, attended by several celebrities including Charles Chaplin, Rex Ingram, Eddie Laemmle as well as the new-comers John Gilbert, Rudolph Valentino and Ralph Graves.

After the banquet there was a very lively dance. And later, they all went to Venice where they continued to dance at the Ship's Café. Rudolph, like the host, was dedicated to dancing mainly with the two older women attending the party; the mother and the aunt of Pauline Frederick. This generated so much attention that someone, who apparently had a good opinion of him, said to Douglas,

"That little Italian can be whatever you want. But, at least, it seems he has gentlemanly instincts."

The following Saturday, Pauline Frederick hosted another big party at her home in Beverly Hills and, of course, she invited Douglas. He asked her, by telephone, if he could bring Rudolph.

"Of course. My mother and aunt are very pleased with him. He is a nice boy and an admirable dancer."

Two things occurred at that party which left Rudolph deeply affected. The actor, Thomas Meighan called him aside and spoke with him, in a low voice and for a long time. When Rudolph returned to Douglas, he had tears in his eyes. Meighan told him he was well aware of Rudolph the dancer's bad reputation and went on to say even more humiliating things to Rudolph. How could anyone imagine that in the future, when innumerable friends would turn their backs on Rudolph in one of the most critical moments of his life, it would be the benevolent Thomas Meighan who would be the first to reach out to help and with the most timely effectiveness!

But just as Rudolph tasted the bitterness of being so condemned by such a stern man at that party, the actor would meet one unforgettable female discovery. There, he met a woman who as an actress was nothing more than a simple "extra", but who attracted Rudolph Valentino with such force that he would pay no more attention to those elderly ladies who were so anxious to be with him.

Her name was Jean Acker and soon she became Rudolph Valentino's first wife.

Installment

V

The Triumph

It is often said that marriage is the stimulus which makes a man prosper. The first marital adventure of Rudolph Valentino is a curious case regarding just such prosperity as sometimes the married man was completely broke[24] before beginning his marital life.

Rudolph met Jean Acker, as mentioned, at a party held in the home of Pauline Frederick. This was in the beginning of September 1919. It would take a few weeks before Rudolph would see that pretty brunette again; a young woman he could not forget.

They would meet again in the Metro studios, where he was working in a movie starring Dorothy Phillips. Jean worked for the same company but with more regularity and with more profit as well. According to Rudolph himself, the moment he saw Jean again, he felt suddenly in love with her. Not only was Jean Acker beautiful, but she looked to him to be one of those women especially gifted for the constitution of a home; a woman who would bear a family and give him all that he was longing for incessantly.

They met several times within a few days and Jean, in turn, seemed to accept his unconcealed homage. At the end of two months, they met on the afternoon of November 4, to join in a horseback ride through the rugged hills and canyons of Beverly Hills. It was one of those warm, poetic days in late autumn which serve to embellish life in California. It reminded Rudolph of the splendid days of his beloved Italy and filled him with yearnings and suggestions.

The allure of romanticism permeated the countryside, in the mountains, in the sky, in the distant, foggy horizon behind which the waves of the mysterious Pacific sighed. But this was nothing in comparison to the romantic feelings in Rudolph which were already bonding him with the

---

24 t.n.: *Ser a la cuarta pregunta* - (to be at the fouth question) - to be broke, out of money.

brunette riding beside him; young, beautiful, vivacious, modest, affectionate and sweet.

Jean was twenty-three years old[25] and she had never been married, nor had she much fondness for men. Alla Nazimova brought her to Hollywood and Jean lived with her for a while. It was said that both women abhorred men. The 24-year-old exotic Italian, so young, handsome and gallant, just seemed so different from the others. At least, he impressed Jean in a different way than the others.

They stopped their horses in the shade of a grove of trees where the sun filtered through the branches, drawing arabesques on the grass and creating a sort of luminous, rustic carpet. With great emotion, Rudolph helped Jean down from her horse. How he relished in prolonging the ceremony, as if he were celebrating it with excessive care. But in reality he was guided by the manly purpose of making the enjoyment last longer; the pleasure he found in gently pressing his loving fingers into Jean's young flesh throbbing under her dress!

In the shade of those trees every moment felt delicious for him. Jean was amused by the unusual phrases of her Latin suitor and watched with no less interest his dreamy expression when, at times, he was silent. Under the spell of Valentino's beautiful words and mysterious silences and his magnetic eyes, the panorama of California transformed by assuming appearances and significance which Jean Acker had never before contemplated. The foliage swaying in its gentle, warm ripple of breeze left her serene yet overwhelmed; from the clouds and out to the sea.

That supple panorama seemed to become a symbol of modern life for her. The bleached houses perched along the slopes of the ravines appeared as shipwrecked homes rocked mercilessly by some storm. Jean gazed at those "shipwrecked homes" she perceived of as being immobile instead of being rocked. She looked up towards the face of her suitor who, at times, seemed to raving.

Swayed by the fantasies of his Latin spirit, Jean came to understand the comforting presence of the Californian panorama and this despite her mentality being hopelessly influenced by the practical reasoning of the movie world. She perceived those homes on those ravine hillsides as shipwrecked only for a lack of love. Only if loving couples lived in those homes, she thought, could they survive the stormy social sea.

---

25 Jean Acker was born on October 23, 1893 and was two years older than Rudolph Valentino.

Rudolph accomplished a miracle in the soul of Jean Acker, who seemed to so detest men. He made her interested in poetry, in love and even in family.

The two remained silent for a long time while their hands played with the grass and their eyes roamed the countryside. As if in the few sentences exchanged and their looks and caresses, their souls had already said everything. From time to time, however, they stared at each other as if to search each other's souls and this resulted in their approving smiles.

At last, Rudolph felt he had little more to say and that he was repeating the same thing he had already said. He spoke of his ideal home, of the sentimental coldness in which he felt they were both living, of men and womens elevated mission in the world. Both Jean and Rudolph sighed.

"How romantic this all is, Rudy!" exclaimed the beautiful brunette full of emotion.

"Very romantic, little Jean! But don't you think it would be better if we went down to Santa Ana to get married right now?"

"Do not say it so seriously, Rudy, because you run the risk of me taking you up on that."

"I'm telling you very seriously, little Jean," Rudolph said anxiously.

Jean did not like the idea of driving rashly to Santa Ana to be married. She preferred to return to Hollywood, share the news with her friends and marry in full view the next day and without haste. She wanted to marry as God intended. What a good girl! That is how Rudolph wanted her to be and as his little wife he wished for her to respect the sacred institution of marriage. He squeezed her in his arms and covered her with real kisses.

At the Hollywood Hotel where Jean lived, they found several of her friends and told them of their intention to marry the following day. Metro studios manager, Maxwell Karger and his wife, were hosting a farewell party that night in honor of the president of the company, Richard Rowland; this on the occasion of his return to New York. They proposed that the bride and groom take advantage of the gala party by turning it into their wedding reception.

The couple went immediately to Los Angeles in search of a marriage license. They woke the official who would issue it to them, a Mr. Sparkes. Then, they went in search of the Pastor, James I. Myers of the Christian Church of Broadway and took him to the house of Joseph Engel (treasurer of the Metro), which was located at the corner of Hollywood Boulevard and Mariposa Avenue. It was there the wedding was held shortly after midnight on November 5.[26]

They then dined, danced and toasted as newlyweds. Rudolph was careful to follow the European custom of shattering glasses after the toasts.[27] This was done to ensure their conjugal bliss would last for many years; as many years as the pieces into which the glass was broken. The nuptial party lasted until two in the morning and a few hours later, Jean Acker would leave her brand-new husband, Rudolph Valentino.

After the party, they went to the apartment Jean occupied in the Hollywood Hotel. Very early that same morning, just six hours after the wedding, Jean entered Mrs. Karger's room, she who helped organize the marriage. Jean confessed openly that she felt her marriage was a big mistake and she was not sure she could continue in such a state. She then threw herself on a bed and began sobbing. Shortly after this she disappeared from the hotel.

Rudolph was perplexed over the situation which did not seem real to him. It was not even a good plot for a movie. A few hours earlier, when Jean gave him her hand in such a romantic setting, he felt happier than ever before. When it was time to consummate the desired union, he sighed happily as one who has managed to realize his most dear ideal. And now, when Fate had just given him the taste of that unusual bliss after so many years of cruel bitterness, it suddenly took everything back; leaving him newly married, in love and yet abandoned by his beloved wife.

He had no idea what happened to Jean and was ashamed to ask the hotel management where his wife of only a few hours could have gone. He waited, pacing back and forth in the bedroom. He was nervous, exhausted, worried and wondering what happened.

He napped for a while to calm down and then went to the hotel lobby to find some distraction with his friends. He was chatting with them when he was mysteriously called on the phone. It was his wife calling!

"But where are you, beautiful?" he asked in an affectionate tone.

---

26 The marriage was recorded on November 7, 1919 in the California County Birth, Marriage & Death record.

"On the beach!" she replied, sounding washed away in grief.

"And what are you doing there? Why do you not come here?"

"I'm watching the waves."

Jean would return to Rudolph later, throwing herself on a sofa and bursting again into tears. Between sobs, she told her husband she had made a mistake and that she did not expect to find happiness in marriage. Rudolph begged her to give him a chance to see if he could make her happy. He argued they had only been married a few hours and how could she judge whether she would be happy or unhappy in married life in such a short time?

Rudolph's affectionate words managed to calm her to a certain extent. Moments later, as they walked together into the dining room of the hotel, Jean was apparently smiling and happy. But after the meal and again alone with her husband in their room, the newly-married woman returned to her strange pessimism. She told Rudolph she wanted the marriage annulled. To which he replied he would not do so because he had been married only for a few hours and intended to build a lasting home for them.

"No, no, no! I made a mistake. I could not stand this kind of life."

In vain he begged her to give him an opportunity to show her they could be happy. Despite this, his wife left for the home of her beautiful friend Grace Darmond, in whose company she spent that night.

With great difficulty, Rudolph managed to speak with Jean the following day, only to hear again how she was determined not to continue living with him. His pleas were fruitless.

However, Rudolph did not lose hope. He simply refused to believe what he was seeing with his own eyes and hearing with his own ears. There must have been some reason for his wife to assume such an incredible attitude. What could have taken her away from him? Was it, perhaps that Jean preferred her friend, Grace to her husband? But then why had she married him the day before? How was it possible that her fickleness made her solemnly sign a life-long obligation when after a few hours she

---

27 The tradition of breaking a glass after the bride has been given the ring or at the end of the ceremony, is a Jewish tradition and not a general European tradition.

disowned the commitment in favor of a simple friendship? No, Rudolph believed that was not possible.

After pondering, he believed he found a satisfactory explanation. Perhaps his wife was not satisfied with the wedding ring he gave her as it was none other than the one belonging to his deceased mother. To please her, he bought her another platinum ring and when he gave it to her, she put it on with visible satisfaction. But when her husband asked her to return to live with him, Jean answered glibly,

"No, Rudy. Go on alone as a good boy."

Rudolph left without being able to speak to his wife alone, because her friend Grace Darmond and her mother would not leave Jean alone with him.

In the days that followed, he tried daily to speak with her by phone or to see her personally. Jean rejected him on every occasion. On November 22, that is, a little more than fifteen days after the wedding, Rudolph wrote Jean a loving letter which in part read;

"My dear Jean:
Since I can not force you to meet me, either at the hotel or at Grace's house, which is where you spend most of your time, I suppose I must leave everything for peace. I am always willing to provide you with a home and all the comforts that can be achieved with my modest resources and faculties, as well as all the love and solicitude of a husband for his dear little wife.
Please, dear Jean, my life, reconsider and give me an opportunity to show you my sincere love and my eternal devotion to you.
Your unhappy and loving husband,
Rudolph. "

During this same time, Jean Acker went to the office of Maxwell Karger and told him that the best thing she and Rudolph could do would be to separate permanently. It would be one full month since their wedding before Rudolph and his wife would meet. Rudolph approached Jean and kissed her. He was so full of joy to find her respond lovingly that he invited all their friends to accompany them to celebrate the unexpected reconciliation. After this celebration, Rudolph and Jean went together to his residence. The next day Jean left again to go to live with her close friend Grace Darmond.

Jean was then working with Fatty Arbuckle in the movie *Round-Up*, and was required to travel to Lone Pine, (California) to do some locations shots. Rudolph was then working with Norman Kerry in another film titled *Passion's Playground*. When he finished his work, Rudolph decided to travel to Lone Pine to see if he had better luck seeing his wife there than in Los Angeles. Upon learning of his intentions, Jean sent the following telegram to Douglas Gerrard,

"Rudolph threatens to come and see me, make him stay, I do not need him here."

Instead, Grace Darmond went to see Jean in Lone Pine and would stay with her in the same room. (It should be noted, however, that when this detail was brought forth in the divorce proceedings, Jean Acker explained there were two beds in the bedroom where she and Grace slept). But Rudolph, not knowing his friend Doug Gerrard received the telegram from Jean, embarked on the trip to Lone Pine. When his wife learned of this, she left Lone Pine to return to Los Angeles guaranteeing she would not cross paths with her husband.

As soon as Rudolph returned to Los Angeles from his fruitless journey, he went furiously in search of his wife in the house of Grace Darmond. Mrs. Alice Johnson, Grace's mother, opened the door. Rudolph asked about his wife and Mrs. Johnson told him Jean was upstairs. He pushed the gentle lady aside and rushed up to the second floor. His wife was bathing.

Rudolph began knocking excitedly on the door; threatening to break it down if his wife did not open it. Jean opened the bathroom door and they began arguing. And then, as she would declare before a judge in the divorce trial, her husband hit her in the face. Grace Darmond and her mother both declared they heard the blows and the screams and witnessed Jean's swollen face.

When Rudolph realized what he had done and saw his wife crying, he begged her forgiveness. Jean dressed and the two of them walked down to the hall, where he told her he would always be her friend but that he no longer wanted to remain her husband. He proposed a plan that she hire detectives to spy on him. He would allow himself to act surprised and the detectives would catch him with some other woman. This would give her cause for a divorce. Jean rejected his idea.

The following day, Jean asked her husband for money by saying she was sick and without resources. She would later say her husband replied he would lend her money but that he would not give her a single dime. Rudolph then traveled to New York where he immediately found work as a villain in the movie *Stolen Moments*, starring Marguerite Namara, the famous singer of the Chicago Opera Company.

It was about this time, Rudolph read in the news how Metro purchased the filming rights to *The Four Horsemen of the Apocalypse*. He learned there was a role in the film which was perfectly made for him. He read the book and then went to see his mentor, Maxwell Karger who promised to keep him in mind when it came time to cast the film.

What Rudolph Valentino could not then imagine was that he had a godmother in Hollywood who, without ever having spoken a word with him, was waging a campaign in his favor. At last she secured a role for him; a role which he would have begged for on his knees and one which would bring him a fame he had never dreamed of.

One day Rudolph was at the Metro studios in Hollywood, surrounded by a group of "extras" when the screenwriter June Mathis and her secretary, Florence Heinz (today the secretary of Pola Negri), happened to pass by. When seeing Rudolph, June Mathis said in a low voice to her secretary,

"Where have I seen that boy?"

Immediately, without giving her secretary time to say a word, June Mathis slapped her forehead and exclaimed, "Ah, it's Julio!"

"What Julio?"

"The character from *The Four Horsemen*, woman."

At the time, June Mathis was studying the novel by Blasco Ibáñez, adapting it for the screen and developing the characters of the play. As she imagined the lead character of Julio, she envisioned him to be exactly like Rudolph Valentino. When Mathis first saw him, she did not know him, yet she believed she was in the presence of the imaginary character, Julio. From that day on, June Mathis began to study Rudolph, albeit with some guile.

She watched him dancing in Los Angeles and wanted to see how he appeared on screen; first as a dancer and then as an actor. She convinced Metro to give her film clips of his appearance in their films; doing all this without Rudolph knowing she was considering him for the role. Satisfied

70

with all these secret tests, June Mathis began her campaign to convince Metro that Rudolph was the true incarnation of Julio from *The Four Horsemen*.

She then took a step to facilitate his being cast in the role. She managed to have Rex Ingram appointed as the film's director. Until then the now famous Irishman had not completed much important work and this was precisely why the president of the Metro, Richard Rowland, rejected him as director of *The Four Horsemen*. But June Mathis convinced Rowland of her choice of director and thus helped to discover one of the geniuses of cinematography.

Unexpectedly, Rex Ingram did not help Mathis in her campaign to have Rudolph cast as Julio. The director had another actor in mind for the role. Ingram was also a bit hostile towards Rudolph, because it seems both men once had eyes on the same woman; Alice Terry. Rex Ingram had just discovered her as an "extra" at Metro and Rudolph knew her long before as an "extra" at Universal when Alice Terry was still Alice Taffe.

After lengthy discussions, Rex Ingram and June Mathis arrived at an agreement in which each one got their way in regards to what interested them most. Alice Terry was cast in the main female role and Rudolph Valentino in the lead male role. June Mathis then traveled to New York to convince Richard Rowland and find Rudolph.

In Chicago she met with Blasco Ibáñez, who was somewhat worried because he did not know of an American actor who could satisfactorily play the role of Julio; his most important character. June Mathis reassured him by saying she was going to give the part to Rudolph Valentino.

"And who is that?" asked the Spanish novelist.

June Mathis described Rudolph for him and assured him the tests to which he had been subjected to as a dancer and as an actor convinced her he was perfect for the part. She concluded by telling him,

"But in any case, we will use a Latin type; in no way an American."

Hearing this, the author was satisfied. Richard Rowland was initially opposed to giving the two most important roles to two unknowns, Rudolph Valentino and Alice Terry. But June Mathis argued,

"The film will be so important by itself that we do not need names to make it great. On the contrary, we are going to make important names with it because it is more than sufficiently powerful for that. And in exchange for the popularity we are going to give these two young artists, they will work for reasonable pay."

Thanks to these economic considerations, Richard Rowland was convinced and it was then June Mathis wanted to meet Rudolph personally. She avoided the meeting until that time because she was afraid Rudolph had some personal appeal which might make it difficult for her to be impartial. If there was some powerful reason which prevented him from playing Julio she would have been sorry to take him out of the cast.

Valentino was working at the time with Eugene O'Brien in a film called *The Wonderful Chance*, directed by Archainbaud. One day it occurred to him to go back to the Metro offices and there a friend told him,

"Miss Mathis wants to talk to you."

"And who is she?" asked the as yet still unconscious godson of such a good godmother.

"She is the one who wrote the scenario of *The Four Horsemen* and she will be manageress of the filming. Everything about the cast is up to her."

Rudolph timidly entered Miss Mathis' office. When she told him why she wanted to see him, he began to jump with joy like a child. He signed the contract in which he would earn $350 a week, or $50 less than what they gave him in the occasional jobs he had at that time. June Mathis returned to Los Angeles feeling very satisfied and Rudolph ran to tell director Archainbaud what just happened to him. The director accelerated the work on his film so the lucky Italian would be free as soon as possible. A few days later, Valentino left for Hollywood where the film which led to his triumph and subsequent worldwide fame was filmed.

As testimony to exactly who Rudolph knew to thank for the success he achieved in this way; in the living room of director Silvano Balboni's house,[28] whose wife is June Mathis, there is a beautiful portrait of Rudolph

28 S. Balboni was a cinematographer and directed only two movies.

greeting the visitor with this significant inscription dated December 14, 1922. This when the artist was reaping the fruits of victory,

"To my dear and intelligent
June
THE ONLY ONE
I owe my triumph and the position that I occupy
in the life.
Always grateful,
RUDY"

The Four Horsemen brought other consequences to Rudolph's life. Among them was a solution to the conflict with Jean Acker. When the devious wife learned about the salary her husband was earning, she demanded it be shared with her. She filed a lawsuit in which she had the nerve to accuse Rudolph of having abandoned her when they were married and she asked the court to order him to pay her a monthly allowance for her support. She also stated Rudolph married her without having a penny and that she herself supported him and even bought him his underwear. Rudolph responded with a counter-accusation, to which he added a demand for divorce.

It would be one year before the divorce trial came to an end. But on January 10, 1922, the judge ruled in Rudolph's favor, to the point of not granting Jean Acker even the monthly allowance which was usual to assign.

Upon his new screen triumph, Rudolph was asked if he planned to marry again and he answered, raising his hand in a gesture of solemn promise,

"Not until I find a woman who is willing to give me a home and children."

He was asked that question because at that time there were rumors linking his name to Natacha Rambova, whom he met during the filming of *The Four Horsemen of the Apocalypse.*

Installment

VI

The Sly Natacha Rambova

Natacha Rambova was working as the artistic director for Alla Nazimova when Rudolph saw her for the first time at the Metro studios. At that time, the artist with the Russian name was designing the famous work of Pierre Louys, *Aphrodite*; and in these plans she acted as a collaborator with her close friend.

From the first moment Natacha caught the attention of the Italian actor Rudolph, it had more to do with curiosity than admiration. As he declared later, in privacy, Nazimova's art director seemed at first glance to be masculine. Her clothes had a certain masculine air and her shoes also looked like men's shoes. In her very behavior, nothing seemed to reveal the soul of a woman. Despite this, that rather mannish woman left a strange impression and attracted with mysterious magnetism.[29]

What Rudolph least imagined at that time was the mystery that was hidden in this impassive woman; who barely looked one side to the other. At the most, he would recognize her affiliation with the extraordinary Madame Nazimova. Perhaps he would have heard the rumors bandied about through Hollywood studios about the friendship uniting those unusual women. He would have also heard similar rumors about the relationship between Nazimova and Jean Acker. But Rambova came to be the successor of that first wife of Rudolph Valentino.

He did not know at the time, that behind the sphinx-like coldness of the stepdaughter of the multi-millionaire perfumer, Richard Hudnut, there was a mythical past which not only served to impose an expression of indifference on her face but also served to attract men with her peculiar style.

---

29 Natacha Rambova was not a stereotypical woman in regards to her dress. She was a cutting edge designer in the style of French designer Paul Poiret who emphasized loose-fitting designs and the draping of fabric for the uncorseted woman.

Natacha Rambova's original name was Winifred Shaughnessy. Her father, deceased by the time Rudolph met her, was the Colonel M. Shaughnessy. Her mother, the magnificent Mrs. Edgar De Wolfe was a member of New York's high society. She married a second husband, Richard Hudnut, who was happy to adopt his extraordinary stepdaughter. All this explains the different names Natacha often uses after her first name; Shaughnessy, De Wolfe and Hudnut. She preferred to use the pseudonym Natacha Rambova as according to authoritative persons, this exotic name brought her succeess and fame.

Besides being a spiritualist, Natacha Rambova has been fond of art since adolescence; above all of dance. In 1916, she attended, as a disciple, the classical dance academy run by the Russian dancer Theodore Kosloff in New York. Natacha admired the method of this teacher and decided to pursue a career as a dancer. Her mother of course screamed loudly in protest[30]. What would the world say if a Miss De Wolfe went about kicking her legs in the air and in those hellish theaters[31]! Impossible! But the girl assured her distinguished mother that Theodore Kosloff was the only person who could develop her artistic abilities which she indeed possessed and she insisted on continuing studying with him against her mother's will.

As her mother continued to protest Winifred's vocation, one day young Winifred disappeared from her home and for months. In vain, numerous detectives searched for her throughout the world. In vain, several senators, diplomats, politicians, bankers, etc. intervened in the extensive investigation. In vain, the mother spent a fortune paying for the laborious effort to find her daughter.

Winifred De Wolfe was finally discovered dancing on stage in Chicago, already a dancer in Theodore Kosloff's company. When Winifred De Wolfe resurfaced, she explained her prolonged absence to her mother by saying she went to England to educate herself and traveled to other European countries to study classical dance. Theodore Kosloff testified Winifred was telling the truth.

It is clear the dance instructor of the distinguished Miss De Wolfe referred to her in a gentlemanly way and denied categorically there was any love affair between him and her. But the aristocratic dancer, Winifred rejected her high social position to dedicate her life to dance and her love of art. It would be this love which would unite her with Theodore Kosloff.

However, the authorities thought it appropriate to further investigate their relationship and detectives spent a few nights in

---

30 t.n.: *Puso el grito en el cielo* - (put the scream in the sky) - screamed loudly in protest.

31 t.n.: *Teatros de Dios* - (God's theaters) - hellish theaters.

Winifred's hotel. Kosloff was then summoned to the offices of the Department of Justice where he endured a lengthy interrogation. Whether he was right or wrong, the investigation suddenly ceased. The splendid Mrs. De Wolfe became convinced her daughter Winifred had a future as a dancer and consequently considered it appropriate to reconcile with her. This is how Natacha learned not only dancing but the art of attracting men by observing them without being noticed; in this she slyly led them to believe she was indifferent to them.

Rudolph Valentino returned to see Natacha when he worked in the movie *Uncharted Seas* with Metro. That second encounter was due to Natacha herself and was not accidental.

At the time, Madame Alla Nazimova needed to urgently resolve the problem of casting the young gallant for her film, *Camille*. At the last minute, she realized that the actor she intended to cast was not available. Searching through the young actors roaming the Hollywood studios, she could not find a suitable candidate. She searched for a dark young man, slender, beautiful, passionate and especially one who would be convincing in love scenes. Upon hearing these characteristics, Natacha recalled an Italian actor she saw in the Metro studios.

"I know of an Italian young actor who I believe would fill that role perfectly. His name is Rudolph Valentino," the aloof young woman said to Nazimova.

"But does he know how to make love?" Madame Nazimova asked.

"I do not know! Judging by his appearance, however, he should know. Why not test him?"

The Russian artist Nazimova summoned Rudolph Valentino and after a brief interview she cast him in the role. It was then he was formally introduced to Natacha and enjoyed his first chance to chat with her. This conversation served to confirm his previous impression of her which had left him speechless.

After that unexpected exchange, they continued to meet often and little by little, the sphinx became more communicative. So much so that by the end of the filming of *Uncharted Seas*, Rudolph invited Natacha to go out with him. She accepted his invitation. It was just by chance they went to the house of the Russian doctor Samuel Levin, where a party was being held. There Rudolph and Natacha danced together for the first time.

It was also there the ice was broken. Although Natacha did not effuse greatly over the Italian, he felt a hint of friendship from that woman whom he thought previously to be cold. This allowed him to go to sleep that night full of illusions.

A few days later, the shooting of *Camille* began and Rudolph and Natacha, as collaborators, met daily. It did not take long for them to enjoy a certain degree of intimacy. Natacha deigned to become a humble groomer as she fixed Rudolph's hair befitting his film character of Armando Duval. Very soon the ardent lover and the aloof woman were good friends.

Many nights as they left work, they would spend a few hours together, reading, or walking or driving. They discovered they had similar passions; above all with regard to literature, music and art. Natacha also intrigued her new friend in the phenomena of spiritualism. Gradually, their friendship evolved into love. That woman who seemed so cold, so indifferent, knew how to stir her mystery in the heart of the man who would soon be known to the world as the greatest lover of the screen.

At last, it seemed that good winds were beginning to blow into the stormy life of Rudolph Valentino. In his intimate life, a woman provided consolation for the cruelty of his past full of vicissitudes and in his professional life he began to savor the first fruits of triumph. It is true that in *Uncharted Seas* and *Camille*, he worked for the same salary which was still relatively low. This was three-hundred and fifty dollars a week, the same as he received for *The Four Horsemen of the Apocalypse*.

As the most famous work of Blasco Ibáñez was being exhibited across the United States, Rudolph's reputation grew. When June Mathis appointed him as lead actor in *The Conquering Power*, the young actor dared to ask for an increase of $100 a week. After a great deal of arguing with Rex Ingram, with whom he would never establish a friendship, Rudolph was granted $400 weekly. His awareness of his success was already taking root and this, by itself, filled him with happiness.

When work on *The Conquering Power* was complete, Rudolph recognized that the initially important role assigned to him by his great friend June Mathis was being considerably reduced. He then left Metro, and signed with the Famous Players-Lasky studios to film *The Sheik*, earning a salary of $500 a week.

In his next film, *Moran of the Lady Letty*, his salary was raised to $700. Then, in a movie titled, *Beyond the Rocks*, his paychecks reached $1000. He was then contractually obliged to continue to provide his services for that same salary, during a period which was deemed mandatory. As agreed after *Beyond the Rocks*, he would film, *Blood and Sand* in Spain and under the direction of George Fitzmaurice. These conditions, however, were excluded from the contract signed on January 22, 1922, and the exclusion of those conditions would soon cause much trouble.

Under such increasing prosperity and while falling in love, Rudolph could not help but think of creating the home he dreamed about for so many years. If he did not marry Natacha right away, it was because he had not yet been able to legally divorce his first wife. As we have seen in the previous chapter, he would not succeed in this until January 10, 1922; and even then he was granted the divorce in such a way which required him to wait one year for the divorce to become final before being able to marry another woman.

Meanwhile, Rudolph and Natacha adapted to the circumstance to the best of their ability by living together just the same as they had been doing before the aforementioned ruling. They were so intimately linked in the divorce proceedings that a "Miss Winifred Shaughnessy" was named as co-respondent; she, it will be remembered, was none other than Natacha Rambova.

In search of a solution to their love problem which was causing them so much worry, they learned it was a usual practice in similar cases to travel to Mexico to be married according to a more liberal law. Many consultations were completed by Rudolph and Natacha to verify the legality of the procedure and ensure it would be satisfactory.

On May 13, 1922, Rudolph, Natacha, Dr. Floretta Mansfield White and Douglas Gerrard arrived by car to the home of Mr. Otto Moller, mayor of Mexicali, Mexico. They were received with open arms by the representative of that city's citizenry who immediately dictated orders for the wedding to be celebrated as befitting the now famous movie star, Rudolph Valentino. Both Rudolph and Natacha asked several officials if the ceremony celebrated in Mexicali would be considered legal in California. There was no one present who did not answer them satisfactorily.

Champagne was being served from the time of their arrival. Judge Tolentino Sandoval arrived and an orchestra was set up along with a government band. General laughter ensued. With the pronouncement of the technical legal sentences, Rudolph and Natacha were declared husband and wife; after which the couple christened their official union with a kiss full of love.

The band played a nuptial march which was accompanied by the tinkling of champagne glasses as the wedding party participants toasted the eternal joy of the bride and groom. The couple received the congratulations of the prominent local officials, including the governor. Meanwhile, beautiful ladies presented bouquets of flowers to the bride. This was followed by a great banquet and speeches both in Spanish and English.

At the end of this animated party it was announced that the music, flowers, food and champagne was a generous gift from the municipal authorities. The guests did not have to pay a single penny. Several years later, Rudolph remembered with sincere enthusiasm how generously the Mayor of Mexicali entertained him and his wedding party and he was full of praise for Mexican hospitality.

At one o'clock in the morning on the following day, May 14, the wedding party arrived in Palm Springs (California), where the couple settled into a cottage to enjoy a few days of tranquility. The husband and wife had not yet risen from their country beds when the press in Los Angeles, and that of all the United States, began to generate the furor which turned that modest and innocent ceremony, held in the hospitable house of the mayor of Mexicali, into a national scandal.

According to the Los Angeles District Attorney's office, Jean Acker alleged Rudolph had just committed bigamy, as according to the law he was still married to her. As soon as the scandalous news in the press reached Rudolph and Natacha's tranquil retreat in Palm Springs, they suspended their barely begun honeymoon and hurried back to Los Angeles to contest the terrible accusation. Natacha then headed to New York in the comforting company of her favorite Pekinese puppy "Ruddy", whose name should not be confused with Rudy or Rudie, as she was familiarly calling Rudolph.

In almost every town during her arduous transcontinental voyage, Natacha received a loving telegram signed, "Your Bambino", which she answered immediately with no less affection. After several days of traveling, Natacha's curious traveling companions would have debarked and left her sphinx-like presence without even knowing her voice, if she had not pronounced energetically,

"I will never give up on him, never, and I'm going back to Hollywood soon."

After legal consultations, Rudolph was summoned to the District Attorney's office on the afternoon of May 20. He was charged with the crime of bigamy and upon his appearance there he ran the risk of being kept in jail for two days. This because it was a Saturday and all the banks and their offices were closed. With most of his friends outside the city for the week-end, it was difficult for Rudolph to raise his $10,000 bail. Without that sum, he could no longer continue to enjoy his freedom and Rudolph did not possess that amount of money by any means.

As he himself told me a few years later, the Famous Players-Lasky studio executives refused to provide his bail. And at the time his friends whom he most confidently could ask for such a favor, were nowhere to be found. It was Thomas Meighan who arrived to help before anyone else. Thomas Meighan; the same person who made Rudolph Valentino cry at the house of Pauline Frederick as he reproached him for the embarrassing sins attributed to him during his unhappy New York life.

Thomas Meighan arrived with a certified check made out in the amount of $10,000 in case a real estate bond was not considered sufficient. Soon after, the director George Melford arrived and also as always, Rudolph's opportune friend, June Mathis. They all prepared to free their friend Rudolph. Subsequent offers of help arrived from movie industry mogul, Joseph M. Schenck, the playwright Richard W. Tully, director James Young and others. A few months before dying, Rudolph told me about this event in his life, speaking with great pride and gratitude,

"After having been so impatient awaiting the arrival of the first $10,000, it turned out that a few hours after my arrest, I had a large fortune at my disposal."

And then, in concluding his praise for his friends,

"Good grief! I will never forget that act by Tom Meighan because, in reality, he was the one I would least expect. We were not close friends and actually much less."

During the ensuing legal process, the authorities intended to demonstrate that Rudolph and Natacha lived as husband and wife in California after the wedding held in Mexicali. This meant they had broken California law. This legal interpretation was unusual because the alleged crime was then considered usual and commonly practiced. Rudolph's defense lawyers accused the District Attorney's office of forcing this interpretation of the law in this particular case as it had never been done in similar cases. They attributed such an interpretation to the desire for notoriety to gain political advantage, demonstrating that the theoretical caretakers of society were not hesitating to charge an innocent and honorable man with a crime.

During his trial on bigamy, the only testimony against Rudolph and Natacha was the statement of the waitress Romualda Lugo. She said she saw them in their cottage in Palm Springs having breakfast and wearing their pajamas, these being, for the most part, purple. Those infamous pajamas "starred" in this curious legal process, somewhat dousing it in comedy.

Fortunately, the defense lawyers rose to the situation and showed clearly that the clothing described in court as pajamas to suggest intimacy, was nothing more than a light clothing in the Chinese style which could be used decorously around the house at any time; especially in a warm climate such as Palm Springs. Thanks to this argument, Rudolph was exonerated by the judge on June 5. The judge further warned him that he did not have the right to live with another woman until the legal deadline necessary for his divorce had passed.

When the judge finished reading his decision, the numerous flappers present rejoiced and rushed towards Rudolph with the intention of congratulating him more closely. The great lover was forced to sneak away to avoid their loving grasps.

A few weeks later he began work on the film, *The Young Rajah*. Meanwhile, Natacha waited impatiently at Foxlair, the country house of her stepfather, in North Creek (New York State).

The following letters (shared with me by Rudolph) shed no little light on that time in the life of the great movie lover. All of them came from Foxlair and were written by Natacha during the summer of 1922.

(A letter addressed to "Gerry", Douglas Gerrard)

"Dear Gerry,
You say in your telegram that you can not understand my point of view, this proves that you do not understand me in any way, because otherwise, you would not have send me such a message. He was not the only one who suffered hysterical attacks because of that phone call. It seems that you two believe that I have nothing to do but distrust him and believe that he is out there with other women, while the truth is that I do not even think about that anymore.

One woman or a hundred it does not matter anymore. I do not care. If you could try to understand instead of jumping to conclusions. All I want or care about is having him with me again and I can not stand the continual setbacks. Every time I make a plan or shelter any hope, everything comes down once more. When a letter arrives from you, I will return it unopened, since I don't know, by your telegram, what it contains and I can not take any more.

If you do not understand this, it is just too bad. I'm too tired to try to explain myself better. If you were not such a good friend, I would not care what you think. But I will still love you, anyway, for what you have done for Rudie, even though you have made me suffer more than you imagine.
N. "

(A second letter to Douglas Gerrard)

"Dear Gerry,
Thank you very much for your more than appreciated letter, which came to me last night. Of course, you had a lot of reasons to be angry when you received my letter. As for me, Gerry, please do me the favor of believing that I fully trust you and that I know that you have been my best friend, as well as Rudolph's, and that you are helping us in everything so that we can see each other again.[32]

I am currently terribly worried about what I think I should do and want to do most of all in the world. Rudolph will probably have received my letter by this date and he will have told you how things are, as you will understand, I am dying to return home, but I can not ignore the advice of all or run the risk of ruining the future and the career of Rudie. I would never forgive myself; and it would remain between him and me for a lifetime, even if the fault was not mine.

After the stupid advice that G.[33] *gave us before, it is natural that your opinion does not inspire much confidence now that everyone advises me otherwise. G. is a good lawyer, but he does not realize how much the public opinion and the press opinion matter to Rudie. Perhaps the best thing I could do is go abroad with my mother and convince Rudie to make his next film in Europe.*

But I hope everything is fixed in no more than a week. The idea of having to leave makes me feel weak. I know that you will continue to help us and that you will advise him what suits him the best. But his career must be considered first of all since that will mean his happiness. Nothing else for now. Do not stop giving me news of you when you have time. With all my love for my dear and loyal friend Gerry.
N. "

(A letter addressed to "Rudie" regarding his Daydreams poetry)

"Beloved,
I received your poems last night. According to what I telegraphed you today, I think they are good. Actually, very good and to be commended even if they lack in that something in which you shine.

With them, we should go far; so it seems better to wait, another eight or ten days, for a few others with better themes in order to present them as advantageously as possible. "The Fickle Boat" is really splendid, but the

---

32 This letter seems to contradict Cué's previous statement that Natacha forbid Rudolph's friendship with Douglas Gerrard.

others, although good, are not extraordinary enough to serve as samples. We need some with more fantastical imagination, some passionate, some whose value lies more in the plot and others which are more oriental.

Do not forget the idea which the public has formed of you and which should guide us; this being the unusual and something useful for a few out of the ordinary illustrations.This volume must be very rare and exceptional as well as appealing to the general public. Do you remember the story which I once told you; the one about women-orchids? I think it would serve to make a fascinating poem with a wonderful opportunity for an unconventional illustration.

The story, in a few words, refers to a gardener whose hobby and passion consisted of collecting orchids. He learns that a mysterious orchid is found in the undergrowth of an African region. He moves to Africa and, at last, runs into a tribe telling him of a gigantic flower which grows in the bush, not far from there. They tell him it is a cursed plant and that in the night it emits a strong odor and whoever smells it loses his mind. The gardener laughs at this, considering it only as a superstition of an uncivilized tribe.

Then he tries to induce them to guide him to that place; but they are afraid and refuse, limiting themselves to orienting him so he can go there alone. After wandering through the undergrowth for a day or two, one night he is attracted by a wonderful and subjugating perfume as well as by an iridescent light shining through the dense vegetation.

Guided by the light, the gardener comes to find the magnificent orchid which appears as a flickering flame. It is about three feet in diameter and consists of all the colors of fire; scarlet, orange, yellow, etc. In addition to this, from the center of the flower radiate tentacles, like fingers of various lengths which are endowed with life and extend outward. It also has luminous virtues, which emits the faint light which at first attracted the gardener's attention.

He is full of joy at his wonderful and beautiful find and takes the plant with him. He then places his trophy in a special corner of his garden. As the days pass, the flower fascinates him more and more and he believes he sees in it the soul of a woman. At last, he only lives to wait for the sunset and go to spend the night uner the spell of the fragrance, light and beauty of his flower. It seems to him that a woman breathes and lives in the flower. In the heart of that flower you could see the soul and the face of the woman-orchid. The long, flame-colored tentacles, always in motion, seem to caress him and hold him in a passionate embrace. One morning he is found dead in his garden

---

33 Referring to Rudolph Valentino's lawyer in Los Angeles, W. I. Gilbert.

with the tentacles of the flower tightly wound around him. I think the story is fascinating.

And I could suggest or bring to mind the vision of a beautiful woman carrying an orchid or the view of the Florida undergrowth. You can do something wonderful with this and I'm sure Adela St. Johns[34] will agree with me. This could become the top poem and I have an idea for a truly amazing illustration. It depends on how it interests you.

You must put extraordinary things in the poems and the topics must be fascinating as well. Last night I received your letter written after receiving that terrible telegram from me. My beloved child, I know you are having a lot of patience and that you do what you can to understand me when my exasperation overwhelms me. I also do everything I can to control myself and not to worry you, little boy.

You do not know how the strain exhausts me; it's so hard! And it seems that I'm going from bad to worse. Instead of correcting myself, despite what I do. Nor does it ever leave me, the fear that this will separate us in the end. If you could hurry up and come before it's too late!

Try to have a little patience and I will also try to master myself as best I can. My imagination seems to be always active and exaggerating and I can not stop it. I anxiously await your letter telling me of your plans. I hope that this time we can make them. Things are getting so discouraging! That's all for now, my life. I must close, because A ... is waiting to take the correspondence.

All my love is for you, little boy. If I did not love you, I would not be so excited, nor would it excite you either; but I can not manage life without you. A million kisses of love and tenderness.

Your naughty – LITTLE DOLL. "

(The volume of verses referred to in this letter is the one with the title *Day Dreams*, published by Rudolph Valentino in 1923. In this, however, the poems, "The Fickle Boat" and "The Orchid Women" to which the letter particularly refers are not included. In any case, the strange mention of the writer Adela St. Johns in relation to Valentino's poems is not without interest.)

Despite the name of Rudolph Valentino circulating around the world because of the fame established by *The Four Horsemen*, *The Sheik* and *Blood and Sand*, the Italian actor was struggling in a sea of difficult setbacks.

---

34 Adela Rogers St. John (1894-1988) was an American journalist, screenplay writer and novelist.

Besides living apart from the woman he loved, he was tormented by the anxieties she was suffering as a result of being his love. His financial arrangement made with Jean Acker cost him a few thousand dollars and the accusation of bigamy also cost him no small amount of money. His employers, Paramount, who had not helped raise his bail, also refused to assign him a salary which corresponded to his rapidly growing popularity.

Blood and Sand was not filmed in Spain or directed by George Fitzmaurice, despite Rudolph's request. Far from helping him to increase his professional prestige, the film company put him to work in a new movie, *The Young Rajah*, which they felt could not diminish him in the eyes of his public.

During that time frame, when Rudolph was envied by so many actors who witnessed his sudden rise, I present one of his checks for a miserable $17.50, which I have in my possession. This was returned with a note reporting that the account was overdrawn. Rudolph had to mortgage his house in Whitley Heights (Hollywood) for the amount of $5,000.

However, rather than being exploited by Paramount or allowing his name to be used in mediocre movies designed just to exploit the public's interest, Rudolph had the courage to go on strike. The formidable movie company then took the matter to court and obtained a ruling prohibiting him from working for any other film company for a long time.

Despite the difficulties such a situation implied, the actor did not give up.[35] He waited patiently for the time to pass before he could marry. And finally, Rudolph Valentino and Natacha Rambova were legally united as husband and wife in Crowne Point (Indiana), on March 14, 1923, with Mrs. Werner (aunt of the bride) and two or three other friends present. One wedding guest occupying a preferential place, was the beloved Pekinese dog of the popular lover's second wife.

---

35 t.n.: *No dio su brazo a torcer* - (did not give his arm to sprain) - did not give up.

Installment

VII

Honeymoon

Shortly before Rudolph and Natacha married in Crowne Point (Indiana), they met Samuel George Ullman, a businessman who was destined to play a role of great importance in the life of Rudolph Valentino. Ullman, at that time, was working with the manufacturing company of the famous Mineralava clay, which was advertised at that time as an effective means of beautifying the skin.

As a businessman, Ullman knew Rudolph Valentino was overwhelmed by debts and responsibilities and discouraged by the difficulties preventing his professional and economic development. The legal triumph of Paramount tied Rudolph's hands. According to the judicial mandate, he was prohibited from acting professionally and this referred to both silent and spoken scenes.

Despite the social position to which his artistic fame elevated him, Rudolph could not offer his wife the one gift which even the humblest couples usually enjoy when they get married; a honeymoon. Additionally, Rudolph's lawyer charged him no less than two-thousand-five-hundred dollars a week for legally orchestrating his financial break down.

In such a grievous state of affairs, Rudolph, whose imagination had adapted to the practical habits of the Americans for ten years, found only one resource worthy of his artistic soul; to write poetry.

Here follows the prologue of his book *Day Dreams*, published shortly after, in the same year of 1923.

"PREFACE

To you, gentle reader, I wish to say a few words of warning before you read the contents of this volume. I am neither a poet nor a scholar. Therefore, you will find neither poems nor prose. Only dreams - reveries - a bit of romanticism, a bit of sentimentality, a little philosophy, not studied, but acquired through the constant observation of the greatest teacher: Nature.

While I remained idle, not through choice but because forcibly kept from my preferred and actual field of activity, I took to dreams to forget the tediousness of worldly struggle and the boredom of jurisprudence's pedantic etiquette. I will be happy, indeed, if my Day Dreams will bring you as much enjoyment in the reading as they brought me in the writing.

Rudolph Valentino - New York, May 29, 1923. "

Rudolph's compositions are, according to what he himself says in one of them, "ultramodern rhymes", and are dedicated collectively; "To J.C.N.G. and my friends here and there", with many of them having individual dedications no less mysterious.

Here, translated into a humble prose format, are some of those ultramodern rhymes.

" To M.

The serenade of a thousand years ago, the song of a hushed lip, lives forever in the glass of today. Wherein we see the reflection of it if we but brush away the cobwebs of a doubting faith.

You

Your eyes. Your eyes, mystic pools of beauteous light. Golden brown in color, deep, yet amber clear. Unshadowed by a frown, fathomless, wherein my senses drown. Your eyes. Your lips. Your lips, twin silken petals of a dewy rose. Altar of the heart, where love, kindling desire, worships unafraid. Crucible of the passions. The rose in masquerade. Your lips. Your kiss, your kiss, a flame of passion's fire. The sensitive seal of love. In the desire, the fragrance of your caress. Alas, at times I find exquisite bitterness in your kiss.

Morphia

I am the ingrate Morphia. You hold the brimming cup of your life. To me, athirst I am, and drink my fill, of strength, until the cup is drained dry. Then, satisfied I care no more. The cup, I cast away, crunch 'neath my heel, its doom I seal, as I walk on my way.

Mirage

Happiness! You wait for us just beyond, just beyond. We know not where, nor how we shall find you, We only know you are waiting, waiting, waiting, just beyond.

Three Generations of Kissses

A Mother's kisses are blessed with love, straight from the heart of heaven above. Love's benediction, her dear caress, the sum of all our happiness. Til' we kiss the lips of the mate of our soul, we never know love has reached its goal. Caress divine, you reign until a baby's kiss seems sweeter still. That beloved blossom, a baby's face, seems to be love's resting place. And a million kisses tenderly linger there in ecstasy. Were I told to select just one kiss a day; oh! what a puzzle I would say. Still a baby's kiss I'd choose, you see, for in that wise choice I'd gain all three."

While Rudolph so beautifully solved the arduous problems preventing him from developing in his earthly life, more practical daydreaming forged another solution which while not exactly spiritual, could also have the honor of being described as ultramodern.

Ullman tells in his interesting work titled, *Valentino As I Knew Him*, how in regards to the interests of the Mineralava Company and the situation of Rudolph Valentino and Natacha Rambova when he met them, he devised an original idea which seemed to serve both the troubles of Rudolph and Natacha while generating a substantial advertising campaign for the clay which improved the skin.

Ullman realized Rudolph was, above all, a famous dancer and that dance was also Natacha's original profession. He made sure the court ruling, which forbade Rudolph to earn a living as an actor, did not prevent him either expressly nor implicitly, from performing as a dancer. Rudolph and Natacha could, therefore, create a program of attractive dances and tour the theaters of the United States. In this way they could obtain more profit than any other pair of dancers. And if, at the time they made such an extensive tour, they publicized the clay, the Mineralava Company, represented by Ullman, would benefit from the project.

The proposal was so tempting, Rudolph and Natacha accepted Ullman's idea instantly and they were soon booked to perform in theaters in prominent American cities on a tour of about four months. They would earn seven thousand dollars a week. In exchange for this fabulous salary, the couple would perform exotic dances in every show and announce to their audiences, and in a convincing way, that the beauty of Natacha's skin was due solely and exclusively to the use of the Mineralava clay.

There is no doubt Rudolph took great pleasure in writing those poems he shared with the public in the form of a book. But it was not a great sacrifice for him to give up that pleasure in order to undertake the advertisement of the clay which supposedly beautified his wife's skin. Such an activity could be useful in forgetting the annoyance of his worldly struggles and the boredom of the pedantic formulas of jurisprudents; all while providing abundant and welcome dollars.

On the other hand, Natacha, while helping her husband achieve such goals in which she herself was no less interested, pursued other goals whose success would be facilitated by the dancing tour which Ullman proposed to them. One of Natacha's purposes, apparently, was conquering Rudolph's will to the fullest extent. She had in her favor, to subjugate him, the love he professed to her, his eagerness as a disciple in spiritual matters and the desire to preserve at all costs his conjugal bliss.

Natacha faced other challenges, as Rudolph's friends also exerted a great influence on him and threatened her efforts; both with their witty remarks on the subject of Natacha's dominant character and with their constant invitations to conjugal infidelity.

Most of Rudolph's closest friends were single and accustomed to carousing in their daily life. They were not able to understand how a newlywed should have more wise intentions and live with such utmost honesty. They could scarcely respect such a commitment.

Rudolph used to visit the homes of some of these friends, where more than once he received visits from his female admirers. Notwithstanding the care he placed in being punctual to fulfill a commitment with Natacha, it was not unusual for some fortuitous circumstance to force him to arrive very late. His secret adventures with these friends would often been revealed by the smell of alcohol on his breath, by some strange perfume or by some other indication which could be recognized by an intelligent and strong woman like Natacha.

As a woman of her temperment, she often gave advice to her husband and drove away from his company those who represented a threat to their conjugal harmony, as she herself perceived it to be.

The following letter was sent at that time by a beautiful woman to one of those very friends of Rudolph Valentino. This gives the idea of the situation which forced Natacha Rambova to isolate her husband from those who called themselves friends, mainly because of their continual carousing.

"Sweet D,

I regret very, very much that I have not seen you once again. I was with Rudolph when you telephoned him and I told him to give you my affectionate memories. But when he gave them to you. . . there was no answer.

One of two; either you did not want to receive my love or you had already hung up the telephone. I hope the latter is true. Rudolph is so charming! But he is so excessively and terribly married, that he has not a minute left to dedicate to me and I do not even have the right to condemn him for it. But it does make me suffer. Really. Do you understand?

I like to be the main lady occupying his center stage. I need to always be "the best friend", "the best lover" or "the best enemy", and it is clear as far as Rudolph is concerned that I am now not able to play any of these roles.

Anyway, it is certain that there is nobody in the whole nation who can stop me from loving him. Is that not true? As for you, young man, I think I should warn you that the next time I trip over to New York, I will tear you physically out of all your conferences and all your commitments, whether they refer to business or anything else. Then, between you and me, we'll kidnap Rudolph!

Well ... at least for a little while. We will ruthlessly break the ties that bind him to that family and home. I've promised myself a dance with him and I want you to help me get it.

Cheer up!
K. "

The advertising of the virtues of the Mineralava clay could be profitable from many points of view, so much so that Natacha would accept the proposal with the same enthusiasm as Rudolph. Just married in Crowne Point (Indiana), they traveled on to Chicago where they rode to the luxuriously customized train car awaiting them. They then launched the famous tour, which at the same time acted as an unusually productive honeymoon.

They began their intriguing artistic and commercial campaign in the city of Omaha, where years before Natacha Rambova reappeared after having been sensationally lost for some months. In Omaha's main theater, as they did in all the others in which they were exhibited during the seventeen week tour, they danced the Argentine tango which Rudolph popularized in *The Four Horsemen of the Apocalypse*.

They also performed another dance choreographed for them with elements derived from Russian and Indian dances. As the crowning element of the program, Rudolph delivered a short speech in which he praised the virtues of Mineralava Beauty Clay. The dancer solemnly swore that the beauty of his beloved wife's skin, which the world admired and which was then affected by a slight and enhancing blush, was due to the miracle of the mud.

The words of the dancer, deliberately pronounced as a solemn oath, convinced more than a few listeners of both sexes to buy the praised clay and slather it on their faces. They then confidently awaited for their complexion to become as admirable as that of the beautiful Natacha Rambova. And sometimes the Mineralava Beauty Clay converts obtained convincing results.

By then, those two fervent apostles of the virtues of the clay were already many miles away, performing before another audience no less admiring and easy to convince. They were again dancing the tango and the Russian and Indian dances, preaching with exemplary faith the wonders of the magical clay while enjoying another seven thousand dollars in payment for their week's work. They were also remedying the economic damages caused by the series of calamities which until then plagued the Italian actor's American life.

In addition to the material benefit, which alone would have sufficed to satisfy both dancers, the tour helped to realize Rudolph Valentino's enormous popularity both in the United States and in Canada, where they also performed as if they were Mercury and Terpsichore. Rudolph was welcomed as a popular hero everywhere. It became a holiday when the dancer arrived for the first time in any town and in some towns the schools were closed to allow students to participate in the reception.

Rudolph then realized the importance his name had for the American people. Ullman was also convinced and because of this he decided to accept the position of manager of Rudolph's interests. This, despite his rejecting the job offer when the dancer offered it to him two and a half months earlier when the tour began .

Meanwhile, Natacha was consummating her conquest of her popular husband. As she developed her own spiritual strength, so this accentuated a certain weakness in her husband's soul. Before his lady, this manifested in the form of an increasingly affected chivalrous behavior. With her husband's dangerous friends far away, Natacha moved him further away from those who, without providing any of the gifts characterizing true friendship, expected to be treated as perfect friends.

Those estrangements, initiated by Natacha Rambova, gave rise to disagreements and bans which caused displeasure even with people who truly held their marriage in high regard. It is clear these troubles were increased by the intrigues of those who were less worthy of esteem.

The following is a fragment of a letter, written during the middle of the dancing tour. Rudolph admonishes his friend, Douglas Gerrard, about his friendship with a certain banned person. In addition, he refers to other interesting points, namely Paramount, as being fundamental in his concerns at the time.

"Frankly speaking, if I was in your place, I would have remained neutral, instead of favoring one side or the other. You say I was wrong in judging M ...... I wish it were so! But as you know, I've known him for a long time and I know very well what I'm saying. I think I've devoted too much time to an issue as uninteresting as this one so I'll put a period on it and move on to something else.

I'm really glad you came back to California and I hope that when this letter reaches your hands I will find you very busy in the direction of a film. By the way, I saw Dick Roland in Chicago and he told me that he did not understand how he has not seen you again. After having told you that his company did not like the kind of plotline you had chosen, he also told me that if you're going to see him again, he would find you a scenario and give you a chance with First National.

He told me he would have given you the opportunity with First National, not because of Rex's recommendation (since, judging by what I gathered from our conversation, he gives it as little importance as I do), but by June's recommendation and by mine.

My tour progresses very satisfactorily and I have no more than nine weeks, because I have no interest in committing myself for a long period of time, given that the Paramount issue can be resolved at any time. "

And in fact, Valentino's conflict with the powerful company which caused so much trouble to him and which introduced radical changes in his life, did not take long to settle. During his tour as a dancer, he signed a contract with J. D. Williams, agreeing to make films under certain conditions and for a company which would be formed with the special objective of filming and distributing his films.

The film's scenarios would be selected by Rudolph and his wife, who, in this manner could pursue in a practical way, her secret ambition to influence the movie business and her ascendancy over her husband's career. The company came to be formed as the "Ritz Carlton Pictures, Incorporated"; but far from being an independent company, as Rudolph dreamed, it was a subsidiary, well disguised, of the powerful Paramount. Mr. Williams was sent to secure the services of Rudolph Valentino in any way possible.

Before filming the movies for Paramount and those for Ritz Carlton, Rudolph and Natacha wished to enjoy a true honeymoon as the one they spent while touring the United States was far from satisfying the requirements of a classic honeymoon. At the end of July 1923, Rudolph and his wife, accompanied by Mrs. T. K. Werner, aunt of Natacha, embarked for Europe on the steamship "Aquitaine". It was the first trip Rudolph made to his homeland since he said goodbye some ten years earlier in the month of December 1913, to try his fortune in North America like so many other young emigrants.

What Rudolph least imagined in those distant moments as he sailed west on board the steamer "Cleveland", was that he would return as an idol of the screen. He would also return as a great dancer at the peak of the enormous popularity which he had just enjoyed on a tour of North American theaters. And yet, despite all he suffered in America, despite all the setbacks preventing the realization of his innocent ideals, it was indisputable that his return to his homeland was one of the happiest periods of his life.

That adoration of the vast population of American Yankees was not only a satisfaction for his exagerrated vanity as a man and as an artist but a flattering promise for his future ambition and well-being. It was also a vindication of his wretched name; a compensation for all the troubles he confronted in his emigration. In addition, his success removed the most burdensome part of his debts and launched various businesses which would allow him to soon be in a position of happy economic relief.

And as if this prospect did not provide enough happiness, he had at his side a proud wife; beautiful, cultured, loved, whom he was convinced was the right partner to build the healthy and cheerful home his romantic spirit dreamed of. He was perfectly ready to undertake, after brief wanderings, new struggles to achieve greater triumphs.

In such conditions, Rudolph Valentino set sail on the Atlantic again with fewer illusions than when he crossed it years before in pursuit of his first adventures in a new world. He returned as a conqueror who, in full youth, was returning to his motherland to give a report of his conquests and find renewed vigor with which to undertake future ones.

There was only one sad memory marring his happiness. He would not find his mother whom he left sobbing when sailing first for America. His mother had been dead for five years having past away before he triumphed. Rudolph left Italy in 1913 with the illusion of making a fortune and hoped to reward his mother with gifts. When he returned, he was saddened by the sorrow of not being able to include her as a participant in his happy venture.

The beginning of August, the three travelers arrived at the sumptuous chateau of Juan-les-Pins which the stepfather of Natacha owned in the surroundings of Nice, over-looking the luminous panorama of the French Riviera, the Côte d'Azur .

Soon after, the couple and aunt set out on a trip by car through Italy. In Milan, Rudolph's sister joined the caravan. They then continued on to Florence. Then, in Rome, Natacha contracted a slight cold which alarmed her and this prompted her return to Juan-les-Pins to be cared for by her mother while the others continued the excursion. It was during that brief stay in Rome, Rudolph met the colossus of the screen whom he sincerely admired, Emil Jannings. At the time, Jannings was filming the movie *Quo Vadis*.

From Rome, Rudolph, his sister María and Mrs. Werner made a special trip to Campobasso to visit his brother Alberto; who was at that time the city clerk. For three unforgettable days, Rudolph enjoyed the company of his brother, his sister-in-law, Ada, and above all his nephew Jean. In addition to finding satisfaction because of his love for children and his longing to see his family, Rudolph was particularly flattered to see how very much his nephew, Jean resembled him.

In those three days, despite Rudolph's great American triumphs, he envied the state of supreme happiness of fatherhood which his older brother achieved. His brother had done so without so many victories, but also without so many sacrifices and while living a quiet life in the homeland.

After having received this gentle balm of homemade happiness, Rudolph went on to Castellaneta and Taranto where he spent his childhood and adolescence. He also went to Perugia, where, in addition to visiting the Collegio della Sapienza, in which he received part of his education, he placed flowers on the tomb of the poetess Vittoria Aganoor Pompilj, his cultured and affectionate counselor when he was a teenager.

Rudolph traveled those locales with his spirit saturated with a mixture of joy and sorrow found only when one returns from the harsh realities of life to familiar locations which are imagined so differently. The deft American idol, cried and laughed as if he had returned to the innocence of his childhood, embued even more with the pleasure of a loving man rather than of just an actor.

After reveling in those memories and feeling stung by his natural reactions, he was motivated by good intentions which stimulated him to undertake even more arduous enterprises. Rudolph left his beloved homeland, where he was barely noticed, and would never return.

He spent Christmas in the chateau of Juan-les-Pins, in the company of his wife, her parents and aunt. He passed a few more days in the midst of that Mediterranean beauty which his soul always enjoyed. In that sumptuous chateau, Rudolph passed some of the happiest days of his life.

That happiness was not only caused by his stay in the palace of his wealthy father-in-law. It was inspired by the beautiful and comfortable residence, the dear and affectionate company he enjoyed and at the same time, the flattery of the people surrounding him, the tranquility of a well-earned vacation, the memories of his homeland, the contemplation of a home, the consciousness of triumph, the caresses of love and the hope of a child; which would be his greatest dream.

Overflowing with happiness, on January 3, he returned to embark with Natacha. The end of their prolonged and interesting honeymoon was approaching and it was necessary to return to his life of conquests.

Installment

VIII

Another Marital Failure

As soon as Rudolph and Natacha arrived in New York, they began filming *Monsieur Beaucaire*. The couple's determination reigned supreme during the making of the film, with Natacha in command despite her having no experience either as a director or as a film producer. Her previous experience was only in artistic direction, that is to say; all aspects concerning decorations, clothing, furniture, etc.[36] Because of this, her frequent ideas, observations and orders were not as relevant as they should have been. The underlings were then in a bind as they sought clearer direction and in doing so faced the temperament of the lady of the actor playing the lead role.

If an argument did arise because of those differences of opinion, Rudolph always corroborated with Natacha's reasoning. In this constant tribute to his wife, he enjoyed the same result both in his professional work and in the intimacy of his home. It was usual for him to assume the characteristics of the roles he played by manifesting, in the activities of his private life, certain features of those characters he played.

During the filming of *Monsieur Beaucaire*, the courtly Versailles courtesy displayed by the noble protagonist inspired Rudolph's behavior in real life. This added to his natural humble disposition in regards to his lady, making the great movie lover's constant homage to his lofty wife even more profound. She, in turn, received those tributes as something due.

Fortunately, Natacha was aware she still lacked the knowledge to impose whatever directions she wished. She extended herself as little as possible and tried, rather, to take advantage of the situation as an apprentice; hence, the film could be finished in a presentable form. As work on *Monsieur Beaucaire* ended, they made one more film for Paramount,

---

36 As an art director, Natacha Rambova was responsible for a film's artistic vision and this included costume design, set design and all artistic aspects of production.

The Sainted Devil, in which Natacha, with more experience, imposed her direction with more confidence than in the previous work.

However, in *The Sainted Devil,* Natacha would not contend with actress Bebe Daniels, whose disposition worked perfectly in harmony with her. Rudolph co-starred with the headstrong Jetta Goudal, with whom Natacha soon had a conflict. The hostility was so serious it resulted in the vehement French actress being replaced with the beautiful Helena d'Algy from Madrid.

What took place between Natacha and Jetta Goudal has been the cause of speculation. Some say it was all caused by the jealousy of the first; and perhaps it was Jetta Goudal who contributed most to propagate those rumors. Others attribute this to the intolerable waste Jetta expended on her elegant costumes. Perhaps both reasons have equal merit. There was additionally the explanation of the obvious incompatibility between the pride of Natacha and the genius of Jetta Goudal; who is well known in Hollywood. It is rare the film in which she is cast, in which she does not have some disagreement, in the least, with the director.

The fact is that the film was completed and Natacha became convinced that, thanks to her talent and culture and the experience she had just acquired, she was then an accomplished director of films. She began to forge great plans for super films that, according to her dreams, would greatly influence the evolution of film as art and place her on par with the Hollywood moguls.

She seemed to then care more about herself, considering Rudolph the instrument by which she could reach her goals. In this she considered herself superior. But now, seeing her own faculties so fully developed, she had more reason to be proud of her accomplishments and show them to the world. At last, the occasion arrived to share her art with the public. According to Rudolph's contractual commitments, after completing the two films with Paramount, he would dedicate himself to those films made with Ritz Carlton Pictures, which, as I have mentioned, was the same company in disguise.

According to his contract, Rudolph was authorized to personally choose the works he wished to film. Therefore, Natacha decided upon *The Hooded Falcon,* a film about the Moors in Spain. This was slated to be a major movie with the company authorizing a budget of almost a half a million dollars. Natacha's designs guaranteed it could not be adequately brilliant for less than a million. In order to complete this film in a thoughtful manner, Natacha and Rudolph traveled to Spain to immerse themselves in the Moorish environment by acquiring clothing and furniture worthy of the film's huge budget. The company advanced them forty thousand dollars to carry out that mission.

They arrived in Europe in August 1924, traveling as royalty. They bought whatever they desired and they desired almost everything they saw. Natacha was even more lavish than Rudolph as she spent an enormous amount of money on her dogs. One of them, an insignificant little dog, cost no less than fifteen hundred dollars. They spent another enjoyable season at the Juan-Les-Pins chateau with Natacha's mother and stepfather. And it was then Rudolph's wife met his brother-in-law Alberto, who visited the chateau in return for his brother's visit to Campobasso the previous year.

In those moments, Rudolph was happy. He loved his wife and her family and he was loved by them. He triumphed in the United States as no one could have imagined and after two years of moving away from the cinema, the films he had just made proved he still enjoyed a huge popularity. This fame brought him great financial gain with which he could realize the fantastic projects he envisioned. All, of course, was meant to dignify and enthrone the majesty of his lady and mistress; his Queen Natacha.

However, Alberto Guglielmi Valentino relates how during the intimate talks which the two brothers used to enjoy in those happy days, Rudolph told him about his American life. He told him about the most important episodes of his career as a dancer and a filmmaker. During these talks, he excitedly evoked the memory of that South American beauty he fell in love with during his first stay in New York, and confessed that this woman, Blanca, was the one he loved the most in his life.

In the month of September, Rudolph, his wife and his mother-in-law traveled to Spain to visit Madrid, Seville and Granada. They searched everywhere to find the needed costumes, furniture, weapons and jewelry. They spent a great deal of money on old, or what was thought to be old, objects. Spanish antique dealers and antiquities counterfeiters conducted a very profitable business with them[37]. They spent a fortune on mantillas, shawls and ivory objects. Needless to say, each artifact they bought came with its own history, which Rudolph used to explain to his guests at length. This when, according to his amusement, he invited them to visit the interesting museum which was his Beverly Hills mansion. He shared explanations about his collection with his visitors with the certainty of a

---

37 t.n.: *ponerse las botas* - (put the boots on) - to take a lot of profit from something.

museum docent[38]; speaking with familiarity and repeating by rote and by heart[39] . Rudolph added the pride of being possessor of those garments related to such ancient characters. But perhaps they were made by counterfeiters shortly before his arrival in Madrid or Seville.

Among the more valuable pieces he brought from Spain and which he wore more than once in Cinelandia, was a magnificent and traditional bullfighter suit.[40] It was claimed by the man who sold it to him that it once belonged to a close friend of the bullfighter who inspired Blasco Ibáñez to create his character of Juan Gallardo in *Blood and Sand.*

After such extensive preparations for the film, *The Hooded Falcon* and after having spent far more than the authorized $40,000, and having shaved off his beard which was necessary to play the protagonist of his wife's work, the couple arrived in New York and rented an expensive apartment on Park Avenue. Then, under the pretext that the Long Island studios were not a suitable place to shoot such a great movie as *The Hooded Falcon*, they moved immediately to Hollywood. There, after a short time, they were told that it was necessary to postpone the filming of this epic movie in order to make another of less pretensions chosen by the company, and according to the agreement.

The movie would be titled *Cobra,* as the play from which it was taken. Natacha Rambova's direction was already beginning to have ramifications and *Cobra* was made under the authority of the star's wife. When this film was finished, the couple went to rest for a season in Palm Springs; with the sad memory of having been there when they were forced to separate as he was accused of bigamy. It was still an attractive place for them because there lived their good friend Dr. White and because on the edge of the desert they were far away from the hustle and bustle of city life.

The tranquility they enjoyed there was disturbed on this occasion by a letter from Ritz Carlton Pictures, inspired perhaps by Natacha's interference in *Cobra.* This stated the company was not willing to invest money in *The Hooded Falcon.* Thus Natacha's dream of being a great reformer in the realm of cinema began to fall apart. The contract was then canceled and a new one signed, this time, with Joseph M. Schenck. This

---

38 Cicerone - Marcus Tulius Cicero Roman statesman, orator, lawyer and philosopher, docent.

39 t.n.: *de coro* - (as a chorus) - by heart.

40 t.n.: *traje de luces* - (suit of lights) - traditional bullfighter suit.

contract stipulated that the actor's wife would not have any interference as far as Rudolph's performances with this new entrepreneur.[41] This was a terrible blow for the pride and ambition of Natacha Rambova and for the conjugal bliss of Rudolph Valentino.

The first film the actor made with the new company, United Artists, was *The Eagle,* based on a Russian novel by Pushkin. The lead actress in the film was the beautiful Hungarian Vilma Banky; with golden hair, complexion of rose and eyes of heaven. Natacha, who compromised her husband's career[42] by contributing to their extensive spending and the quality of his films, did not accept her new mission as a housewife.

She did not wait patiently for her husband to recover by earning more money and conquering more admirers. Natacha thought for herself. It occurred to her to make a film on her own as funded by her husband yet in this she risked wasting more. It was then Rudolph's gallantry towards his wife waned; but even so he did all to preserve domestic peace.

He authorized Natacha to film a scenario she devised, with the title *What Price Beauty* which would cost her husband a fortune. He used to say later, with irony, he had no "more memory of that than if he sat on a rickety chair."[43] It was then when Natacha began to stray and a coldness began to fall on the home where Rudolph dreamed of forming a loving family. He worked on *The Eagle* and she on *What Price Beauty* and when they finished their daily work, each one sought and in their own way, for the joy which should be found at home.

At that time, Natacha was living almost independently. She often went out for long car rides without saying where she was going and sometimes she was absent for several days. Rudolph, as a true Latino, began to show jealousy. It took a little while for him to become fully exasperated, because of the influence of his characteristic gallantry and by the frequent and timely intervention of Mrs. Teresa Werner, Natacha's aunt. She loved Rudolph as a mother would and he also loved her dearly.

---

41 Natacha Rambova was not mentioned in the United Artists' contract which is included in S. George Ullman's Appeals Case, The original contract dated March 30, 1925, and submitted as "Executor's Exhibit One", filed under the case of the Estate of Guglielmi, #83678.

42 Under Natacha's direction, Valentino's career was developed successfully and her elevating his onscreen persona provided him with new levels of artistic opportunity such as the United Artists' contract.

43 t.n.: *Una silla de mala muerte* - (a chair of bad death) - a rickety chair.

The jealous husband wanted, however, to find out what was behind the enigmatic behavior of his wife and he hired detectives who followed her mysterious steps. Soon they discovered that the proud Natacha Rambova held frequent meetings, possibly for professional reasons with her film's editor, who, by the way, was married and had several children.

As Rudolph was not sufficiently modernized in his character as a husband, nor one to tolerate such a relationship between his wife and another man, the serious conflicts between him and his wife were inevitable. To make it brief,[44] the real cause of the conflict was something both spouses kept secret for very different reasons; she, because it was not convenient to confess the friendship she had with another man and he, because he did want to hinder his detective's investigations as he was finding out the truth and this interested him greatly.

One day, after Rudolph was advised as to Natacha's location by his skilled detectives, he arrived to discover what she was secretly doing. If it was not for the providential presence of a good friend of both, a tragedy could have occurred at once and columns of reportage would have told of the events which were instead kept secret.

From that day on, Rudolph did not return to lead the usual marital life with his wife. They lived, yes, still a season, under the same roof. He wanted to avoid a scandal and if possible a separation from a woman in whom he held so many illusions after his first marital failure. But the haughty wife was not so grateful and continued to look with defiance at the magnanimous husband while still carrying on with her life as if nothing happened.

Soon after, the same detectives discovered Natacha rented a small beach house where she could retire when needed. They also discovered that in addition to her modest cottage she was utilizing their yacht in order to isolate herself even more. One day, Rudolph arrived at the dock just when she, in pleasant company, was about to undertake an excursion by sea.

A remedy was then deemed necessary and the most acceptable thing occurring to the two was to distance themselves and announce they were going to take a year as a "marital vacation".

Upon this generosity, Rudolph accompanied his wife to the station to be portrayed smiling next to her and to kiss her in plain sight of all. He also advised her that instead of staying in New York, she should travel to

---

44 t.n.: *quítame allá esas pajas* - (Take those straws away, simple thing to be done fast) - today this phrase is of scarce colloquial presence and is applied to something of little difficulty or importance that is done quickly.

Juan-Les-Pins, where she would receive good advice from her mother. Several letters and telegrams were exchanged between the two from New York and Hollywood, but one response from Natacha made the separation final.

Under the pretext of making purchases for a film *When Love Grows Cold,* for which Natacha had just been cast as a star in New York, she went to Paris where she established her residency in order to file for a divorce. Meanwhile, Rudolph resumed his relationships with his carousing friends whom Natacha dispatched. He returned to surrender, in such company, to the happy and yet ruinous lifestyle of before.

Professionally, he was then linked to Vilma Banky, with whom he made a very good friend. Besides working together in the filming of *The Eagle*, they ate together in the bungalow which Rudolph had built inside the studios (he was the first of the movie stars to enjoy such a comfort), and they attended social gatherings together. This led to more than a few rumors being spread about in Hollywood. However, as soon as the filming of *The Eagle* was finished, Vilma and Rudolph left each other on their own while retaining a friendship which never ended.

Rudolph was again fully living the bachelor life and the public often witnessed the accompaniment of a lady actress he might be dating. But the women who would truly gain his attention were, of course, the ones the public did not see. There was one woman one day and another the next, countless women who disputed the honor of being intimate with him. Whether in Hollywood or in the surrounding area; in his house or in the ladies' homes or his friend's homes, in hotel rooms, in cabarets, in his yacht of such sad history; here these affairs took place to fill him with joy. But everywhere he was left disappointed, because he was only seeking distraction to mitigate the pain of his heavy-heart.

It was around that same time Rudolph began to court Pola Negri. Or did Pola Negri woo him? He met her at a party at Marion Davies' house and it did not take long for the press to comment on the battered conqueror's new love affair. But no sooner had the two big stars begun to understand each other, he would leave for New York and London to attend the premiere of *The Eagle* in both cities.

During his stay in Europe, he and his wife were granted the divorce she filed for in Paris. Immediately, Rudolph dedicated himself to continue, and with even more enthusiasm, the hedonistic lifestyle which he had already resumed in Hollywood. He often passed several days in a row without sleeping and he was drinking like never before. He surrendered completely to pleasure.

One day he was with Jean Nash, the following one with Mae Murray and another day with an American millionairess or with some European noblewoman. There was much talk that he would marry Mae Murray, the current Princess Mdivani, whose wedding Rudolph would act as best man a few months later. Mae Murray denied the rumor in Paris with her famous mouth by saying,

"As I've always said, we're just good friends. Too good friends to get married. And the fact that we traveled together from London to Paris and had fun together here and there, does not mean anything. Au revoir."

Mae left the reporters with this statement because she said she had to take the train for Berlin at half past eight, where she would spend a few days. On the other hand, Rudolph was also saying he had to take the same Berlin train at half past eight, where he would spend a few days.

Close to Christmas and New Year's Eve, Rudolph received two telegrams sent by Natacha, which brought him, along with the best wishes, very intriguing invitations. At this point Rudolph did not accept them.

Natacha returned to New York, where, responding to questions from the press claiming Rudolph accused her of not dedicating herself to the home or to being a mother, she made this statement,

"I am sure my husband did not state that, because he is not capable of descending to such a level. If my married life were happy, I would have had great pleasure in remaining at home."

It took a while for Rudolph to reply to those declarations and others which were pronounced before and after. Actually, he did not answer, publicly, until a few days after his death. Here is what happened in this respect.

On July 12, 1926, two days before Rudolph began his last trip from Hollywood to New York, he issued a statement regarding his latest marriage failure. During his stay in New York, the same carefully typed statement was sent to him from his Hollywood office so he could sign it if he had nothing to amend.

Rudolph found it satisfactory and signed. But when he returned them to Don Eddy, then his advertising agent, he warned him not to release the statement for the time being because he did not think it appropriate to publish it yet. After Rudolph died, his declarations were made public by the newspaper *The Los Angeles Examiner*. In this statement, Rudolph clearly alludes to his last wife and dedicates no little irony to her; but the immediate cause of their separation is not mentioned. Here are some important paragraphs from his posthumous manifesto.

"I will be forced to disappoint the reader who expects something sensational. I did not hit Natacha and she did not throw an iron at me. I'm sorry, but we have not done anything like that nor did I oppose her pursuing her own career. I did not ask her to have children.

I wanted her to have whatever she wanted as long as I could be with her. I wanted her to do what she wanted and if I could not help her to do it, I was not in any way bothering her. In other words, I wanted her to be happy and I tried to make her happy, as much as any other man could. It was never a matter of discussion for her to stay at home and do housework. In Los Angeles, the wives have their own cars, as a rule, and they come and go as they please. Fortunately, I was able to free my wife from the housework and all kinds of domestic tasks.

The dissatisfaction in marriage, as in the rest of family life, is usually cumulative. It is not a sudden, capricious or dramatic offense that determines one's leaving home in order to get rid of the presence and influence of relatives and to get out of their environment at all costs. There is often a constant decline in mutual interest, in sympathy, in estimation."

Rudolph then refers to a young man, "who is too tightly constrained by an ambitious girl."

"At first, she encourages him to do great and better things, is truly generous and useful and is excited and flattered to see how she devotes herself to his ideal; how she dedicates herself to what he is interested in. Both of them form, enthusiastically, the young man's career plan and he welcomes the girl's advice and following the advice, he sees that was rational. Rational, because, in the first flowering of love, while she is very much in love with him, she thinks with her heart rather than with her head and arrives intuitively at the right conclusions.

She has inspirations and divination faculties which the calculating woman can never put into play for the man she wants to push only for utility and self-aggrandizement. They get married, she gives up her career, if she has one, to help him at her best and most completely. Almost imperceptibly, but slowly and surely, the attitude of the girl changes. Little by little, she realizes that although if it is true that she abandoned her own career, she has not given up the idea of having a career.

She begins to manage and take her husband to victory. Now, you will tell me that man should be deeply grateful for that. Yes and no. Wait a moment. In the periods of friendship and courtship, she considered him, weighed and advised him with regard to the profession or art that he tried to dominate, in relation to the public or to the companies he sought to serve, satisfy, attract, preserve.

With marriage and the routine of daily living, servants, household budgets, clothes, his friends, her friends, his family, her family, and the rest, she inevitably started to consider him and them in relation to herself. Would they intervene, would they pretend to advise and do projects before consulting her, in other words; would they usurp her position as friend, guide and philosopher? Your job and your powers are in danger, then the essential question of money arises just as a lot of money comes in. When you have a residence, it is so necessary to give parties and all that! And if one does not make money, more and more money, one stays in this situation.

Relationships must be valued according to the place they occupy in the progression. They must be culled or discarded in direct proportion to the help or hindrance they contribute to the desire to prosper socially, professionally or financially. I am not by nature, what you Americans call, practical.

The Latin man can find friends who apparently are not worth much and will never be worth much. But they bring a lot of distraction to his life and relief from the stress of work. So it happens that a Latino may want to take such a friendship as he would carry a beautiful flower; for itself, because it is beautiful and fragrant, and is tuned with his best.

This is an experience that I believe I share with the North American husband. That after a few years of marital life, he retains only those friends that his wife has approved. He is visited only by his or her relatives, which she approves, and all the friends of the wife will be invited to the house at all times whether he likes them or not and whether they like him or not.

Well, what happens when a man discovers he is being handled in all aspects of his life: the same in those in which he may need direction, than in those in which, for the sake of his own development, he should have freedom of desire and choice?

The result is that all that management comes to annoy. Suddenly, it manifests as energetic as before it was weak. He decisively decides to be himself and do what he likes. He discovers he can hire a competent counselor and guide in business, and living his own life, so to speak, what does a wife do when the government of her husband's career gets out of hand? She can return to her own career or be only a wife.

The business manager does not have a soft, feminine chest over which a weary actor can recline his head when night comes in. If she is more loving than proud, she will fix it necessarily and start over on a new basis. If her pride predominates, she will probably whip her husband's face with divorce papers.

The world knows what happened in my case and I do not have regret or remorse. I enjoyed my marriage to Natacha and did everything I could to make her happy. Say it or think what you want now, she also drew much from our coexistence: the same in material things as in happy times.

I am neither distressed nor homeless. I have a secretary and a few trusted servants to take care of me. This summer I brought my brother and his wife with me from Europe. They watch over my house and I can entertain myself with whom I want, when I want, and I have that feeling of 'monarch of what I can embrace', which is so invigorating to the masculine self.

Perhaps this account of my second shipwreck in the pitfalls of marriage belies the reputation which I so unjustly enjoy; that of being a 'great lover', the same on the screen as outside of it. I suppose this is said of me with the best intentions, but it does not flatter me.

However, I must admit that I am never indifferent to the attraction of the beautiful sex.

Signed,
Rudolph Valentino".

This is how Rudolph explained his last marital failure just a few days before he died. Later, according to reports Natacha shared with the world, Rudolph sent her interesting messages from beyond the grave, full of love, (which reveal that he changed some of his ideas) and it is useless to expound upon them here.

But this otherworldly retraction does not affect in any way our story, which refers only to the real Rudolph Valentino; that man of flesh and bone, who thought and worked so humanly.

Installment

IX

About Pola and Other Trivialities

Before Rudolph left for Europe to finalize his divorce, he began his famous relationship with the fiery Pola Negri. The incidents to which this latest adventure of the great conqueror gave rise are so well-known, it is difficult to bring forth something new relating to it. But, on the other hand, this story would seem insufficient and partial if I omitted elements pertaining to this most famous lover.

To solve the dilemma with some novelty while avoiding running the risk of being accused of repeating my own articles; some of which are published in *Cine-Mundial*, I will turn to the words of two Latina women who helped me in an unusual way.

The first woman is one of Rudolph's many fans, who has honored me with fine letters in response to my articles about the deceased actor. She is a French woman living in Buenos Aires, who some time before *Cine-Mundial* began the publication of these installments, read other works of mine in one of the magazines in which I have described faithfully and dutifully scenes of the relationship between Rudolph Valentino and Pola Negri. Those scenes which I myself witnessed. After some time, I thought it appropriate to publish them because the sad outcome of my ill-fated friend came to embue them with special interest and a romantic color which made them, to my eyes, worthy of publication.

This letter came from Buenos Aires and was written by a woman unaware that when a journalist is hired to write about a certain topic, he does not have to include everything he knows. He must be discreet in what he has to say or else confuse the main subject with data which has not a thing to do with the subject. These are the privileges of other people, among whom I include the woman from Buenos Aires. She, who in addition to her repeated observations made about Pola and Rudolph, felt it necessary to describe in her own way; not only my supposed moral character but also my physiognomy.

Despite this, this lady who clearly considers herself as a rival of Pola Negri, exposes a version of the love of Rudolph, which regardless of the obvious defects it contains, is an approximate representation of what countless women feel and believe with respect to the last gallant adventure of Rudolph.

(The following words were sent to me in English as I share here the original. Apart from a slight modification and the deletion of a pair of offensive words targeting a third person, the letter has been respected even in its spelling.)

"Buenos Aires, January 10, 1927
Mr. Baltasar Fernández Cué
New York

I have read with enough annoyance your "interview" with Pola Negri, and believe me I could not help but send you these lines in the name of the honor and memory of dear Rudy.

Do not think that now that the divine and beloved Negrito[45] does not live, you can say whatever you want with your kind of blurbing. No! That could never be, because there are still some souls in the world who loved him dearly, who want and will love him and they will defend him even at the cost of their own lives. One of those people is me who will not allow the money of that woman who pays for this advertising, to spread her lies throughout the world and to destroy the reputation which he enjoys and the delicacy he possesses like no other man.

How did you (You... well I don't know you as I do know my little Rudolph) dare to speak about that woman as if she is the fiancée of the adored Negrito? How did you have the audacity to invent that he thought to marry this woman when he denied this would happen until his last moment. He aspired to another kind of woman who would make him happy and know the delights of a home, a home he so much lamented he did not own. All of those who showed him affection were liars, because what those stupid people craved was his fame, his money and his name above all.

I ask, why did you not publish an "interview" about Pola with all the details about the dreadful kick that Charlie Chaplin gave her after she was his

---

45 "Negrito" would be a term of affection in Argentine vernacular denoting someone with black hair or dark skin.

girlfriend and which left her so disappointed? Now she makes public this with Rudy, saying he was the only man she loved; and the painter where did she leave him?

I would like to read that "interview" because it must be very interesting. Because it is about living people. Stop profaning the memory of the deceased so mourned and so loved by those who know how to cry and love. Why does that woman say so much how she loved him when all her affections vanished by magic when she learned that to the adored Polita or Polititita he left in his 'Last Will and Testament' a nice nothing[46]! How funny! What a sincere affection. How much she longed for fame, money and beauty. But God did not allow that woman to wrap him up as she wanted, in her idiotic cunning, so he would give her his name, which the famous and intelligent Charlie Chaplin denied.

I'm surprised that in exploiting publicity for her fame, that Politita, to gain a little favor from the public, uses an idiot like you. So therefore she remains before the eyes of the world, famous; but people are not as stupid as you are and not about to swallow such a little pill. Her false groans, covered in silk crepe, and assisted needless to say by strong sex, well I laughed a lot during that sad funeral ceremony. I was confused, because there were no religious rites but only advertisement and a farce from which the self-titled fiancée, her friends, etc., etc. all profited.

Why did you not publish the first interview in that magazine when my beloved Negrito, my precious kid was alive? Why? Oh! You must fear a big punch because I would smash your face in like a fried cake and leave you "knocked-out" for the rest of your life! What cowardice!

Take care, understand it well, to honor the memory of the one who was in life the most perfect of knights and remember there are women worthy to defend his name and his honor which is worth more than all worldly ambitions and richness.

I think you have enough doses for the rest of your life, and before writing any more infamy, cut your hand so you do not sell yourself out for the money. I send my compassion to you and to all the false people, and pity is what such venomous people deserve, especially an "angering" person like you. "

---

46 t.n.: *Una cuarta de narices* - (a quarter of nostrils) – nothing.

Some of the adverse opinions about Pola Negri's love, included in the preceding letter from the French woman in Buenos Aires, were reinforced later, because of her love story and new marriage to Sergio Mdivani. There are other aspects which the press subsequently revealed but there are at least two not-so-well-publicized omissions; which if not mentioned could easily vanish.

In the first place, the fabulous wealth of Rudolph Valentino was a myth.[47] If his heirs receive something by virtue of the rights granted to them in his will, it will be because the premature death of the actor came to grant a higher value to his movies. Rudolph owned a considerable share of the profits from two movies. And Pola knew well her lover's scarcity of resources and she herself provided him with a large sum of money to continue the expensive works in his house in Beverly Hills.

And as for the good name people believed she was looking for in lovingly linking herself to Rudolph Valentino, the following documents clearly demonstrate how different his fame was a few months before he died and when he was associated with Pola; the fame that was then given, very humanly, by the sad events which suddenly cut short his brilliant professional career.

Shortly after beginning a relationship with Pola Negri, but before she publicly expressed her enthusiasm over her new love, Rudolph became aware of the bitterness against him and his films in his own country where loud demonstrations were organized against him. He was then being scorned by the government and the Italian press itself, who refused to acknowledge his messages sent in defense of his own dignity.

It was then he found himself in Germany, unable to leave because his passport was missing a small legal requirement which was being ignored by the embassy representative. He would not have been able to return to the United States and would have lost, therefore, his magnificent professional position if it were not for the support of a diplomat from another foreign country. This diplomat illegally provided him with the solution. In this regard, it is helpful to read the following documents Rudolph Valentino himself put in my hands upon returning from Europe to Hollywood.

---

47 Although Valentino's estate was heavily-indebted at the time of his death, he was a wealthy man by any standard of the day. His estate settlement court records reveal, cite, "Executor's Inventory", filed four years after his death on January 31, 1930, record his estate worth $325,779.36. Currency exchange rate to 2019 as x13 = $4,235,131.68.

Here follows a clipping from the newspaper, *II Popolo d'Italia* of Milan, dated, January 30, 1926, which was titled, "The Sense of Beauty and of ... the Vileness".

"Along with a photograph and an interview with the famous cinematographic artist Rudolph Valentino, the most beautiful man in the world, 'Le Petit Niçois', from Nice, says:

'Rudolph Valentino, who is the main character in an interesting film titled The Sheikh, was considered in Italy, until recently, an ace of cinema. In addition, The Sheikh obtained a colossal success in Genova; in part because of Valentino's fame. But did the pure gold turn into vile lead?

It has been known that Rudolph has renounced his homeland and adopted American citizenship, but there is something more serious; he was bragging about that. Why? We don't know. Anyway, it's a fact that the day before yesterday, in Genova, in front of the "Cinema-Teatro Olimpia", where as every day a poster of The Sheikh, was posted; a hostile crowd gathered whistling and shouting; "Down with the renegade!" The manager of the theater was forced to change the poster. In the classic country of art, fascism makes the people lose nothing less than the sense of beauty.'

No, dunderheads! The fascism, in the long-established country of art, makes people lose only the sense of vileness to train them in the love for the motherland, the nobility, the value.

This explains why after the news appeared how Rudolph had renounced his Italian citizenship to be an American, the popular demonstrations, as well in Genoa as in Bergamo and elsewhere, did justice to the renegade and his works."

The following is the telegram sent by Rudolph Valentino to Mussolini:

"Your Excellency Mr. Benito Mussolini,
Minister of Foreign Affairs.
Rome

I am very sad because of the position of the Italian press and the public against me and for the accusation of my supposed disloyalty towards my motherland.

Allow me to submit to your Excellency my open letter addressed to the Italian press. I trust in your competent judgment, your Excellency, in dealing with internal and external business and that you will intervene to clarify this situation which in my opinion could be misinterpreted to the detriment of the interests of Italy.

In effect, it is important for me not to contribute to the American public opinion by giving the impression that it is considered disloyal for Italians living in North America to take American citizenship.

In making my request for American citizenship, I thought to interpret your Excellency's opinion you already expressed in Parliament. I hope your Excellency will take the necessary measures to prevent a repetition of this first unjust, unfounded, insidious manifestation. Clarifying my most respectful tributes and feelings of admiration for my Italianity, I remain a devotee of your Excellency.

Rudolph Valentino."

The Italian dictator left the dignified message of his compatriot unanswered. When Rudolph then returned to Hollywood, he read how the most respectable newspaper in Los Angeles was treating him; and in an editorial. This because of a car accident he was involved in which took place in a deserted area and caused only slight damage to himself with the only harm being done to his luxurious Isotta-Fraschini.

The clipping from the newspaper *Los Angeles Examiner*

"Put a Stop to Such Reckless Racing"

"Put a beggar on horseback and he will ride to the underworld," says the old adage. Putting it in more modern terms, "Give a car to a fatuous upstart, and it will not be long before he breaks his head or the one of someone else". Mr. Rudolph Valentino is an example of this. His last feat was to suddenly wrap his car around a pole in San Luis Obispo while driving at breakneck speed.

This reckless, irresponsible individual is always driving his car at dangerously high speeds which frequently results in accidents. His dangerous run should be swiftly punished by the strong hand of the law. The police and justice system should stop bothering those who commit petty faults and innocent violators of secondary traffic laws, to severely punish the insane who run at a rate of seventy miles per hour and who are a threat to the peace and safety of those who respect the law. This would provide a great benefit to the community.

We want people to come to visit our country. We want them to have fun while they are here and to reside permanently with us if they wish. We should not annoy our visitors or our own fellow citizens with an endless tangle of laws and traffic rules; but at the same time we should punish the true delinquents, those who deliberately infringe liberal laws; those reckless, brainless, dangerous motorists who rush madly down the roads at a speed higher than that of an express train.

The perfect place for these vain and selfish fools who seek notoriety is the municipal jail or the madhouse. If they want new thrills, they should try the unusual sensations that isolated confinement and useful work provide."

Shortly after this, *The Chicago Tribune*, one of the most important newspapers in the world, published, on July 18, 1926, the following editorial, which contained ideas already expressed in the same newspaper some months before. This is believed to be one of the causes which accelerated the outcome of the sickness so well concealed under the robust appearance of Rudolph Valentino.

"PINK POWDER PUFFS

A new public ballroom was opened on the north side a few days ago, a truly beautiful venue and apparently well run. The pleasant impression lasts until one steps into the men's washroom and finds there on the wall a contraption of glass tubes and levers and a slot for the insertion of a coin. The glass tubes contain a fluffy and pink solid, and beneath one reads an amazing legend which runs something like this: "Insert coin. Hold personal puff beneath the tube. Then pull the lever."

A powder vending machine! In a men's washroom! Homo Americanus! Why didn't someone quietly drown Rudolph Guglielmo, alias Valentino, years ago?

And was the pink powder machine pulled from the wall or ignored? It was not. It was used. We personally saw two "men"- as young lady contributors to the Voice of the People are wont to describe the breed- step up, insert coin, hold kerchief beneath the spout, pull the lever, then take the pretty pink stuff and pat it on their cheeks in front of the mirror.

Another member of this department, one of the most benevolent men on earth, burst raging in the office the other day because he had seen a young "man" combing his pomaded hair in the elevator. But we claim our pink powder story beats his all hollow.

It is time for a matriarchy if the male of the species allows such things to persist. Better a rule by masculine women than by effeminate men. Man began to slip, we are beginning to believe, when he discarded the straight razor for the safety pattern. We shall not be surprised if we hear that the safety razor has given way to the depilatory.

Who or what is to blame is what puzzles us. Is this degeneration into effeminacy a cognate reaction similar with pacifism to the virilities and realities of the war? Are pink powder and parlor pinks in any way related? How does one reconcile masculine cosmetics, sheiks, floppy pants and slave bracelets with a disregard for law and an aptitude for crime more in keeping with the frontier of half a century ago than a twentieth century metropolis?

Do women like the type of "man" who pats pink powder on his face in a public washroom and arranges his coiffure in a public elevator? Do women at heart belong to the Wilsonian era of "I Didn't Raise My Boy to be a Soldier?" What has become of the old "caveman" line?

It's a strange social phenomenon and one that is running its course not only here in America but in Europe as well. Chicago may have its powder puffs; London has its "dancing men" and Paris its "gigolos". Down with Decateur; up with Elinor Glyn. Hollywood is the national school of masculinity. Rudy, the beautiful gardener's boy, is the prototype of the American male.

Hell's bells. Oh sugar."

To make the situation worse, one of the best known chroniclers of Hollywood life, dedicated the following lines to Rudolph which were published in the all-important newspaper *The Los Angeles Times* on July 22, 1926 and signed by Harry Carr.

"This is a little free advice for Mr. Rudolph Valentino. If he would stop riding in automobiles with silver snakes crawling around the hoods and take off his gold bracelets; and stop kissing the hands of visiting ladies; and generally stop trying to show himself off as a 'Latin Lover' for the benefit of over-awed telephone girls, he would last longer as a screen star.

As it is, the beauteous Rudy is, I fear, sunk forevermore. By issuing a 'challenge' to the author of that Chicago Tribune editorial about powder puffs and gold slave bracelets, he has made himself ridiculous all over the world.

Other 'Latino lovers' of the screen are fortunately of a different type. Ramón Novarro is a modest, retiring boy, who spends all his leisure hours studying music; and Tony Moreno is a vigorous real estate agent who likes to go to Chamber of Commerce banquets and ardently studies the financial page of the paper."

These were the opinions of Rudolph Valentino which were published very shortly before his death; or rather before his idolization.

Now the second Latina woman who told me something about Rudolph Valentino, provided a story which permits us to look at his relationship with Pola as something very natural and very human. This had nothing to do with Pola's greed of a wealth which did not exist nor her desire to take advantage of a name which held no more prestige than her own.

Here follows, along with reports from other sources, the accounts of the second Latina, who was an eye-witness at key moments. A woman who also acted an intermediary in the beginning of the love affair of the two great artists. A great deal of the data she provided to me was confirmed by other sources.

Rudolph Valentino and Pola Negri were attracted to each other from the first moment they saw each other on screen. When the first was far from being a famous actor and just beginning to have any prominence above the immense flock of "extras", and while Pola enjoyed a worldwide fame after appearing as the character of Dubarry, Pola recalls how she received a letter from a certain Rudolph Guglielmi asking for her portrait just as would any other screen fan.

Pola soon watched her admirer in his Hollywood movies and admired him in turn; but much more as a man than just as an actor. In time, both were seen in Hollywood as being triumphant in the same profession and both very popular; he as idol and seducer and she as idol and seductress.

Apart from the natural desire with which they were attracted to each other as man and woman, pride also brought them together. Rudolph had plenty of women and she had plenty of men. But Pola would take a special pleasure in conquering such a coveted young man. Rudolph, in turn, would feel more flattered with her attention than by any other woman who fell into his arms. This mysterious, magnetic and ruthless woman who although she gave joy to some fortunate men, seemed to delight in tormenting most of them.

However, neither of them wanted to sacrifice their pride to the point of revealing the eager disposition of their spirits. At last they met at a party held at the house of Marion Davies. But they made very little progress in this initial contact. They did spend time casting glances at each other to test the interest which each guessed in the other.

I, myself, heard them afterwards from the height of happiness together, how he and she talked and observed and proceeded in that preliminary period before their relationship began. They used to look at each other out of the corner of their eyes while searching for some encouraging sign. They used to show indifference when there were signs of their longed for attraction. They used to still be effusive with a third party, as if to inspire jealousy which would serve to pique more interest.

Occasionally they enjoyed certain expressive glances which opened the door to the amorous adventure both were strongly desiring. Rudolph said he would never have surrendered[48] if Pola's signs of a favorable attitude had not given him the security of success. Pola, in turn, was convinced Rudolph responded exactly as she calculated as a result of her natural female diplomacy.

Among the ploys she used to achieve her goal, was this Latina actress whose close relationship with Pola inspired not a few spicy comments. The aforementioned confidant of the Polish actress came to work in the filming of one of Rudolph's movies just at the time when he and Pola were courting discreetly.

Rudolph also used to speak about Pola with the Latina intermediary, while Pola talked about him to her; the Latina was careful to tell the Italian what the Polish woman was saying and then made sure, in turn, to tell the Polish actress what was said about her.

At that time the writer Michael Arlen, author of *The Green Hat* arrived in Hollywood to be entertained by the film community. Among his admirers, Pola Negri distinguished herself prominently and she hosted a banquet at the Biltmore Hotel in honor of the writer. When making out her list of guests, Pola hesitated before including the name of Rudolph Valentino because she feared he would humiliate her by not accepting the invitation. But the aforementioned Latina matchmaker assured her,

"He will jump for joy if you invite him."

And thanks to this invitation, the Italian appeared at the banquet hosted by Pola in honor of Michael Arlen. Others present were Gretta Nissen, Agnes Ayres, Malcolm Saint Clair, Sid Grauman, Dorothy

---

48 t.n.: *Nunca habrìa dado su brazo a torcer* - (never would have given his arm to bend) - surrender.

Cummings and a certain gentleman named, Tony, who was then the beau and intimate lover of the hosting actress, Pola Negri.

Pola Negri's party at the Biltmore Hotel was a very happy one and after the banquet the guests danced until late into the night. Pola danced with many gentlemen and Rudolph danced with many ladies. That happy night passed by quickly and Pola and Rudolph had yet to dance together. Thus a sort of game began between them which for some time was played quietly, but would be deeply effective.

At last, a favorable moment arrived for Pola to make a move in that sweet, muffled war. Rudolph was dancing the tango with Pola's trusted friend (the Latina), while Pola was distracted and turning around on the dance floor in the arms of an elderly gentleman named, Schultz. Between the two women there were constant eye messages being shared.

Pola, with a wink, told her friend that the right time had arrived and little by little the two dancing couples approached each other. They turned one around the other without the two men having noticed the cause of such closeness. The music paused and Pola and her partner stood next to Rudolph and her friend. A few steps were taken. Who would make the first move? Who would determine when? Who knows! Moments later Pola was in the arms of Rudolph Valentino, whereas the elderly Schultz was listening to the Latina's words.

Later, when the dance was over, the two couples went to a private sitting room in the Biltmore where they continued to be even happier despite Prohibition. Soon, however, the elderly Schultz wished to retire and the three young people remained alone with the same blissful disposition; until a few hours later.

Rudolph was so thrilled with this first intimate encounter with Pola Negri, he began to sing his favorite tunes. Sitting on the floor, at her feet, this man so admired by millions of women all over the world, sang and sang to the delight of the no less admired woman. She, from the height of her narcissism, listened to him sing joyfully, much as a Queen receiving a tribute which she had long, longed for and which had been very difficult to realize.

He sang "Little Princess" with special care and as the lyrics were timely in that circumstance, he sang it translated from the Spanish. Pola felt she had finally arrived at the height of the triumph hearing those lyrics pronounced by the lips of the beautiful, manly and proud Rudolph, whose words to her after his song were,

"Little Princess. . . Butterfly! ... Look at the man who sighs at your feet! .. Love the one who would die leaving you! ... Kiss me!"

Around three in the morning the three cabbed to Pola's bungalow at the Ambassador Hotel. In the cab, Rudolph, seated between the two women, placed his virile arm around Pola, therefore, in a gallant gesture.

By the time they arrived, the ease of their friendship was extraordinarily. Rudolph no longer hesitated to speak about the most intimate things. He spoke, with utmost frankness of Natacha Rambova, of how much it cost to have that marriage on the eve of it being legally dissolved, about how cruelly his wife seemed to prefer the closeness of her friends to the company of her husband.

At four o'clock in the morning, their first encounter ended and Rudolph escorted their common friend to her home. On the way, he disclosed to her how attracted he was to Pola. As soon as Pola's friend reached her home, her phone was already ringing. It was Pola, demanding to know exactly what Rudolph said about her on the way home. Then, to discuss this further, she invited her friend to have tea with her that afternoon.

Meanwhile Tony, that poor man who was Pola's boyfriend at the time, also arrived about tea time to his beloved's home. He arrived in a furious state, because Pola paid no attention to him at the Biltmore party. As soon as he entered the room it was clear he was very upset. Pola's mother then arrived with an equally as angry disposition and spoke to her daughter in Polish, claiming a great scandal because Tony had passed by her in the foyer and had not deigned to even acknowledge her.

Pola, of course, immediately scolded Tony because he did not show her mother the respect she deserved. But she had to interrupt this severe admonition to answer the phone, which was ringing incessantly. It was Rudolph. They chatted for a while and he invited her to take a horse ride with him. When the actress returned to the living room, she threw Tony out of her house in a bad manner[49]. The poor man did return to Pola's house the next day; this time with a revolver in his hand and intent on killing his cruel beloved. However, the servants shoved him out to door and he did not bother Pola again.

---

49 t.n.: *Con gaitas destempladas* - (with untuned bagpipes) - to be sent away in a bad manner.

Meanwhile, the relationship between Pola and Rudolph was developing so quickly that news of their affair were already rumored in the press by the time he left for Europe; the destination to finalize his divorce.

The day before his departure, Pola's Latina friend arrived to Pola's home for lunch and was surprised to see Rudolph deeply asleep on the sofa. He looked like a corpse. The newcomer tiptoed across the room and went in search of Pola, whom she found having a massage before dressing for lunch.

During that meal, the three engaged in a prolonged and interesting discussion. Candid stories were shared which were told with a frankness barely surpassed by the confessions of Jean Jacques Rousseau. The artists remembered certain pastimes they used to participate in while at school, and which, according to them, were but symptoms of their future and respective temperaments. And this, which over time, correspondingly manifested in their older age: in Rudolph the strong impulse which pushed him towards women and in Pola, the irresistible force with which she was attracted to men.

Over that lunch, Pola expressed her sadness in even thinking about Rudolph's upcoming trip. She said to him with great melancholy,

"I can't believe that I have been looking for you my entire life and now that I found you, you're leaving me. . . But maybe that's better, because that way you can divorce and we'll be free to love each other without creating gossip."

Despite her attempts to be positive about Rudolph's trip, Pola began crying and Rudolph began to wipe away her tears. Their friend understood it was time to go and left the lovers alone, being sure this would facilitate the comforting mission of Pola's lover.

The next day, the same three rode Pola's Rolls Royce to Pasadena where Rudolph preferred to board the train. He hugged Pola the entire way to the station. They then embraced and kissed and were both crying when it was time to say goodbye.

He implored Pola's friend to take care of her and to never leave her alone. As the train left and with Rudolph still throwing kisses to his beloved, Pola returned sobbing to Hollywood. According to her, at that moment Rudolph was the man she loved most and as proof of her love, she promised to not have a single drink until he returned.

Installment

X

The Idolization

During Rudolph's last stay in Europe, in addition to divorcing and enjoying the company of his brother Alberto, his sister Maria, his sister-in-law Ada and his nephew Jean, he surrendered his body and soul to pleasurable things; as if in bliss he could drown all the sorrows troubling his soul. Of all the women everywhere who gazed at him with suggestively amorous eyes, whether in steamers, trains or cities; there are many who can boast of having savored even a few of his last thousands of kisses.

Those who most flattered his vanity as a conqueror and as a novice in all things of England during that trip, were two women who shared with him, each in turn, moments of intimate yet ephemeral joy. One was said to be the mistress of the Prince of Wales and the other enjoyed the same honorable social status. There has been a lot of talk about his love affair with one, Peggy Scott; who committed suicide in London upon learning of his death.

It has been said that moments before Rudolph died, he whispered some secret words as a message in the ear of his great comrade Frank Mennillo. Mennillo would then, in turn, only whisper them in the ear of Alberto Guglielmi Valentino. It has also been alleged such mysterious words were a message for the young Peggy Scott. But that remains a secret; a sacred one, which was not revealed by either of the two men in charge of protecting it. Such discretion would be compatible with the discretion regarding other details pertaining to Peggy Scott.

I asked Alberto Guglielmi Valentino if there was any truth to the rumors of a love affair between Peggy and Rudolph as the press reported. Alberto, who was in London with his brother, said he never heard of Peggy Scott. Others who were very close to Rudolph did not know a word about that girl either. When Alberto read the news coverage about this English woman's love of his brother in articles which included several letters, he sent a protest to the newspaper which published the article in Los Angeles. The reply was that this kind of reportage was formed from outside their offices, and that, since the newspaper was not responsible for its veracity, Alberto should contact the news agency first broadcasting it.

To everyone else, Peggy Scott seemed to be cultivating in her spirit certain memories of a past already growing distant. Moments before committing suicide, Peggy Scott, more precisely, Margaret Murray Scott, a 26-year-old widow of Captain Pat Scott, killed in the World War, wrote a letter to a friend saying, among other things, the following,

"To live looking at the past when the future does not give us hope, I ask you to do me the favor of taking care of Rudolph's photographs. He helped me in many ways without knowing it. I had many admirable moments and I have a lot to tell you. But with the death of Rudolph the last remnant of my courage has vanished and in 1922 Rudolph helped me to move forward when he told me of his own suffering."

Nothing in that letter presents any hypothesis that there was a love affair between them or even a recent relationship of any other kind.

Of all of Rudolph's adventures during his last stay in Europe, only one reveals something of what was hidden in the depths of his heart. Although he no longer belonged to the Hudnut family, Natacha's mother and stepfather invited him to spend Christmas with them at the chateau in Juan les Pins. Natacha was then back in New York and Rudolph did not want to spend those Christmas holidays in the house where he passed "the happiest days of his life." They would have been too bitter for him.

But he accepted the invitation for the first days of the new year. And he went, in effect, to make a brief but affectionate visit to his in-laws; during which he did not allow himself, even for a moment, to be dominated by his profound sadness. He spent long moments sitting alone in the bedroom he shared with Natacha and he approached his ex-mother-in-law, kneeling down at her feet and resting his head on her lap to cry like a child.

The carousing, the love affairs, the apparently careless statements, everything which Rudolph publicly manifested in Europe is eclipsed by that silent detail of his private life; this is how one knows what was in the soul of the famous "Sheik".

Indeed the roar of Bacchanalia faced a futile mission in silencing the formidable feeling that, even after his divorce, his love for Natacha survived in his heart. However, Rudolph insisted on being a free man and left Juan-Les-Pins to return to the world, to the pleasure he enjoyed being with many women.

To fill the void in his own mansion and give it a more of a homey atmosphere, he convinced his brother and his sister-in-law to come, with their son Jean, to live together as a family in Hollywood. He took great satisfaction in providing this for his relatives, who were accustomed to a life so different from that of Hollywood. They agreed with pleasure to help him solve those sentimental problems which, above all others, worried him most.

He would return, then, to Cinelandia with conditions in place which he thought to be ideal to ensure his happiness. On the one hand his house was going to be a home; thanks to his brother, his sister-in-law and his nephew. On the other hand, he was free to openly revel in the company of Pola.

Because, despite that intimate scene in Juan-Les-Pins which manifested one of the most important aspects of his soul, Rudolph would return to Hollywood as if he belonged completely to Pola Negri. And this would continue day by day, except for some passing clouds which often obscure even the most harmonious relationship, until the moment he made his last trip to New York.

Pola Negri left secretly to welcome Rudolph in Albuquerque (New Mexico) on his return to Los Angeles; but the press discovered her presence and she had to invent a pretext to return to Hollywood without her beloved. But it did not take her long to retaliate for the loss of those first moments she thought she would be enjoying on the last stretch of Rudolph's return trip. As soon as he arrived in Hollywood, they were reunited and continued to be seen together, at all times, as two inseparable companions whether in a car or on horseback.

And when they were not out and about, they used to spend time together at home; mainly in her home, hour after hour and constantly. There they talked about love, their common profession and everything happening to them in their lives. They did as they wished as they were both free to do so. They were a couple who, in the midst of a society foreign to both of them, created a small piece of Europe without the restrictions the puritanical dictatorship in the United States tries to impose. And they enjoyed the extreme independence which usually governs the union of artists abroad.

Incidentally, they dedicated themselves to spiritual entertainment by applying the powers Rudolph developed thanks to Natacha. Together Rudolph and Pola used to explore the mysteries of the afterlife and ennobled their male and female coupling with the presence of other higher souls.

What would have happened between them if Rudolph had not died? This is not possible to know. Among the most intimate friends of the couple, more than once I heard how Pola told Rudolph to "get away"[50]. On

---

50 t.n.: *Mandar a paseo* - (send for a walk) - close a relationship.

the other hand, others believed they would soon marry. Charles Eyton, a great friend of both, told me that Rudolph disclosed to him, before leaving for New York; saying he planned to marry Pola on January 1, 1927.

On the other hand, Mrs. Eyton, the filmmaker Kathleen Williams, one of Pola's best friends and a person fond of communicating with spirits, received at that time a message through automatic writing. This message told her Pola and Rudolph would never celebrate their wedding; and both believed in such communications.

What can not be denied is that, for many months, Rudolph devoted himself body and soul to Pola and Pola with the same enthusiasm, to Rudolph. They both decided to leave aside, with some rare exceptions, their respective admirers. And what I can myself say in good faith, is that on very few occasions did I ever see them separated for very long.

They were almost always together and very loving, until the day I said goodbye to Rudolph; July 12, 1926, two days before he left for New York. We were in the living room of Falcon Lair, where he and Pola, in my presence, shared a beautiful discussion about Pola's portrait which he would take with him on his trip. It was set in a little silver frame which Valentino had on his night table with the image of his beloved, as one of three portraits of her kept in the bedroom of the "Sheik".

It was on that occasion, after Pola Negri left to her work in *Hotel Imperial,* which began that same day, that I said to Rudolph,

"Now I am convinced that you are in love like a donkey."

I explained to him that the evidence was the adolescent tone with which he just discussed the picture frame; pleading and showing jealousy over such a trivial detail. He smiled a satisfied smile and then the great conqueror of the screen nodded.

However, what he was not enjoying as much as Pola's love, was the company of his relatives. Despite how much he and his brother and sister-in-law cared about each other, despite the pleasure with which he gazed upon his nephew who looked so very much like him, despite the good will with which they all hoped to be happy, their attempt to build a home together was a resounding failure. It seemed that the Destiny, in which Rudolph so blindly believed, was determined to prevent the realization of that great life ideal.

The interests of friends and the general dynamic surrounding Rudolph Valentino then were slyly opposed to him being able to organize his domestic life, and they instigated discord[51] which would make the fortunate peace dreamed of by the Guglielmi family, impossible.

Rudolph had, at the time, eight members of his household staff. As a result of the increase in household members, arguments were instigated because of his staff's increased work load. The Guglielmi family presented more work for them and concern as they tried to perform the useful tasks they were supposed to complete. Rudolph's family proved unable to take charge of the government of the home and this manifested in such a way that the household staff lost all respect for said relatives.

Not only did they ignore the orders given to them by the relatives, but, sometimes they did the opposite of what was requested. Alberto and Ada suffered these things in silence as not to aggravate Rudolph's situation. The sister-in-law became sick because of so much discomfort. One day, at last, Alberto decided not to tolerate such grievous disrespect from his brother's staff. He complained to Rudolph who, as the master of the house, summoned one of the servants and asked him to respect his brother. The servant, with unprecedented rudeness, answered that since he was not able to respect Alberto, he preferred to leave.

Another day, one of the maids tried to kill another servant by stabbing him. As she did not know how to wield the weapon for that purpose, she instead went into a cloakroom to unleash her fury by taking the knife and shredding the clothing she found there which all belonged to Rudolph, his family and the other servants.

I remember one occasion when Rudolph and Pola were late for a meeting of fellow artists in which they were to be the guests of honor. When the great lover of the screen explained his delay, some of the people there smiled incredulously. They suspected a more plausible explanation would be that this was a story he invented to hide the fact that the two great lovers, so immersed in each other, forgot the commitment. What they least expected was for Rudolph Valentino to give an explanation so implausibly unexciting.

He said he gathered all his numerous servants in the paddock of his Hispanic mansion and under the light of the stars, he delivered a passionate harangue urging them to cooperate with him. The Servants and the Sheik! He asked them to contribute to his performances in his artistic mission by saying that in order to achieve an accurate accomplishment in this, the contribution of the cook was as indispensable as that of the steward or of the bartender or that of the chauffeur or the one of any other of the numerous servitude.

---

51 t.n.: *Sembrar la cizaña* - to sow the tare, an injurious weed resembling wheat when young (Matt. 13:24–30) - to instigate discord.

He told the servants he needed to have his imagination free to dedicate himself to his art and he could not do so fully and effectively if they came to disturb him constantly with their domestic issues. While he spoke to them, he became so inspired by the interesting subject of the relations between art and servitude, that he said he continued to speak to them until he remembered his obligation and left his staff to hurry towards the meeting where all were waiting for his arrival.

Despite such harangues, Rudolph's sister-in-law was often suffering in such a state of nervousness she could not deal with the domestic life in the sumptuous mansion of Falcon Lair. The building was still under construction and with workers abounding, therefore, this was an unbearable noise for a sick person. Ada went to live in a hotel. About this time, Rudolph's family decided they were unable to adapt to the Hollywood life and would soon return to Italy.

The relations between Pola and Rudolph, of course, were not always good. From time to time some cause for displeasure arose. This might distance them from each other for a few days or hours. During these times, each one of them retreated to their own side and took leave to ponder the trust between them. But it was never long before reconciliation came and, with it, a renewed period of even more passionate lovemaking. And even those times of separation and divergence demonstrated to witnesses, that Rudolph and Pola loved each other.

Once, for example, after one Pola Negri spat, the Polish actress disappeared for a day. It was pitiful to hear Rudolph calling all of Pola's friends asking if they knew where she went or to see him running hither and thither[52] to find where she was hiding. It never appeared, by any means, that this was the behavior corresponding to that of the famous "Sheik," the behavior beloved by thousands and thousands of women scattered throughout the world.

And Pola also used to show a patience that did not seem to comply with her seductive role. On one occasion, after the filming of *The Son of the Sheik,* and after Rudolph's contract with the United Artists expired, Pola devised a wise political campaign to get him to work again for Paramount studios. She managed to arrange a meeting to finalize the conditions of such an association, when at the last minute, Rudolph, instead of going with Pola to Paramount, went to sign a new contract with United Artists. This put Pola in an awkward position with the rebuffed company. This episode could have been cause of serious tension between Rudolph and Pola but they remained close and amused as if nothing happened.

---

52 t.n.: *Correr de la Ceca a la Meca* - (to run from the Mint to the Mecca) - hither and thither.

On July 14, Rudolph left Los Angeles for New York, via San Francisco, where he was scheduled to appear at the New York premiere of *The Son of the Sheik*. The film was released a few days earlier in Los Angeles and hailed as a great artistic and financial success. With some bad luck, as Rudolph was exiting the stage, he stumbled and fell to the floor of the orchestra pit receiving a wound to his forehead. The wound left a mark which was still visible the day of the departure to New York when Pola escorted him to the train.

As you can see, Rudolph never worried about superstition; as it is considered a bad omen to witness the departure of a loved one. He also did not worry a few weeks prior when there were thirteen diners at the banquet Pola and Rudolph hosted at the Ambassador Hotel after the wedding of Mae Murray and Prince David Mdivani at the Good Shepherd Church in Beverly Hills. This said, however despicable the superstitions may be, the curious fact is that a few months after that banquet of the thirteen guests, the strongest of them all died; and a few weeks after Pola bid adieu to her sweetheart, the beloved died.

The day after Rudolph's departure, Alberto, Ada and little Jean also left for New York and Europe. Rudolph spent one day in San Francisco, where he was welcomed by Mayor Rolph and he then continued his journey eastward.

It was then, in those brief hours when he stopped in the city of Chicago to change trains, the famous article entitled "Pink Powder Puffs", published in *The Chicago Tribune* came into his hands.

This article was unfair in the extreme, not only because Rudolph Valentino was virile and manly, but also because he become famous on the screen and outside of it for just that reason. It was understandable then that because of this he experienced the most profound and transcendental anguish of his entire life.

He immediately called a representative of *The Chicago Herald-Examiner*, a passionate competitor of the *Tribune*, and sent them the following letter. The letter was published in that important newspaper and attracted much attention because of the passion with which Rudolph addressed the author of the offensive piece in the *Chicago Tribune* and because of the excessive emphasis the newspaper placed in dispersing it.

"July 19, 1926.

To the man(?) who wrote the editorial entitled "Pink Powder Puffs"
in The Chicago Tribune:
The above-mentioned editorial is at least the second scurrilous personal attack you have made upon me, my race, and my Father's name.

You slur my Italian ancestry; you cast ridicule upon my Italian name; you cast doubt upon my manhood.

I call you in return a contemptible coward and to prove which of us is the better man I challenge you to a personal contest. This is not a challenge of a duel in the generally accepted sense-that would be illegal. But in Illinois boxing is legal; so is wrestling. I, therefore, defy you to meet me in the boxing or wrestling arena to prove, in typically American fashion (for I am an American citizen) which of us is more of a man.

I prefer this test of honor to be private so I may give you the beating you deserve and because I want to make it absolutely plain this challenge is not for the purposes of publicity, I am handing copies of this to the newspapers simply because I doubt that anyone so cowardly as to write about me as you have done would respond to a challenge unless forced by the press to do so.

I do not know who you are or how big you are, but this challenge stands if you are as big as Jack Dempsey.

I will meet you immediately, or give you a reasonable time in which to prepare, for I assume that your muscles must be flabby and weak, judging by your cowardly mentality and that you will have to replace the vitriol in your veins with red blood-if there be a place in such a body as yours for red blood and manly muscle.

I welcome the criticism of my work as an actor-but I will resent with every muscle in my body attacks upon my manhood and ancestry.

Hoping that I will have an opportunity to demonstrate to you that the wrist under a slave bracelet may slap a real fist into your sagging jaw, and that I may teach you to respect a man even though he prefers to keep his face clean.

I remain with utter contempt,

Rudolph Valentino

P.S. I will return to Chicago within 10 days. You may send your answer to me in New York, in care of the United Artists Corporation."

After fifteen days and having not received an answer, Rudolph gave the press this statement:

"It is evident that it is not possible to oblige a coward to fight, as is not possible to draw blood from a radish. The heroic silence of the writer who attacked me, without provocation, in the Chicago Tribune, leaves no doubt about the total lack of manhood in all his being.

I feel vindicated because I consider his silence as a tacit retraction as well as an admission that I am obliged to accept, even if it is not entirely to my liking.

The men and women of the press who I have had the distinction of knowing, either for a short and for a long time, have been so absolutely fair and so loyal to their own profession and to their newspapers, that it goes without saying how rare this exception is inside of the journalistic community. "

Meanwhile, Rudolph said farewell to his family in the port of New York and attended the premiere of *The Son of the Sheik* in the same city, and then in Chicago. In the first, the enthusiasm with which he was acclaimed was such that in order to leave the theater, he had to face a close battle in which he lost his handkerchief, buttons, tie and hat. In the second he was also the object of exceptional expressions of admiration.

During his stay in New York, Rudolph resumed relations with numerous friends from whom Natacha Rambova had advised him to part ways. He certainly devoted himself to having more fun. His reconciliation with his first wife, Jean Acker, was announced by the entire United States press core. Imagine Pola Negri's reaction; she who just said good-bye to him believing Rudolph was hers, when she read in the newspapers how he and his ex-wife were strolling late at night through the so-called "night clubs" of New York.

A witness of these events told me personally that not only were Rudolph and Jean walking together and in harmony, but in front of everyone else present the "Sheik" held his ex-wife's hand in his, caressed it incessantly and from time to time he lifted her hand to his lips and kissed it.

No matter how human Pola Negri was, at that moment she thought about revenge. Being so markedly susceptible and feminine, it did not take her long to imitate Rudolph and this would be with Prince Sergio Mdivani; the most handsome and most sympathetic bachelor around her at the time. It was he who was favored with those sudden effusions from Pola, inspired no doubt by those Rudolph was sharing with Jean Acker.

We know how his illness came to reconcile the two great lovers and death would unite their souls forever. But I remember how, only a few months after Rudolph's funeral, Pola told me very proudly that Malcolm Saint Clair told her how Rudolph placed the portrait of her between two full vases of lilies on his night table in the New York hotel.

In order to understand the complex emotional constitution of Rudolph Valentino, supposing that it has not already been seen in the course of this story, when I spoke with Saint Clair myself about such a detail, he replied,

"Yes, indeed, Rudy placed something romantic next to the portrait of Pola. But the woman he really wanted was Natacha. He confessed this to me."

Saint Clair also told me, and this was confirmed by those who were with Rudolph in New York in those days, that the offensive article in *The Tribune*, which represented him so unfairly as effeminate, contributed to his troubled state of mind.

Rudolph was constantly worried that the accusation could become a permanent part of his legacy. At every moment, when least expected, he would utter some phrase relating to that unmotivated injustice and its author. While his companions talked about other things, he remained thoughtful and suddenly, as if coming to a conclusion after some intimate reasoning, he surprised people with something like,

"Yes, I have to break his nose for that!"

He, Rudolph, who was so virile and who was deservedly respected for this virility in all the world, had to suffer the unspeakable in being represented as something he himself *truly hated*.

Throughout those days, according to those who were with him at the time, after commenting on the unforgettable offense, he used to place his hand on his stomach and complain of pain. And the unpleasant accusation was constantly being repeated wherever he went; his friends, jokingly asking him, "How about the pink powder puffs?" Although he tried to pretend he was enjoying the joke, his disgust grew stronger and corroded his insides.

On Saturday, August 14, Rudolph and the actress Marian Kay Benda of the Ziegfeld Follies, were having fun in the company of another friendly couple, of which the male belonged to the famous and wealthy American family Wanamaker.

After having been in the "nightclub" of Texas Guinan, they retired to the residence of one member of the group. Late that night, Rudolph returned to his hotel, but changed his mind and returned again to that same residence and Marian Benda. He explained his return to her,

"I am depressed and sad. I feel like I'm going to die and I do not want to die alone."

Soon after they all retired to bed. At dawn, Marian Benda, alarmed, rushed from the bed to warn the others of Rudolph's condition. She said he felt very sick and had a cadaverous appearance.

A doctor was immediately summoned, who ruled it was necessary to take Rudolph urgently to a hospital. To avoid scandal, however, Marian Benda dressed Rudolph in his pajamas, a coat, wrapped a scarf around his neck, put his hat on his head and took him back to his hotel. It was from there the ambulance was called. Before the arrival of the ambulance, Rudolph fainted in the hotel. At last, he was taken to the Polyclinic Hospital in the early hours of Sunday, August 15.

At 6 o'clock in the afternoon the surgeons began to operate and at seven o'clock they finished the performance of their mission. By half past ten, Rudolph completely emerged from the effects of the ether and these were his first conscious words, according to George Ullman who was there to hear them,

"Hello! Did I behave like "the one of the pink powder puffs" or as a man?"

It did not occur to the doctors to say then that Rudolph's stomach was full of ulcers. On the 19th, four days after the operation, a medical bulletin reported,

"Mr. Valentino is improving satisfactorily and having passed the most critical period, no more bulletins will be issued unless something unexpected happens."

The next day, the improvement was accentuated to the extent that Rudolph began to feel motivated to "do something" and to forge projects for the period of his convalescence. This was then planned to take place in the summer residence of the President of Associated Artists, Hiram Abrams, who would die some months later. Rudolph then believed he was out of danger.

"I almost died, eh?" he asked Ullman. "But I would rather be missed in about ninety years."

Even then, he was under the illusion he had many years yet to live. And who did not want to join him in such a belief! The illness was already beginning to be considered just a physical mishap which served, among other things, to show how vast was Rudolph's following; from all over the world came messages which revealed the public's general interest.

And then, at this time, the patient made peace with his second wife, Natacha Rambova. This happened thanks to Rudolph himself, the day after the operation. He asked Ullman to cable news to Natacha and from that moment, he and Natacha were in daily communication.

Pola Negri was also notified by Ullman about the patient's condition. But she, like all the others who are accustomed to the exaggerations of the news regarding the "stars", did not believe the illness was serious. She limited herself to saying she was involved in the filming of *Hotel Imperial*, which was keeping her tied in Hollywood, and instead sent messages and flowers to her beloved. After an encouraging period, on the 21st, Rudolph relapsed due to an inflammation of the pleura cavity in the lungs, followed soon by pneumonia and endocarditis.

The medical bulletin of day 22 read,

"The state of Mr. Valentino is critical, there has been a slight extension of the inflammation in the left side of the thorax, it is impossible now to make a prognosis. His temperature is 104 (Fahrenheit); the heartbeat 120, breathing, 30."

Rudolph was not even aware of this seriousness. To the few friends who could visit him, he greeted them with a smile and spoke to them with a tranquility that magnified the tragic aspect of his appearance and his condition.

Flowers were arriving in piles; letters and telegrams too. The superintendent of the hospital received two hundred missives just to suggest many other healing procedures that might save the "Sheik". The believers were sending him relics and amulets, whose only contact they alleged, would be enough to save him.

It was then Pola Negri began to be alarmed. She was visiting, one evening in the home of Mae Murray and Prince David Mdivani; with several other friends present. In a secluded corner, Pola Negri and her friend Sergio Mdivani were seated; Sergio being David's older brother. Pola was waiting anxiously for a phone call from New York to learn more about her lover's condition.

To make the wait more pleasant, she enjoyed an intimate conversation with her young and beautiful friend, Sergio. At last the phone call came from New York and Pola rose from the sofa where she had been waiting so coyly. She answered the phone. Sergio Mdivani, in turn, then approached the other visitors and opined about Pola. He wondered why, with a boyfriend so ill in New York, would Pola isolate herself to chat so intimately with him. This gave rise to comments from those present, who would not today receive the approval of the man who instigated those comments. This because a few months later, he, Sergio Mdivani would become the husband of the woman they all spoke so bitterly about at that time.

After that phone call, Pola was well convinced that her lover, Rudolph was seriously ill. It was also in those moments, or a few hours later, when her friendship with Mae Murray ended; this when just a few months earlier Pola acted as Mae Murray's Maid of Honor.

In the early hours of August 23, Rudolph expressed a great desire to go fishing during his convalescence and invited his doctor to go with him. Then, revealing that his imagination might be making him delusional, he asked the same doctor,

"Do you have enough rods and hooks?"

However, shortly after four o'clock in the morning he began to speak incoherently and mainly in Italian. At about six o'clock, Ullman entered the room. Ullman had been on duty all night long with the doctors and Rudolph's great friend, Frank Mennillo. Rudolph opened his eyes, recognized Ullman, and said,

"It was terrible how we were lost last night in the woods!"

Ullman, shaken by that statement, caressed Rudolph's hair. Rudolph continued,

"On the one hand, you do not realize how funny that is. True?"

"Of course I do, Rudy, of course," said Ullman, forcing a smile.

"On the other hand," Rudolph resumed, "you also do not realize how serious that was."

Then Ullman went to close the blinds so that the sun, shining so brightly, would not prevent the patient from falling asleep. Rudolph whispered, smiling, his last words,

"Do not close the blinds. I feel good and I want the sun to greet me."

At eight in the morning Rudolph was in a comatose state. He only opened his eyes from time to time if he heard someone calling his name.

Father Leonard placed a crucifix on his lips, a crucifix in which a splinter of the true cross of Calvary is kept.

Jean Acker arrived distraught to find Rudolph so extremely emaciated and unconsciousness. She left his room distressed, leaving her ex-husband with George Ullman, Joseph M. Schenck, two priests and four doctors. Shortly after noon, his childhood companion, Father Congedo, administered the last sacraments. Keeping the crucifix on those lips so expert in profane kisses, when everyone present realized the moving event taking place.

Joseph M. Schenck, deeply afflicted, went to the room where the journalists were waiting, and, in a voice broken by grief, said weakly,

"He just died."[53]

The news broke, bringing to the whole world the deepest despair which only the "Sheik" could give it. With the crucifix on his smiling lips and without the slightest suffering, Rudolph Valentino exhaled his last breath ten minutes past twelve on the twenty-third of August 1926. A moment later, as the news reached the immense crowd that, hour after hour waited as vigil outside, one woman uttered a shriek of anguish which was the starting signal for many others to begin shedding copious tears.

Then, of course, the body was embalmed. Such was the devastation caused by nine days of pain to his athletic body, that the embalmers asked for a portrait of Rudolph to model the dead face so it resembled as he was in life.

Then there was no doubt that the illness of the "Sheik" was very serious. Until then many of us did not believe it possible. I remember when I presented my condolences to the staff of the publicity office of Rudolph Valentino, they told me that they themselves were skeptical until the last minute. Upon receiving the news their boss was ill, they telegraphed to New York recommending that the disease be "prolonged", so the press could take advantage of it.

A few days later, they were admiring how well George Ullman was handling the advertising. Then arrived the day when it began to look that George Ullman was exaggerating the seriousness of the illness. This was just when they were thinking to recommend reporting the "beginning of the improvement", this when they suddenly realized Ullman's grievous reports were real.

---

53 George Ullman breaks news to the press room and J. Schenck visits day prior to
   Valentino's death, cite *The S. George Ullman Memoir*, p. 228-229.

It was no doubt due to the unlikelihood that a man so strong and so healthy became so ill and this coupled with the mention of the word "poisoning" in the last medical bulletin which gave rise to the rumor that Rudolph had been poisoned.

To dispel these alarming rumors, Dr. Harold Meeker of the Polyclinic Hospital declared; that the actor was suffering from the stomach problems for some time, that he never took care of himself, and that in the last six weeks, he had resorted immoderately to the use of bicarbonate of soda which aggravated his situation. According to the same doctor, Rudolph's stomach was full of holes the diameter of a finger, through which food passed into the abdominal cavity, giving rise to the blood poisoning. This determined the fatal outcome.

As soon as the terrible news reached Hollywood, Pola Negri began to faint and shed tears. She spent hours in the hall of Falcon Lair standing before the two great portraits of Rudolph. She claimed for herself the one she had seen being painted; the one which represents Rudy as a Jerez-born gentleman. Then the filming of *Hotel Imperial* was suspended and she went urgently to New York on a pilgrimage which constituted perhaps the longest series of faints, tears and sobs recorded in the history of contemporary widowhood.

Alberto left Europe to return to New York and, replying to the telegram of condolence from Pola, he contributed to her sorrow by saying, "Only you and I can appreciate this loss."

The entire world was extraordinarily moved with manifestations of grief pouring in from everywhere. Even Mussolini sent his wreath, the fascists fighting against the anti-fascists the be honor guard of Rudolph's coffin.[54] Mussolini and the fascists, who so despised the compatriot a few months before!

An immense New York crowd assaulted the funeral home in which his body was lying in repose. Several tens of thousands of devoted admirers mingled with prying curiosity seekers who paraded in the front of his coffin. There was one platonic lover, a curiosity seeker, who fainted upon seeing how cruel death ravaged the beautiful face of her beloved. Another woman acted as an advertising huntress and collapsed to be revived as soon as a journalist asked her for news with their camera set.

Next to her, another woman, whose legs buckled with emotion, and another whose profane feet dared to stir in jazz movements. She stood beside another more discreet woman who barely managed to keep her serenity and yet another woman who was crying great tears, thanks to a

---

54 The Fascist honor guard by Valentino's coffin was later exposed as a hoax perpetrated by Sterling Wyman, *Affairs Valentino*, Viale Industria Pubblicazioni, p. 348.

piece of onion she had hidden in her handkerchief. Despite the imposing nature of the public demonstration, the irreverence of a minority forced Ullman to close the funeral home to the public to avoid such an unprecedented desecration.

The most famous Hollywood actors sent Alberto Guglielmi Valentino the following message,

"We, members of the Hollywood film colony who met Rudolph Valentino and worked with him and loved him, urge you to arrange for his mortal remains to rest forever here, where his friendships were formed and where he established his residence. Signed, Charles Spencer Chaplin"

Natacha asked that Rudolph's body be cremated and the ashes deposited in the Hudnut mausoleum. But this was contrary to the religion in which Rudolph had been raised and dismissed from the living.

Jean Acker went to view the corpse, and stayed for a few moments. After leaving such a sad visit, she said to the journalists,

"I have always loved Rudy, we have always kept the love we professed, at least I have kept it, and his friends told me that he did too. My affection for him was like that of a mother or a sister. We did not think of getting married again. Just two weeks ago, he gave me a portrait of himself, I will keep it with affection, forever."

The New York funeral was celebrated on August 30, shortly after one o'clock in the afternoon, in the church of Saint Malachy's; known as "The Church of the Actors" with the officiating Father Edward Leonard. Adolph Zukor, Marcus Loew, Joseph Schenck, Douglas Fairbanks, Ben Lyon and Richard Dix were also at the funeral. Three women knelt before the coffin; first Pola Negri, then Jean Acker, then, Mrs. Shaughnessy Van Horn, Natacha's stepsister.

After the funeral, Pola Negri received the press at her hotel with no cameras allowed. Pola entered the room as the visitors waited, leaning on her secretary and a nurse and there collapsed on a sofa. The nurse put her feet on a footstool. With her eyes red from so much crying, she sighed deeply. At last, she began to say,

"If you knew what I have in my heart, none of you would be so cruel again ... I have not eaten. The only thing I do is cry, cry, cry."

And she began to shed tears again.

"Will you come to find consolation yourself one day?" asked a reporter.

"Consolation? Comfort for me? Who knows! ... Maybe ... It can be. . . But I will never love again."

Then, still shedding tears, she continued,

"I'm going to read you a letter; and if you knew what it means to me you would all be kinder to a disconsolate woman."

Stopping frequently to sob, Pola Negri read the following letter which Dr. Harold D. Meeker sent her by way of Mary Pickford.

"Dear Miss Negri,
I asked my former friend and client Mary Pickford to deliver this letter to you because I am about to leave for my camp in the State of Maine.
At about 4 o'clock in the morning on Monday (the day of his death) I was sitting next to Rudy's bed. I was alone in the bedroom. He opened his eyes, pulled out a hand and said; 'I'm afraid we won't be going fishing but maybe we'll meet again and who knows if we'll ever go fishing.' That was the first and only time he realized he would not heal. Then he talked about you, and said, 'If Pola does not come in time, tell her I think about her.'
Immediately, Rudy fell asleep, beginning the long sleep from which he never woke up. I feel obliged to make this message known to you.
Most sincerely,
Dr. Meeker. "

Then the secretary and the nurse, assisted by George Ullman, escorted her to her bed. A moment later the nurse returned to tell the journalists,

"She fainted."

The first of September, Alberto arrived from Europe. The day after his arrival, Rudolph's body left for Hollywood in a $15,000 coffin, and escorted by Alberto Guglielmi Valentino, Pola Negri, Ullman and wife and two or three other people. Respectful crowds flocked everywhere to pay homage to the fallen idol.

On the 6th, Rudolph's body was secretly off-loaded in Los Angeles and on the 7th, at ten o'clock in the morning, the Requiem Mass was said at the Church of the Good Shepherd of Beverly Hills. Rudolph's body was then taken to its final resting place in the cemetery of Hollywood.

To give an idea of that memorable farewell, I will share the following sincere description I made of the mournful ceremonies, moments after having witnessed them myself.

"THE LAST NUPTIALS OF
VALENTINO

In this same church of the Good Shepherd, where the catholic actors and actresses of Hollywood usually congregate in their spiritual duties, we attended, little more than two months ago, to the happy wedding of the star Mae Murray and the Georgian prince David Mdivani. Rudolph Valentino and Pola Negri joyfully sponsored that union. Father Mullins blessed it. And only eleven friends of the couple joined the little entourage.

The temple seemed huge to us on that occasion and it sounded empty. We remember very well when the bride and groom and the wedding witnesses were ready for the ceremony, next to the balustrade of the presbytery and while the priest leafed through the holy book in search of the required sheet, Rudolph Valentino and Pola Negri, the two great seducers of the screen, smiled lovingly behind the nuptial couple; in a mute, but flattering allusion to their common desires and purposes. Pola Negri recalls on that happy occasion, within this very church and during the wedding of Mae Murray and Prince Mdivani, that her lover announced to her, very significantly, that they would soon return to the same sanctuary.

A little more than two months have passed since then and today the forecast of the perfect lover is fulfilled. There are Rudolph Valentino and Pola Negri, again close to the balustrade were they witnessed the happy wedding of Mae Murray and David Mdivani. Within the presbytery, the same Father Mullins who blessed the union. Here and there, lost in the crowded seats, some of the members of the brief cortege; Agnes Ayres, Cathleen Williams, Alberto Guglielmi.

Wrapped in black crepe and kneeling, Pola Negri kneels next to her beloved. Her tragic emotion would not be noticed in such a thick blackness, if it was not externalized by her frequent shaking and sobbing. To the side of the plaintive actress, lies the body of the beloved; imprisoned forever in a sumptuous coffin. It is covered by a wide mantle, a cross of lilies from Alberto Guglielmi, brother of the deceased; that hapless man who knelt next to the mourning actress. He is also moaning.

The Reverend Mullins repeats the words of St. Paul then delivers the Requiem Mass. The Temple of the Good Shepherd does not seem as big to us today as on that joyous day of the wedding; it no longer sounds empty to us.

It is full of people. The brightest stars of the cinematographic firmament are part of the mournful entourage. But today they are only extras in a real life tragedy.

Here and there, muffled sobs whisper and handkerchiefs flutter to wipe tears from the eyes or to contain outbursts from the lips. There are so many souls feeling widowhood before that sumptuous coffin! There are so many women who, in real life or in a fictional one, received the kisses of Valentino! He was twice married, a hundred times lover, a thousand times seducer.

Poor Rudolph! A few weeks ago on the eve of his fateful journey, how full of life, of projects, of illusions! And how much in love! It seems we still see him debating with his girlfriend about the portrait of her which he would take with him to New York. He preferred a certain photo. She wanted him to take a different one. They discussed like two silly adolescents those two great seducers of the screen. They were reveling their whims, their jealousies, their love. Who would have thought, at that moment, that a few weeks later that pictorial man of life and optimism would lie cold in a coffin or that his happy lover would be crying by his corpse!

The organ resonates its funeral sobs as the coffin leaves for the cemetery. An endless row of luxurious automobiles forms the slow escort to the hearse. On both sides of the road, thousands and thousands of worshipers who were mainly women. Some were throwing bouquets which could not be kept on the coffin; these from the unknown lovers of the beloved. Above the convoy, graceful airplanes groove the warm Californian air and hum, in their own way, a funeral song while festooning the air by dropping flowers on the hearse.

We arrived at the imposing mausoleum where only a few companions could approach the niche of the actor. While the priest murmurs the last rites, the dead man's brother and girlfriend moan their farewell. A pathetic "Addio, Rodolfo, addio!", from the devastated Alberto Guglielmi, breaks through the hardest of hearts. Clumsily and calmly, the coffin penetrates the square hole. The metal on the marble makes a horrible screech, as if it had heard a complaint from the dead man. Hearing this, the bride utters a savage cry and collapses again.

For a long time they groan inconsolably, seated on the same sofa, Guglielmi and Pola Negri while a chorus of sobs accompanies them. There are no eyes, in this sad moment, that do not shine with sincere tears.

Mary Pickford, Agnes Ayres, Marion Davies, Cathleen Williams and June Mathis stand out among the tearful group. Neither the strong Douglas Fairbanks, nor the comic Charlie Chaplin can at this moment contain their tears. We leave our great friend in his final bed: the beautiful gallant, a thousand times conqueror, conquered in the end by death, the most disdained mistress, in whose cold arms he'll rest forever."

A year of Rudolph's idolization has passed[55] and we have not yet learned just who was the woman who most wanted him or who was the woman he loved the most. Two indispensable traits sketch the soul of a beloved lover. Who did Rudolph Valentino want more?

He bestowed his last amorous messages upon Pola. As he said to some, he never stopped loving Jean Acker. As he told others, there was no woman he wanted as much as Natacha Rambova. But he also said, sometimes in moments of privacy, that it was "Bianca," the proud South American aristocrat who inspired the purest love of his life. And it is pure love, the love which never materializes, which is the one that most often grows and lasts in sentimental and idealistic souls like that of Rudolph Valentino.

The "Sheik" perhaps loved, above all, Woman; and it is logical to suppose "she" occupied in his soul the preferred place where she gave him the greatest illusions perhaps as the Unknown Mistress, the result of the countless admirers who offered him enjoyment everywhere. The other women, except "Bianca", were those he loved as his ideal: the women who never brought him disappointment. Who was the one woman the great lover loved most?

Pola, the one who wanted him as "the greatest love of her life", saying she could never love again, is today the wife of that young man she was with when she received the phone call from New York telling her of Rudolph's serious illness. Jean Acker, Natacha Rambova. . . they remained quite discreet, so respectfully, we now pass them by.

"Bianca" has always been too loyal to her husband to encourage a suitor. There remains, then, the same "unknown lover" who, even after a year has passed, continues to remember Valentino with love. Even today, most of the letters the mail brings me daily come from women who love Rudolph Valentino.

Not long ago, while Pola Negri was absent from Hollywood a few days before the anniversary of the death of her "beloved", a young woman from Lima honored me with the task of depositing flowers on the tomb of Rudolph. That same young woman honored me with an equal mission on the birthday of the "Sheik." That "unknown lover", far from everywhere, is the one that most loved Rudolph Valentino, the one determining the grandiose spectacle of his now thrilling idolization.

---

55 This installment was published in February, 1928.

And it is that same "unknown lover" who will put the last words to this humble story of the real Rudolph Valentino, because of one of the last letters I received from Barcelona, from an anonymous lover of "Sheik". I share the following as a prophecy concerning the post-summoning glory of that great lover, who suffered so much with his most fortunate loved ones, while thousands and thousands of women, less fortunate, were willing to sacrifice themselves to make him happy.

Says the loving Catalan woman in her letter, she who is not yet consoled for the loss of her beloved,

"Unfortunately, the beautiful pedestal on which only he alone knew how to stand, will crumble by itself. Most of it was formed by something very fickle; women's hearts! Until recently, those hearts beat almost in unison for a Rudolph Valentino whom they worshiped as a God. But how many now are already disunited and are feeling reborn with another new idolatry! Vile world, full of envy and baseness; where only the material triumphs!"[56]

The End

---

56 It appears this prophecy of Valentino's Catalan lover would not come true. Almost one hundred years after his death, Rudolph Valentino's continued and revered presence in the hearts of many women worldwide, proves they are not as fickle in their idolization as she projects.

Cine-Mundial
January 1927

The Consolation of Pola Negri

By Baltasar Fernández Cué

Pola Negri's bungalow seems to smile from its corner of the Ambassador Hotel garden. The immaculate patio and privacy walls are covered in red terracotta tiles and the flowers seem to be whispering like gossiping neighbor women. The trees provide their hiding places and the bungalow windows invite their amorous conversations[57]. Only the barking of an occasional aggressive dog sounds as interference.

We just left behind us, there outside this little patio and on the other side of this comforting garden, the dark gray mass of the imposing hotel which is animated by the light of innumerable suggestive windows. Inside that immense building life bustles in a thousand ways. Outside; a beautiful, yet rather desolate panorama.

The last time I saw Pola Negri, she was standing before Rudolph Valentino's coffin. Then she was so blinded by her tears, she noticed no one. I am curious to know what could have happened in the soul of this actress since that mournful scenario; and my visit today represents the scene following that very sad moment. I come in the company of Alberto Guglielmi Valentino, who was with Pola in that last scene, as she moaned before the coffin of the ill-fated Rudolph.

A Swiss maid, wearing the black and white uniform typical of a waitress, escorts us into a luminous room. According to what she tells us, in French, we will not have to wait a long time.

"Madame viendra, tout de suite."

As Alberto and I step into this great room, we see how the space is presided over, from above a delicate night table, by a huge portrait of Rudolph Valentino in which he stares forward, hypnotizing us with his dark magnetic gaze. This was his most characteristic pose.

In this bright room, in addition to the furniture which is as joyful as the

---

57 t.n.: *A pelar la pava* - (plucking the turkey) - to engage in amorous conversation.

space itself, we see large books scattered about and some small books, which seem to doze here and there on various pieces of furniture. We see two fine flowerpots which visually fill the entire space with a striking display of two pompous bouquets of yellow chrysanthemums. This creates a unique effect.

It was here where, not so many months ago, we as friends used to come to witness Pola and Rudolph recalling, often in loud voices, the love tactics they used to conquer each other. Pola would sit on that flirtatious sofa in the corner, with a thin yellow shawl casually thrown around her shoulders. The contrast such a color created with her black hair made her profile more beautiful than ever. Rudolph would stand a few steps away from her.

Both prided themselves in reminiscencing about the dawning of their idyllic courtship and both demonstrated a certain air of triumph. Then we knew, by how they began looking at each admiringly albeit with deception, how they played out their roles; how they used to feign indifference even if they felt something else. We saw how each one recognized that attitude in the other, even while raging emotionally inside and how one laughed at any pretext so that the other would not recognize a breach in the other's snobbishness. In short, the eternal story.

"But continuing like that, nothing could have happened because I would never give in," said Rudolph, eager to confirm he had not been conquered. To this Pola laughed at his words with feminine diplomacy.

Then, after relating other memories, Rudolph proposed to make a peace which was never undone. Putting his hands in his pockets as if to suggest how clean his game was going to be, he turned lovingly towards Pola Negri, offering his pursed lips for a kiss.

And those two loving mouths touched just slightly while their bodies remained distanced; as two carnation blossoms of two different plants might by chance touch. The contact was so slight that Rudolph bent too low and lacking support, he nearly lost his balance to fall headfirst onto the sofa.

As I remember those blissful days of the Polish actress, a most solemn silence now reigns in her home. Suddenly, we hear some quick and resolute steps sounding in the next room. Then, violently and almost rudely, the door opens. There, dressed all in black and wrapped in a smile, appears the peerless Pola Negri.

She is no longer the distressed woman I saw staggering out on the arms of her friends, leaving the mausoleum where the body of her beloved would remain forever. That day, she poured out in a sad, half-conscious state with all the tears she could shed. Afterwards, faithful to her earthbound commitments, she returned to the stress of her professional life and finished the movie *Hotel Imperial*, which was suspended by the death of her lover.

She then made one other movie and drowned her widow's anguish in a mad drunkenness of artistic activity.

She tells us that just yesterday she finished the movie *Barbed Wire* based on the novel of the Great War, "The Woman of Knockaloe", by the famous English novelist Hall Caine. And she seems very happy because the producer and the director praised her performance and the film in general. In *Hotel Imperial* – of the same theme of the Great War - Alberto Guglielmi tells us Pola's work was so exceptional, in his opinion and that of others who have already seen the completed film, the premiere will be a remarkable one.

"Surely," adds Rudolph's brother, "it is the best movie Pola has filmed in the United States."

"But in the studio they think *Barbed Wire* is even better," she assures us.

"I want to add this," I said, "That finally they cast you in the right roles in the United States; because you would agree that until now they have not taken advantage of your artistic faculties."

Pola agrees with the explanation of her current success, adding that many elements contributing to an important degree in the production of *Hotel Imperial* were European. When it comes to *Barbed Wire* you could say almost the same thing too.

"The amazing thing," I add, "is that after so many mistakes they have made as far your numerous directors, the public continues to recognize you as a great actress. Have you not noticed that anomaly?"

"Yes," she replies, "How could I not notice? But that is probably due to the fact that the public remembers me in the great European films in which the Americans first knew me."

"I think it is rather that the public has not lost sight of your intense personality, which is absolute even despite bad scenarios and bad directors."

Now, animated by her latest personal triumphs, Pola Negri's producers decided to assign her the best minds of their company and engage her in bringing to the screen famously classic works. She will begin, upon returning from her next vacation to Honolulu, by filming *Vanity Fair* by Thackeray.

She assures us that it is not true she plans to do, *Camille*, in competition with her friend Norma Talmadge. The company United Artists has already announced the film based on the novel by Dumas; and in the case of works whose property rights have expired, it is customary among serious companies to announce their intent to film a particular story.

It is after our dinner and after several hours of pleasant talk, when finally we speak about the subject which until then we had discreetly avoided. She speaks of a friend - Mal Saint Clair - who visited Rudolph a few days before his death at the hotel he stayed in while in New York. Suddenly, as if remembering something she was meant to tell me, with her voice and her face growing sad, she says,

"No, I am not yet in a position to speak calmly of these things. But do you remember that small oval picture frame in which Rudy had my portrait next to his bed?

"For sure I remember it!"

And I did remember the discussion he and she had on the eve of his last trip, about which portrait would go in that little silver frame; the portrait she wanted or the one he liked the most.

"At last, what portrait did Rudy take?" I ask her.

"The one I wanted," she continues, breaking into tears after these few words and mourning,

"And Saint Clair told me that in New York he had it by his bed between two little branches of lilies."

Pola is silent for a few moments, because her tears will not let her continue. Alberto Guglielmi Valentino, who cares for her as a sister, is also touched. Then, little by little, Pola Negri recovers her serenity and begins to comment about mysterious circumstances related to her irreparable loss.

"Rudy sensed his end was approaching," she says rising nervously.

She then leaves and returns quickly; bringing a book which she opens and places in my hands. It is a copy of Rudolph's verses *Day Dreams*, in which she wants me to read the handwritten dedication in English by the author penned shortly before his leaving.

"For my beloved, 'Polita'. May you dream of your Rudy when time and space have separated us."

"And it happened. We are already separated," she says, sighing, "It is as I just read in his dedication."

Pola stares into my eyes as she then tells me about the spiritual dialogues in which she and Rudy used to entertain themselves.[58] They, who had so much joy in this earthly life and who received so many favors from Fate, far from giving themselves blindly to unbridled pleasure in such tempting circumstances often devoted themselves to meditating on the happiness waiting for them in the Great Beyond. It was the other life which caused them the most concern. It was the connection with the immortal and the invisible which they felt surrounded them and this was the one they most wished to enjoy.

How different from the image of how the world fantasized about them! Sometimes at night, there in the emblazoned areas of Falcon Lair - where Pola spent many evenings as family with Rudolph and his relatives - the couple used to retire to the calmness of the library where they chatted alone about spiritualism; surrounded by panoplies and armors, the old furniture, the dark paintings and the shelves heavy with books.

Suddenly, they might hear a click or a murmur. Then the couple would stay silent and probe the darkness of the room's corners or peek out at the night through the stained glass windows. But the attention of the lovers was not due to the concern for some possible danger, but to the hope of finding decisive confirmation of their theories.

Other times they engaged in automatic writing. They received impressive messages in that way, who knows from where and who knows from whom, which encouraged them to continue on a spiritual path, even if those messages were contrary to their dearest desires. One of those messages, for example, told Pola Negri she would never marry Rudy.

Then another message was received; this upon Pola's arrival in New York to worship the body of her beloved. It was delivered to her in an envelope which contained a message obtained by a spiritualist through automatic writing. Pola shows me that message which was written in awkward, irregular letters. It is addressed to her and signed by "Rudy". She does not know who the spiritualist was or who received the message from Rudy. But, she says, the message contains phrases and ideas he used to tell her about immortal life.

At that moment, a slight and mysterious noise is heard inside Pola's

---

58 Pola Negri's statement to the press re: Natacha Rambova's spiritual "Revelations" from Rudolph, labeling such activity as, "Profane, shocking and commercial!" Cite, "What, No Movies in Heaven?", *New York Daily News*, December 5, 1926. Also *Astral Affairs Rambova*, Viale Industria Pubblicazioni, 2018, p. 113.

bedroom. She looks towards the door and as if by magic the solemn expression with which she has been explaining the content of the message disappears to be replaced by a glow embellishing the actress' face with the appearance of a hopeful smile. Does Pola hope that the soul of her beloved is about to appear in her bedroom?

In any way, she takes comfort in her remembrance of her lost happiness and repeats the words of her lover,

"We are not to die. We will continue living a more spiritual life when time and space have separated us."

Pola tells us she dreams of Rudy in order to not feel lonely. Despite her suffering the severe loss, she understands the intimacy of his spirit. And perhaps, I hope when least expected, she does receive the confirmation of the predictions of her beloved and of their own beliefs.

It is after midnight when Alberto Guglielmi and I say goodbye to "Polita". We then walk across the garden pathways and lawns of the sleepy Ambassador Hotel; a dance of shadows creates for me the impression of life in a space which before was for me just a beautifully desolate panorama.

That night, after going to bed, I felt a presence in the air which would not let me sleep; a presence charged with an otherworldly consolation.

Los Angeles, California, 1926

Cine-Mundial
November 1926

My Last Visit With Rudolph Valentino

By Baltasar Fernández Cué

It was on the eve of Valentino's last trip from Los Angeles to New York, when I surprised him, somewhat hidden, in his tiny office attached to the rich library of his brand new mansion, Falcon Lair; perched high above the populated city of Beverly Hills. He was writing a love letter by hand and I could not help noticing it began with the eternal words, "My love," in English. It was not inscribed to his beloved Pola Negri. Was, then, the "Sheik", in the disposition which most characterized him, in life as well as on screen?

Valentino, Manuel Reachi and the one writing these lines, chatted for a long time in his library as we had on many other occasions. We were seated in front of the portrait preferred by Pola Negri; the work portraying Valentino in the outfit of a Jerez-born gentleman. The actor was in a very good mood as usual and his appearance seemed excellent. As always, his strength was apparant. Since he had not yet dressed, he was wrapped in a loose robe, with his dark muscles peering out here and there whenever he moved.

On his forehead, a scarred bruise received when he fell from the stage to the orchestra pit after having delivered a small speech upon the opening of his latest film, *The Son of the Sheik.*

In the course of our conversation, Valentino shared with me some most flattering words about my review of this cinematographic work. He said he liked how I praised his acting in the role of the Sheik's father. This because my applause was for the actor and not just for the beautiful young man who was jaded by the applause of others. He also liked the conclusion of my review which said,

"In that nice old age which Valentino feigns, we see not only a revelation and a reason for aesthetic enjoyment. We also discover a reliable promise, which may at the same time, be a warning. By demonstrating in his films, characteristics such as that of the father in *The Son of the Sheik*, it will be easy for Valentino to emancipate himself from fictitious youth when he begins to lack real youth."

That is to say; Valentino tried to evolve, little by little, from good boy to good actor and over the years the public would admire him for his refined art as much as they cherished him for his lively youth. How could he imagine the accuracy of his intelligent prediction!

The actor then gave me a copy of his book of verses entitled *Day Dreams*. After reading the generous dedication and to express my gratitude, I opened the tome at random and read, in English, some verses.

"I do not care the easy gold, because it ends soon ... I know ... ."

Looking at Rudolph with flashing eyes, Manuel Reachi thundered implacably,

"Boy, is that the only truth you have said in all your hectic life!"

The characteristic ironic smile of the Italian actor made me guess he was about to speak,

"If I said a great truth, that charity is for you."

I intervened,

"Don't worry, Valentino! Reachi has already told you those same words more than twenty times in my presence. So you have already said, at least, more than twenty great truths."

However, I could not avoid the usual rowdy discussion between the two friends. As they used to argue like two good brothers and about matters of no importance [59], they often had disagreements. Yet, they always looked for each other and when they were not together, they defended each other.

In order to let them resolve this duel with more freedom, I went into Valentino's little private office and began to write on a portable typewriter. The actor thought to close the door so I would not be distracted by the arguing voices. But through the thick mahogany, I heard the characteristic cries of the resounding Latin brotherhood.

Sometimes, I felt they were about to come to blows. I once saw them pull two swords from the old sets of arms which gave Falcon Lair its air of a

---

59 t.n.: *Por un quitame allá esas pajas* - (For to take those straws away) - because of a matter of no importance.

medieval castle. Surely they were already resolving their disagreement in the manner of those who originally wielded that iron armor which acts as ornament in the hispanic mansion where the "Sheik" lives.

I imagined one of the contenders threatening his opponent by shaking the ancient Spanish sideboard which presides over the furniture in the library. I hear the volumes of the packed book shelves flying about; the English, French, Spanish and Italian classics abound. There where the books about costumes and the habits of people around the earth are all included.

I was obliged to accelerate my work on the typewriter to arrive in time to save at least the valuable content of one of those full book shelves. As I left the typewriter, alarmed by the arguing, I was surprised to find the furniture, the books and the armor all intact. Valentino and Reachi were laughing aloud about a memory of a huge party they enjoyed together in New York eight years before.

Suddenly they ceased in their hilarious remembrance because then appeared, like a ghost and dressed in white, the fascinating figure of Pola Negri. She was, in those days, very busy in the preliminaries of the movie *Hotel Imperial.* But every time she was free, she used that time to fly to her boyfriend's side, assuming he had not already flown to her's. They loved each other with all their souls and I never saw it as clear as that day, on the eve of their eternal separation.

Pola Negri entered her boyfriend's office that day and saw on his desk the letter which began with the eternal words "My love," as it was addressed to another woman. She did not pluck a single hair from the Italian actor's head! She remained as calm as if the epistle was something required as a prop for some movie. Did she know it had a different significance, that it was destined for a real person and that Valentino was not working for any movie at the time? Probably, Pola could not conceive that Rudolph could love another woman and this was the reason for her unheardof trust.

Once, when she visited the studio where the movie *The Son of the Sheik* was being completed, she arrived just at the time when Valentino and Vilma Banky were engaged in an enviously tight and long-lasting kiss. Those around Pola at the time watched to see her reaction to such a situation. Very calmly and with a broad smile showing her confident happiness, the Polish actress told them,

"He kisses Vilma, but he thinks of me."

We had not spoken too long nor had we emptied the golden glasses full of a liquid which tasted like the most exquisite Jerez, when Pola began to delight us with a terrible criticism of a famous film director. He, according to her, understood nothing of photography, of costumes or anything else. She was furious at him, above all, because he wanted to dress her in a suit too tight at the waist. Raising her eloquent hands to her chest, she added,

"Since I'm very gifted here, this was all pushed up and it turned out to be something unsightly, rude. Of course, the photograph was able to prove that the suit was an unforgivable barbarity."

In speaking about photographs, Valentino led the conversation in that direction. He wanted Pola to give him a certain portrait to accompany him on his trip to New York and he asked her to send out urgently for a reduction of said portrait.

"I want it to fit in that frame which Marion Davies gave me. You remember?"

The actor was referring to a valuable oval slide mounting frame he kept on the side of his bed which bore one of the three portraits of Pola Negri which adorned his bedroom.

"But why do you want me to give you another one?" Pola asked, "Don't you like me already in that one?"

Valentino thought maybe Pola was asking too much. For him the only question his girlfriend had to ask was, which size would be necessary to reduce the portrait he requested. And to avoid the inquisition, he ran off to his bedroom and immediately returned with the beautiful frame which held a gorgeous image of his beloved.

"But what does this portrait have which makes you want to discard it? Why do you prefer the other?"

"Because I like you more in that one."

"Because you like me more..." Pola repeated slowly, as if she wanted to be certain of the truth of such an enjoyable thought. She delighted in savoring such an idea while staring into Valentino's eyes; which were glued to hers.

Pola kept laughing while gazing into her lover's eyes, as if searching the depths of his soul for the confirmation of the fondness his lips were revealing. At last, the woman half-promised and half-denied and left, very smartly amid a smiling rain of pretexts. She left without giving the "Sheik" any assurance of whether or not she was going to give him the picture he so desired.

"Hey, Rudy," I commented, "now I am convinced you're in love with her like a donkey."

"Why?" He asked mechanically, but full of smugness because he was convinced being in love with her was an honor.

"Like, why?" I replied, "That intensity, those prayers, those discussions over such a trivial thing. Tell me the truth; do not you feel as if you have turned into a teen-ager again?"

The great conqueror of hearts nodded,

"Yes!"

And thus the man who was receiving daily baskets of letters from women who loved him throughout the world, surrendered completely in Pola Negri's presence.

We then said good-bye and see you "in three weeks". But his stay in New York continued and a month and a half after our farewell, he died so tragically.

Los Angeles, California
August 1926

Baltasar Fernández Cué

Biographical Notes

Baltasar Cué was born in Llanes, Asturias, Spain, on September 9, 1878. He completed his formal education in France and in England and graduated with a degree in civil engineering in London in 1901. It was then he moved to Mexico, where he would hold public office in the Ministry of Development. During this time he began working as a journalist and freelance writer.

Cué's political support of Mexican president, Venustiano Carranza would cause his being deported from Mexico in 1921; this after Carranza's assasination. Cué then moved to Los Angeles where he initially earned a living as a Spanish teacher. With his bilingual expertise a valuable commodity at the time, he began working as a Hollywood reporter for Spanish-language newspapers and magazines around the world (*El Sol* and *La Pantalla* of Madrid; *Excelsior* of México, *World Cinema* in New York, *Mercury* in Chile and the *Excelsior* in Manila).

As a result of his *Cine-Mundial* biography of Rudolph Valentino, Cué was appointed head of foreign advertising for RKO Pictures in 1928. Over the next four years, he would secure employment adapting English language screenplays into Spanish. He worked primarily with Universal Pictures where he became director of the studio's Spanish department.

In 1933, Cué returned to Spain, residing in Madrid. As a member of the Socialist Party, he worked as a contributor to the political party's *El Socialista* newspaper. Cué would live in Madrid during the Spanish Civil War as an anti-fascist, anti-Franco agent of the Socialista secret service known as SIM, the "Servicio de Información Militar", the military intelligence service. With Dictator Franco's victory, Cué was charged as a spy and condemned to death. Through his political connections he was able to have his death sentence commuted to a prison sentence of thirty years which he began serving in the prisons of Toreno and Yeserías in Madrid, Ocaña in Toledo, San Simón Island and Vigo in Pontevedra.

Cué was awarded a temporary and provisional furlough, and used this opportunity to escape Spain and travel to Lisbon where he sailed to America; arriving in New York on October 17, 1945.

There he joined the editorial staff of *World Cinema* magazine and worked as a journalist and translator until his death in Venice, California in 1964.

The Images

The covers of each issue of the *Cine-Mundial* installments are included in this publication along with the first few pages of the article to share the illustrations as they were first presented.

The images are reproduced from: *Cine-Mundial* archives, January-December, 1927 – Volume 12, January-December, 1928 – Volume 13, No copyright found, Chalmers Publishing Company, Digitizing Sponsor: Library of Congress Motion Picture, Broadcasting and Recorded Sound Division.

"Cine-Mundial, the Spanish-language version of Moving Picture World, was published between 1916 and 1948. The magazine documents Hollywood's growing dominance in Latin American markets in the 1920's and the emergence of national film industries, such as those of Mexico and Argentina after the introduction of sound film. Far from being a mere translation of its English-language counterpart, Cine-Mundial focused on issues that were important to its readers in Latin America and Spain-the representation of Latin Americans on screen, the geo-politics of film distribution and Hollywood's short foray into Spanish-language film production in the late 1920's and early 1930's."

Laura Isabel Serna
Author of *Making Cinelandia, American Films & Mexican Film Culture Before the Golden Age – Duke University Press, 2014*

Installment # 1, May 1927.

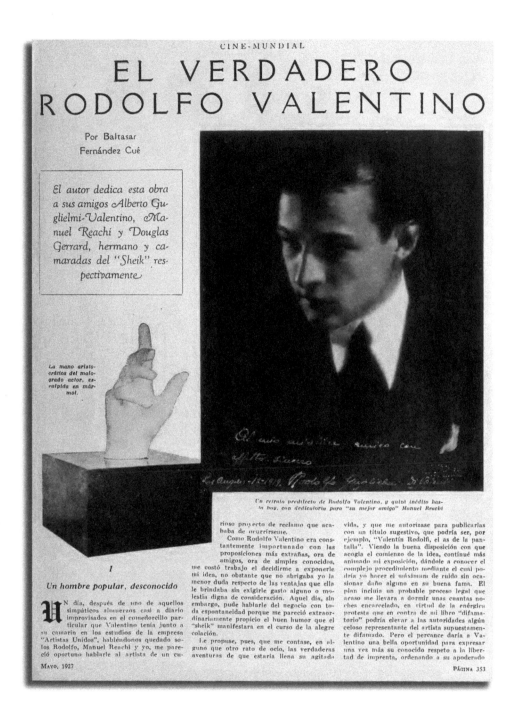

EL VERDADERO
RODOLFO VALENTINO

Por Baltasar
Fernández Cué

El autor dedica esta obra a sus amigos Alberto Guglielmi-Valentino, Manuel Reachi y Douglas Gerrard, hermano y camaradas del "Sheik" respectivamente

La mano aristocrática del malogrado actor, esculpida en mármol.

Un retrato predilecto de Rodolfo Valentino, y quizá inédito hasta hoy, con dedicatoria para "su mejor amigo" Manuel Reachi

I

Un hombre popular, desconocido

UN día, después de uno de aquellos simpáticos almuerzos casi a diario improvisados en el comedorcillo particular que Valentino tenía junto a su camarín en los estudios de la empresa "Artistas Unidos", habiéndonos quedado solos Rodolfo, Manuel Reachi y yo, me pareció oportuno hablarle al artista de un cu-

rioso proyecto de reclamo que acababa de ocurrírseme.

Como Rodolfo Valentino era constantemente importunado con las proposiciones más extrañas, ora de amigos, ora de simples conocidos, me costó trabajo el decidirme a exponerle mi idea, no obstante que no abrigaba yo la menor duda respecto de las ventajas que le brindaba sin exigirle gasto alguno o molestia digna de consideración. Aquel día, sin embargo, pude hablarle del negocio con toda espontaneidad porque me pareció extraordinariamente propicio el buen humor que el "sheik" manifestara en el curso de la alegre colación.

Le propuse, pues, que me contase, en algunos que otro rato de ocio, las verdaderas aventuras de que estaría llena su agitada

vida, y que me autorizase para publicarlas con un título sugestivo, que podría ser, por ejemplo, "Valentín Rodolfi, el as de la pantalla". Viendo la buena disposición con que acogía el comienzo de la idea, continué más animado mi exposición, dándole a conocer el complejo procedimiento mediante el cual podría yo hacer el máximum de ruido sin ocasionar daño alguno en su buena fama. El plan incluía un probable proceso legal que acaso me llevara a dormir unas cuantas noches encarcelado, en virtud de la enérgica protesta que en contra de mi libro "difamatorio" podría elevar a las autoridades algún celoso representante del artista supuestamente difamado. Pero el percance daría a Valentino una bella oportunidad para expresar una vez más su conocido respeto a la libertad de imprenta, ordenando a su apoderado

Installment #1 – page 1.

Portrait of Rudolph Valentino inscribed to his friend Manuel Reachi

que se desistiese de la demanda, toda vez que la obra no se refería expresamente a Rodolfo Valentino, sino a un ser imaginario llamado Valentín Rodolfi. Con lo cual el libro se anunciaría por doquiera y el "sheik" quedaría ante la opinión como un caballero liberal y magnánimo. Los puritanos — coco de toda persona que en los Estados Unidos viva de la notoriedad — no tendrían derecho a hacerle cargo alguno, puesto que sería un juicio temerario el afirmar que ni obra se refería a él. Pero no habría ni un lector que en su fuero interno lo pusiera en duda. Y la responsabilidad de esta sugestión clarísima caería totalmente sobre mis hombros, si bien con el carácter soportable de una provechosa travesura que, lejos de ser reprobada, no podría menos de merecer aplausos en un país en que el culto del reclamo — así en el comercio como en la política, el arte, la sociedad y aun la religión — explicaría por sí solo el enorme desenvolvimiento nacional mucho más convincentemente que todas las teorías hasta ahora aducidas para explicar la tan decantada superioridad de la raza anglosajona.

Arriba, entre escena y escena durante la filmación de "El Hijo del Sheik", Valentino, Vilma Banky, Baltasar Fernández Cué, George Fitzmaurice y Manuel Reachi. Abajo, Jean Guglielmi Valentino, hijo de Alberto — el hermano mayor del finado artista.

Testigo viviente es Manuel Reachi de que, apenas hube terminado la explicación del pro-

vecto, Rodolfo Valentino — el peliculero más amante del reclamo, a cuya magia debió la mayor parte de su talla cinematográfica — dió un brinco, apretó los puños para dar aun más energía a sus palabras, y exclamó muy gozoso:

—¡Caramba, hombre, eso sí me gusta mucho!

Convinimos en que no saldría de los tres la idea de hacer tal libro, hasta que llegara la hora de publicarlo. Lo cual era indispensable para la realización del proyecto, porque la voluntad de Valentino era como una veleta, puesto que siempre apuntaba en la dirección que soplase su último consejero.

En aquella misma ocasión me prometió seriamente relatarme sus más interesantes aventuras. Mas como estaba entonces muy atareado con la película "El Hijo del Sheik" — cuya terminación le importaba muy especialmente para reforzar un poco su situación financiera, tan debilitada por los tumbos de su último viaje a Europa —, y como los ratos de ocio pertenecían por derecho

#1 – 2. On the Set of *The Son of the Sheik*

Left to Right: *Rudolph Valentino, Vilma Banky, Baltasar Cué, George Fitzmaurice, Manuel Reachi.*
Below: *Jean Guglielmi Valentino*

propio a la afortunada Pola Negri, quedámos en que, apenas acabara de hacer la película, me dedicaría todo el tiempo que fuese necesario para enterarme, especialmente, de sus hazañas amorosas.

—Y lo que se me olvide a mí, que se lo cuenten Manuel y Douglas — agregó Rodolfo Valentino refiriéndose a sus dos camaradas predilectos: el mejicano Manuel Reachi y el irlandés Douglas Gerrard, que, como otros tantos mosqueteros, habían compartido con él —si bien con más suerte — el disfrute de jaranas, así en Nueva York como en Hollywood.

Después de aquel día, cada vez que se presentaba ocasión propicia, procuraba yo traer a colación el tema del libro. Nos veíamos con frecuencia durante las últimas semanas de sus trabajos postreros. Después del almuerzo, cuando nos quedábamos a solas los tres mismos amigos, ora de sobremesa, ora sentados en su despacho, ora mientras se retocaba los afeites o se cambiaba la indumentaria árabe ante el resplandeciente tocador, solíamos discutir diversas fases del proyecto.

A veces, contaba Rodolfo algún caso interesante de su propia vida. Otras, metía baza Reachi para corregir algún error o para contar un sabroso incidente olvidado. Otras, el artista tiraba de una gaveta de su escritorio y me entregaba un documento utilizable: una carta, un retrato, un recorte de periódico, una copia de algún mensaje trascendental.

Un día llamó a su secretaria y le rogó

Alberto Guglielmi-Valentino, con cuya colaboración moral y plena autorización, ha escrito nuestro colaborador en Los Angeles estas páginas íntimas. A la izquierda, una de las últimas fotografías de Rodolfo, con motivo del casamiento de Mae Murray: él, Pola Negri, Mae y su marido David Diviani

que me entregase la única copia que tenía del relato de su vida, publicado años antes en una de las más importantes revistas cinematográficas de los Estados Unidos. Miss Margaret Neff me lo entregó acompañado de otros documentos semejantes, pero menos extensos; y, al mismo tiempo, me los recomendó como si se tratase de una joya valiosísima o de algún antiguo pergamino que en modo alguno se pudiera substituir. Valentino, sin embargo, hizo un enorme descuento del valor de aquellos papeles.

El principal de ellos — el que él había rogado que se me diese — era un cuento que se reputaba como autobiografía. Se titulaba "La Historia de mi Vida".

Cómo se escribe la historia

A quien no esté familiarizado con los procedimientos usuales en las oficinas de reclamo de los estudios de Hollywood, le costará trabajo creer que Valentino declarase, aun

(Continúa en la página 397)

#1 – 3.

Above: *Alberto Guglielmi Valentino*
Left to Right Below: *Rudolph Valentino, Pola Negri, Mae Murray & David Mdivani*

158

Installment # 2 – June 1927.

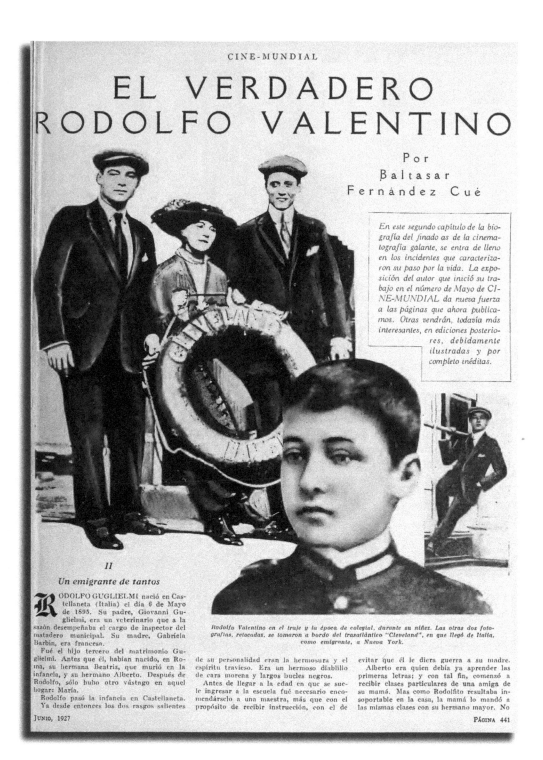

EL VERDADERO RODOLFO VALENTINO

Por
Baltasar
Fernández Cué

En este segundo capítulo de la biografía del finado as de la cinematografía galante, se entra de lleno en los incidentes que caracterizaron su paso por la vida. La exposición del autor que inició su trabajo en el número de Mayo de CINE-MUNDIAL da nueva fuerza a las páginas que ahora publicamos. Otras vendrán, todavía más interesantes, en ediciones posteriores, debidamente ilustradas y por completo inéditas.

II

Un emigrante de tantos

RODOLFO GUGLIELMI nació en Castellaneta (Italia) el día 6 de Mayo de 1895. Su padre, Giovanni Guglielmi, era un veterinario que a la sazón desempeñaba el cargo de inspector del matadero municipal. Su madre, Gabriela Barbin, era francesa.

Fué el hijo tercero del matrimonio Guglielmi. Antes que él, habían nacido, en Roma, su hermana Beatriz, que murió en la infancia, y su hermano Alberto. Después de Rodolfo, sólo hubo otro vástago en aquel hogar: María.

Rodolfo pasó la infancia en Castellaneta. Ya desde entonces los dos rasgos salientes de su personalidad eran la hermosura y el espíritu travieso. Era un hermoso diablillo de cara morena y largos bucles negros.

Antes de llegar a la edad en que se suele ingresar a la escuela fué necesario encomendárselo a una maestra, más que con el propósito de recibir instrucción, con el de evitar que él le diera guerra a su madre.

Alberto era quien debía ya aprender las primeras letras; y con tal fin, comenzó a recibir clases particulares de una amiga de su mamá. Mas como Rodolfito resultaba insoportable en la casa, la mamá lo mandó a las mismas clases con su hermano mayor. No

Rodolfo Valentino en el traje y la época de colegial, durante su niñez. Las otras dos fotografías, retocadas, se tomaron a bordo del trasatlántico "Cleveland", en que llegó de Italia, como emigrante, a Nueva York.

#2 – 1.

Rudolph Valentino on board the S.S. Cleveland and as a child in school uniform

tenía la obligación de estudiar, sino la de estarse quieto, lo que era más difícil. Más difícil, por dos razones: porque su carácter le imponía la inquietud; y porque su natural facultad retentiva le obligaba a absorber conocimientos sin proponérselo.

Desde aquellos primeros años de su vida demostró la facilidad que tenía para aprender con sólo oír, característica que le sirvió siempre de compensación a otra no menos saliente en su carácter: la falta de afición al estudio. Porque Rodolfo jamás fué un estudiante aplicado. Más bien se podría decir que detestaba los libros. Pero retenía cuanto escuchaba; y esto le hacía parecer mejor estudiante que muchos compañeros que acaso se quemaran las cejas procurando estudiar la lección. El mismo hermano Alberto nos cuenta, con plausible modestia, que cuando él salió de aquellas primeras clases de la infancia,

Una instantánea del actor, tomada en el acto en que abandonó su patria para buscar fortuna en los Estados Unidos. No le faltó compañía durante el viaje.

Certificados y boletas de inscripción de la época juvenil y estudiantil de Rodolfo. En el de arriba se notan sus señas particulares, fidelísimas, poco antes de emigrar.

Rodolfo había aprendido, sin estudiar, mucho más que él estudiando.

De una de las más inocentes travesuras infantiles le quedó a Rodolfo una huella física que no le dejaron otras mucho más graves. Un día, cuando contaba apenas cinco años de edad, halló sobre un tocador la navaja de afeitar de su padre. Creyéndose ya un hombrecillo, y tomando el vello de su rostro por barba incipiente, cogió la navaja, colocóse ante el espejo, y, sin perder el tiempo en darse jabón, comenzó a rasurarse. La madre, como tantas otras a quienes la Providencia encomienda la crianza de pícaros de tal jaez, se entretenía lo más de la jornada

en dos grandes y absorbentes preocupaciones: una, regañar a Rodolfo por sus travesuras; y otra, vigilarle a fin de descubrirlas a tiempo. Cuando callaba un gran rato el rapaz, ya estaba la madre corriendo de cuarto en cuarto, apuradísima, temiendo que ocurriese alguna cosa grave. Ahora bien: la iniciación en el hábito varonil de rasurarse, por fuerza había de ser solemnemente silenciosa. Tenía, pues, que atraer en seguida a la mamá. Cuando ésta descubrió a su hijo ante el espejo, no pudo contener un grito de horror. Varios hilos de sangre corrían escandalosamente por la mejilla derecha del chiquillo, en la que el finísimo filo, tan desmañadamente esgrimido, había penetrado sin piedad. El niño que se creía ya hombre, se volvió sonriente hacia su alarmada madre y, con la calma que toda su vida puso en sus palabras, le preguntó:

—Pero ¿qué te pasa, mamá? ¿No ves que estoy rasurándome lo mismo que papá?

Los que se hayan fijado bien en el rostro de Valentino habrán notado que tenía una cicatriz recta en el carrillo derecho. Era el imborrable recuerdo de su primera pretensión de hombría.

María fué la compañera de travesuras domésticas de Rodolfito desde que ella comenzó a despegar las manos del suelo. Alberto, en su calidad de hermano mayor, tenía desde niño la tendencia a considerarse como un

hombre hecho y derecho y, por ende, a mirar por encima del hombro a su hermanito, cuyos entretenimientos le resultaban demasiado pueriles.

Claro está que, a veces, se agregaban a Rodolfo y María amigas de la chiquilla y amigos del muchacho. Y fué así cómo Rodolfo comenzó desde la infancia a estar estrechamente ligado al bello sexo, que tanto habría de hacerle gozar y sufrir.

Desde muy temprano, esas ligas comenzaron a ocasionar amoríos. Y se nota desde luego en las primeras aventuras del futuro "sheik" que no era muy afortu-

#2 – 2.

Various documents relevant to Valentino's life in Italy prior to his emigration

nado que digamos, y que le gustaban preferentemente las muchachas de más edad que él.

Tenía unos seis años cuando se enamoró perdidamente de una mujercita de nueve llamada Teodolinda: pero hallaba dificultad en abordarla, porque carecía él aún de la audacia que suele dar la experiencia, y porque era ella demasiado ruborosa y esquiva, y porque, como si eso fuese poco, la pequeña Teodolinda andaba ordinariamente en compañía de una hermana mayor, tan fea, tan coja y tan irascible, que para Rodolfo hacía las veces de un pavoroso espantajo, a la par animado y agresivo.

Después de una larga temporada de muda y platónica contemplación, a suficiente distancia para librarse de la amenazante furia de la cuñada en cierne, llegó, al fin, una noche propicia que le pareció al futuro "sheik" como deparada especialmente por el cielo para susurrar al oído de la amada las más tiernas frases que le inspirara su pasión. Teodolinda había ido sola al rosario. La aguardó agazapado entre las sombras del vecindario, que era donde se sentía él capaz de mayores arrestos. Preparó bellísimas frases de amor bajo el centelleo inspirador con que le atisbaban las estrellas. Tras largos momentos de inquietud, volvió de la iglesia la muchacha. Rodolfo vacilaba. El pie breve de la amada pisaba ya el umbral de su domicilio cuando, mediante un esfuerzo titánico, salió de entre las sombras Rodolfito, corrió precipitadamente hacia ella, y, olvidando las frases románticas que le inspiraran las estrellas centelleantes, susurró con trémula voz: "¡Teodolindita, te amo!"... La chica huyó escalera arriba; y tras ella, el galán. Fué tal el estrépito producido en la resonante oquedad de los peldaños de madera, que salió alarmada la hermana de Teodolindita y, prorrumpiendo en frases inusitadamente malsonantes, se hartó de dar manotadas en cierta inocente parte del doncel, que tenía tanto que ver con el corazón como con las cuatro témporas. Rodolfo salió de aquella aventura sin ganas de volver a acercarse a la casa donde recibió la primera inolvidable impresión de amor.

Cuando volvió a correr otra aventura importante, ya tenía diez años de edad y contaba con la correspondiente larga experiencia. Vivía en esta otra ocasión en Tarento, a donde se había trasladado ya su familia por haber sido ascendido el padre al cargo de inspector del nacelo de aquella ciudad. El piso en que habitaban se hallaba dividido en dos viviendas. Residían en una los Guglielmi; y en la otra, una familia amiga, que se componía de padre, madre y una bella hija, de quince abriles, recién salida de un colegio de monjas. No había día en que no se visitasen las dos familias. En cuanto a Rodolfo, se había vuelto tan sociable desde el regreso de la colegiala, que no sólo frecuentaba la residencia vecina en compañía de sus familiares, sino que, a veces, los visitaba por propia cuenta. Por supuesto,

(Continúa en la página 486)

Giovanni Guglielmi y Gabriela Barbin, padres de Rodolfo Valentino. La fotografía de abajo nos permite ver al "sheik" trabajando como jardinero, al poco tiempo de haber llegado a los EE. UU.

#2 – 3.

Giovanni Guglielmi and his wife Gabrielle Barbin

162

Installment # 3 – July 1927.

EL VERDADERO RODOLFO VALENTINO

Por
Baltasar
Fernández Cué

III
Rodolfo el bailarín

EN la modesta casa de huéspedes donde, por recomendación de un compañero de viaje, se instaló el recién llegado—allá por la calle 49 Oeste—los compatriotas parecían mucho más dispuestos a interrogarle acerca de las cosas de Italia y de su propia, desconocida personalidad, que a orientarle en los misterios de este país extraño. Bien es verdad que no esperaba él necesitar ayuda de nadie, puesto que traía nada menos que un diploma de la Escuela de Agricultura de Nervi, que no podría menos que abrirle las puertas de la prosperidad en un país donde la riqueza agrícola es uno de los pilares fundamentales. Además, ¿qué dificultades podría hallar él donde tantos italianos ignorantes y torpes en-

Arriba, doña Blanca de Errázuris, de noble abolengo, desgraciada en su primer matrimonio y a quien Valentino rindió hasta el fin respetuoso homenaje. En medio, el propio Rodolfo en una escena de "Conquering Power".

Jack de Saulles, primer marido de doña Blanca de Errázuris.

contraban relativa facilidad para hacer fortuna? El, siquiera, sabía vestir y presentarse correctamente en cualquier parte.

A pesar de estas confiadas consideraciones, sin embargo, al día siguiente de llegar a Nueva York, Rodolfo distaba mucho de acariciar las mismas ilusiones que venía meciendo sobre las olas en aquel momento en que los pasajeros del "Cleveland" comenzaron a distinguir la costa yanqui entre las brumas invernales del horizonte.

Aquella indiferencia de Nueva York era terriblemente desconsoladora. Allá en Tarento era casi imposible andar cien pasos sin hallar una sonrisa, una frase amistosa, una mirada halagüeña. Aquí en Nueva York, ni un amigo, ni un conocido, ni un saludo... nada: como si uno fuese un intruso despreciable. Luego, en Tarento, ¿quién vestía mejor que él? ¿Quién era mejor mozo? En cambio, en Nueva York sobraban los buenos tipos bien vestidos. Hasta entre la gente más vulgar había jóvenes hermosos que vestían relativamente bien. ¡Si parecía que en Nueva York no había gente del pueblo, propiamente dicha! ¡Parecía que aquellos millares y millares de seres que desfilaban día y noche por los caudalosos cauces humanos, que son las calles de Nueva York, pertenecían o a la clase alta o a la clase media! Rodolfo se sentía allí reducido a un átomo insignificante. Allá en su casa, Italia le había parecido chica. Aquí, en el destierro, el pequeño era él.

#3 – 1.

Left to Right: *John L. DeSaulles, Rudolph Valentino in "The Conquering Power" & Blanca DeSaulles*

164

He aquí por qué aquella primera, larga carta que le escribió a su madre desde Nueva York, rezumaba desilusión por todos sus párrafos, no obstante que el joven emigrante quería disfrazar su estado de ánimo con alguna que otra ironía a propósito de la costumbre general de mascar chicle, y de algún que otro rasgo, llamativo, de la vida norteamericana.

Luego, al día siguiente de su llegada a la enorme ciudad era Nochebuena; y al otro día, Navidad. Eran fiestas hogareñas aun para los muchachos traviesos como él. ¡Oh, los villancicos, los aguinaldos, los nacimientos, que tanto le habían deleitado en la infancia, y que ya en los últimos años había comenzado a ver con la suficiencia de quien comienza a creerse hombre! ... Indudablemente, la gente neoyorquina iba a celebrar locamente aquellos días cristianos. En realidad, ya los estaba celebrando. Todo, en las calles y en las tiendas, estaba cuajado de indicios de la fiesta de la Natividad del Señor. Él, sin embargo, pasaría esos días solo, en medio de un frío glacial, lo mismo del clima que de la sociedad. ¡Días cristianos! ¡Y ni una mano que le manifestara simpatía en su soledad! Lo mismo que si se hallara en el Sahara. Sí; en el Sahara. ¿Qué era, para él, para sus sentimientos y nostalgias, todo aquel alud de viandantes, sino despiadados granos de arena humana? Decididamente, Nueva York, con todos sus millones de habitantes, resultaba un desierto: el desierto más populoso de la Tierra.

Esta desolación le arrojaba hacia el hogar. Pero sólo podía ir en espíritu. Y a pesar de la escasez de sus recursos, no vaciló en emplear una parte de ellos en un cable que le mandó a su madre para estar siquiera así con ella en aquellos santos momentos que tantos recuerdos le traían del insustituible cariño maternal, que a la sazón comenzaba a apreciar como nunca lo estimara allá en el terruño. Y, claro está, al compás de tales añoranzas y del vivo deseo de retornar, se hacía los mejores propósitos. Había que trabajar para volver pronto a disfrutar aquella dicha inefable que había dejado al otro lado del mar. Había que luchar. ¿No lo había dicho él ya en la primera carta que acababa de escribir a su madre: "La vida es una lucha. Voy, pues, a luchar. Y he de vencer."

Tres actitudes de Valentino en "Conquering Power" y en "La Novela de un Pícaro", que interpretó para Vitagraph, en los comienzos de su carrera cinematográfica.

#3 – 2.

Rudolph Valentino in *The Conquering Power*

#3 – 3.

Rudolph Valentino in *The Son of the Sheik* & *Cobra* with Nita Naldi

166

Installment #4 – August 1927.

EL VERDADERO RODOLFO VALENTINO

Por
Baltasar Fernández Cué

Valentino con su amigo Douglas Gerrard, a la hora del boxeo. en el Club Atlético de Hollywood.

IV
Contra Viento y Marea

LA compañía de opereta que sacó de Nueva York a Rodolfo el bailarín fracasó en el camino; pero él tuvo la suerte de llegar a San Francisco, donde vivió una temporada, ora del baile, ora de milagro.

Allí, lo mismo que en Nueva York, su figura y sus facultades como bailarín le granjearon algunas provechosas relaciones sociales, entre las que sobresalió la de la distinguida señora de Jack Spreckels, quien fué su mejor amiga en aquel alegre puerto, y le ayudó hasta el punto de conseguir que su propio esposo le recomendase a personas de importancia en la comarca.

Así llegó a dedicarse a la compra y venta de valores, en calidad de corredor; y en esta ocupación estaba cifrando sus ilusiones cuando, un buen día, topó con Norman Kaiser, a quien había conocido en Nueva York como viajante de una fábrica de baúles perteneciente a su propio padre, rico industrial originario de Alemania. Así Norman como su familia habían tenido para Rodolfo muy finas atenciones durante los días malhadados de su vida neoyorquina; de manera que, al encontrar en estas tierras lejanas a

El malogrado actor con la señora de Jack Spreckels, de San Francisco, que lo protegió a su llegada a California por primera vez.

Fotografía de Rodolfo tomada a los pocos meses de su llegada a California en busca de porvenir.

#4 – 1.

Left to Right: *Rudolph Valentino & Douglas Gerrard, with Jack Spreckels' wife*

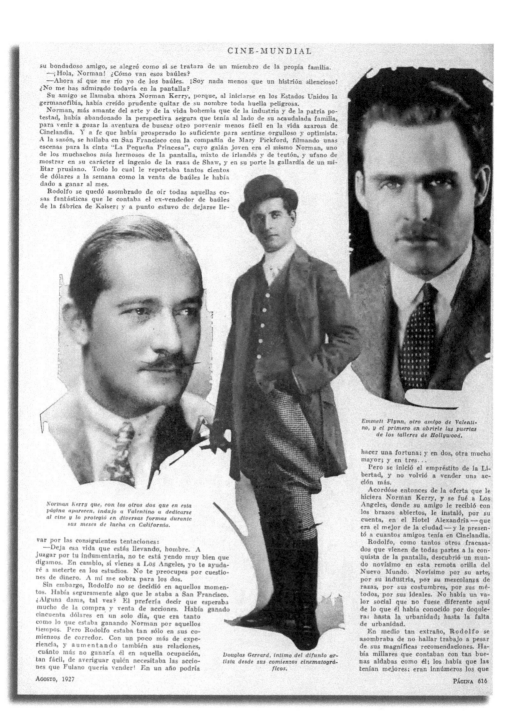

su bondadoso amigo, se alegró como si se tratara de un miembro de la propia familia.

—¡Hola, Norman! ¿Cómo van esos baúles?

—Ahora sí que me río yo de los baúles. ¡Soy nada menos que un histrión silencioso! ¿No me has admirado todavía en la pantalla?

Su amigo se llamaba ahora Norman Kerry, porque, al iniciarse en los Estados Unidos la germanofobia, había creído prudente quitar de su nombre toda huella peligrosa.

Norman, más amante del arte y de la vida bohemia que de la industria y de la patria potestad, había abandonado la perspectiva segura que tenía al lado de su acaudalada familia, para venir a gozar la aventura de buscar otro porvenir menos fácil en la vida azarosa de Cinelandia. Y a fe que había prosperado lo suficiente para sentirse orgulloso y optimista. A la sazón, se hallaba en San Francisco con la compañía de Mary Pickford, filmando unas escenas para la cinta "La Pequeña Princesa", cuyo galán joven era el mismo Norman, uno de los muchachos más hermosos de la pantalla, mixto de irlandés y de teutón, y ufano de mostrar en su carácter el ingenio de la raza de Shaw, y en su porte la gallardía de un militar prusiano. Todo lo cual le reportaba tantos cientos de dólares a la semana como la venta de baúles le había dado a ganar al mes.

Rodolfo se quedó asombrado de oír todas aquellas cosas fantásticas que le contaba el ex-vendedor de baúles de la fábrica de Kaiser; y a punto estuvo de dejarse lle-

Norman Kerry que, con los otros dos que en esta página aparecen, indujo a Valentino a dedicarse al cine y lo protegió en diversas formas durante sus meses de lucha en California.

var por las consiguientes tentaciones:

—Deja esa vida que estás llevando, hombre. A juzgar por tu indumentaria, no te está yendo muy bien que digamos. En cambio, si vienes a Los Angeles, yo te ayudaré a meterte en los estudios. No te preocupes por cuestiones de dinero. A mí me sobra para los dos.

Sin embargo, Rodolfo no se decidió en aquellos momentos. Había seguramente algo que le ataba a San Francisco. ¿Alguna dama, tal vez? Él prefería decir que esperaba mucho de la compra y venta de acciones. Había ganado cincuenta dólares en un solo día, que era tanto como lo que estaba ganando Norman por aquellos tiempos. Pero Rodolfo estaba tan sólo en sus comienzos de corredor. Con un poco más de experiencia, y aumentando también sus relaciones, cuánto más no ganaría él en aquella ocupación, tan fácil, de averiguar quién necesitaba las acciones que Fulano quería vender! En un año podría

Douglas Gerrard, íntimo del difunto artista desde sus comienzos cinematográficos.

Emmett Flynn, otro amigo de Valentino, y el primero en abrirle las puertas de los talleres de Hollywood.

hacer una fortuna; y en dos, otra mucho mayor; y en tres...

Pero se inició el empréstito de la Libertad, y no volvió a vender una acción más.

Acordóse entonces de la oferta que le hiciera Norman Kerry, y se fué a Los Angeles, donde su amigo le recibió con los brazos abiertos, le instaló, por su cuenta, en el Hotel Alexandria —que era el mejor de la ciudad— y le presentó a cuantos amigos tenía en Cinelandia.

Rodolfo, como tantos otros fracasados que vienen de todas partes a la conquista de la pantalla, descubrió un mundo novísimo en esta remota orilla del Nuevo Mundo. Novísimo por su arte, por su industria, por su mezcolanza de razas, por sus costumbres, por sus métodos, por sus ideales. No había un valor social que no fuese diferente aquí de lo que él había conocido por doquiera: hasta la urbanidad; hasta la falta de urbanidad.

En medio tan extraño, Rodolfo se asombraba de no hallar trabajo a pesar de sus magníficas recomendaciones. Había millares que contaban con tan buenas aldabas como él; los había que las tenían mejores; eran innúmeros los que

#4 – 2.

Left to Right: *Norman Kerry, Douglas Gerrard & Emmett Flynn*

169

tenían más experiencia; montones de seres humanos estaban dispuestos a hacer cuantos sacrificios, cuantas humillaciones fuesen necesarios para alcanzar lo que él buscaba fundándose en que había sido bailarín en Nueva York y en que era amigo de Norman Kerry y de los amigos de este artista. Sin embargo, muchos de esos aspirantes a la gloria de la pantalla solían pasar hambre, y, para librarse de tales privaciones, se veían obligados, con no poca frecuencia, a refugiarse en algún hotel o restaurante, donde adornaban con su belleza y con sus ilusiones la humildísima tarea de lavar platos, cuando no tenían que recurrir a medios mucho menos dignos.

Pero Rodolfo, al fin, halló trabajo, como "extra", ganando $5 al día, o sea, mucho menos de lo que solía ganar como Rodolfo el bailarín. Fué Emmett Flynn — el director de "El Conde de Monte Cristo" — quien le dió esa primera ocupación en la película "Alimony" (de la Universal) en que figuraban como actores principales Norman Kerry y Wanda Hawley. Detalle curioso de ese modesto debut de quien había de llegar tan alto en el arte cinematográfico fué que mientras trabajaba en aquella película, conoció a una "extra", llamada Alice Taffe, que, andando el tiempo, había de llamarse Alice Terry y se haría famosa en la misma película que hizo famoso a Rodolfo Valentino: "Los Cuatro Jinetes"

Después de esa tan deseada iniciación volvió a quedar lo mismo que antes: sin trabajo; obligado a recorrer diariamente el mismo calvario, de estudio en estudio, de amigo en amigo, en busca de otra oportunidad, por muy mezquina que fuese; y entretanto, viviendo a expensas de Norman Kerry, si bien ya no en el elegante

Tres artistas que intervinieron en la vida de Valentino durante sus primeros meses en California: Gloria Swanson, a quien él inspiró singular antipatía; Mary Miles Minter, de quien se enamoró sin resultados y Jean Acker, con quien se casó.

bajar en los estudios; pero esta vez, en uno de los principales papeles de "La Virgen Casada". Aquí sí iba a tener ocasión para darse a conocer, en vez de perderse, como hasta entonces, en el montón de anónimos "extras". Le importaba poco que le pagasen tan sólo cincuenta dólares a la semana. Desempeñó su papel lo mejor que pudo, y aguardó confiadamente a que los empresarios de Hollywood que viesen la película viniesen a porfía a ofrecerle contratos fabulosos. Aguardó, en vano. Terminada la cinta, se inició un pleito que retardó su exhibición hasta que Rodolfo ya se había hecho famoso por otros conceptos. Y entonces no fué él quien

Hotel Alexandria, toda vez que, por decoro, se había trasladado a una modesta casa de "apartments".

Logró, a duras penas, trabajar, siempre como "extra", en alguna que otra película; pero desilusionado luego ante la agria realidad de los estudios, tan distinta de lo que uno se imagina antes de conocerlos, volvió a refugiarse en su vieja profesión, que tanto empeño tenía en olvidar. Volvió a ser el mismo Rodolfo el bailarín de Nueva York; pero esta vez, en un cabaret de los alrededores de Los Angeles, y por la modesta suma de $35 a la semana, o sea, lo que ganaba entonces un mísero "extra" de los estudios de Hollywood. Pero siquiera allí tenía la comida segura sin necesidad de pasar por la humillación de que nadie le mantuviese. Y además, tenía la esperanza de que le "descubriera" alguno de los directores peliculeros que frecuentaban el cabaret.

Sin que nadie le descubriese, pasó a bailar al Hotel Maryland, en Pasadena, en compañía de la bailarina Kitty Phelps, que fué la primera mujer a quien amó en California, aun cuando ya antes de eso hubiese tenido ligas de una u otra índole con más de una Eva.

Gracias a una oportuna indicación de Emmett Flynn, volvió a tra-

recogió el fruto de aquel su primer papel importante: fueron los filmadores quienes aprovecharon la fama de Valentino.

De tan poco le había servido aquel ascenso casual, que, después de haber trabajado como uno de los primeros actores en aquella película, volvió a verse en apuros, y tuvo que aceptar otro puesto de "extra" que le ofreció Emmett Flynn, si bien ganando esta vez $7.50 diarios, y recibiéndolos durante todo el tiempo que duró la filmación, en vez de recibirlos unos cuantos días, según los usos de Cinelandia.

Poco después, Bob Leonard y su esposa Mae Murray, que le habían conocido en Nueva York, le dieron el papel de primer actor en "La Gran Personita" con cien dólares de sueldo a la semana. Luego, en la siguiente película de la misma Mae, volvieron a emplearle con la misma categoría. Pero en la otra película, no habiendo papel adecuado para él, fué preferido Ralph Graves, quien acababa de ganar un premio en un concurso de belleza.

Rodolfo trabajó luego a las órdenes de Paul Powell, de James Young, de D. W. Griffith y de Sid Grauman, unas veces como actor *(Continúa en la página 653)*

#4 – 3.

Left to Right: *Gloria Swanson, Mary Miles Minter & Jean Acker*

Installment # 5 – September 1927.

EL VERDADERO RODOLFO VALENTINO

Por
Baltasar Fernández Cué

V
El Triunfo

Retrato del famoso actor en la época en que comenzó a destacarse, gracias a su interpretación en "Los Cuatro Jinetes del Apocalipsis". A la izquierda, Blasco Ibáñez, autor de la novela, hablando con Rex Ingram, director de la película.

SE suele decir que el matrimonio es un estímulo que hace al hombre prosperar. La primera aventura matrimonial de Rodolfo Valentino es un caso curiosísimo de la prosperidad que, apenas casado, puede alcanzar un hombre que siempre había estado a la cuarta pregunta antes de la vida marital.

Rodolfo había conocido a Juana Acker, co-mo hemos visto ya, en una fiesta celebrada en la casa de Pauline Frederick. Fué esto a principios de Septiembre de 1919. Después, tardó algunas semanas en volver a ver a aquella morenita tan simpática, a quien nunca más pudo olvidar.

Se encontraron, al fin, en los estudios de la Metro, donde él estaba tomando parte en una película cuya estrella era Dorothy Phi-llips. Juana trabajaba para la misma empresa, pero con más regularidad, y con más provecho también.

Según contaba el mismo Valentino, apenas la volvió a ver, se sintió súbitamente enamorado de ella. No sólo era hermosa Juana Acker, sino que le parecía a él una de esas mujeres especialmente dotadas para la constitución de un hogar, de una familia,

#5 -1.

On left: Blasco Ibáñez speaks with director Rex Ingram

172

ción a los varones. La había traído a Hollywood la Nazimova, con quien había vivido durante una temporada. Y se decía que ambas detestaban a los hombres. Pero aquel exótico italiano de 24 años, joven, guapo, galante, parecía tan diferente de los demás... Al menos, impresionaba a Juana de un modo muy distinto que los otros.

Detuvieron sus caballos a la sombra de unos árboles: donde Juana quiso detenerse: en un lugar en que, a través de las ramas, se filtraba el sol para dibujar sobre el césped los arabescos de una luminosa alfombra rústica.

¡Con qué emoción ayudó Rodolfo a Juana a apearse del caballo!

¡Con qué fruición prolongó la ceremonia, como si estuviese celebrándola con excesivo cuidado, pero, en realidad, guiado por el varonil propósito de hacer más duradero el goce que hallaba en oprimir suavemente con sus dedos amorosos la carne joven que latía debajo del vestido!

A la sombra de aquellos árboles pasaron momentos muy deliciosos para él, y completamente nuevos para ella. Juana oía embobada las frases inusitadas del pretendiente latino, y observaba con no menos interés la expresión ensoñadora con que, a veces, callaba su interlocutor.

Al conjuro de las bellas palabras de Valentino, y de su silencio misterioso, y de sus miradas magnéticas, el panorama de California se transfiguraba y asumía apariencias y significados que Juana Acker nunca había sabido leer en aquella tibia ondulación de verdura que, ante sus ojos serenos, se precipitaba desde las nubes hasta el mar.

Aquel oleaje campestre era un símbolo de la vida actual. Las casas que blanqueaban en las cumbres, en las laderas, en las cañadas, eran hogares náufragos zarandeados despiadadamente por la tempestad.

Juana miraba, asombrada, ora hacia los "hogares náufragos", que ella veía inmóviles en vez de zarandeados, ora hacia la cara de aquel pretendiente que, a veces, parecía desvariar. Pero, al fin, sugestionada por la fantasía del espíritu latino que a su vera se entretenía en ensoñar, llegó a comprender la exégesis del panorama californiano, no obstante que su mentalidad se hallaba irremisiblemente enviciada en el raciocinio práctico del mundo peliculero.

de todo aquello por lo cual suspiraba él incesantemente.

Varias veces se encontraron en unos cuantos días: y Rodolfo hacía cuanto le era dable por encontrarla todavía más. Se mostró muy obsequioso para con ella: y Juana, a su vez, parecía aceptar gustosa el notorio homenaje.

Hacía apenas dos meses que la había visto por vez primera, cuando, en la tarde del 4 de Noviembre, salieron juntos, a caballo, a dar un paseo por las accidentadas lomas de Beverly. Era uno de esos días tibios, poéticos que aun en las postrimerías del otoño suelen embellecer la vida de California. Le recordaba a Rodolfo aquellos días esplendorosos de su querida Italia, y le llenaba de añoranzas y sugestiones.

Por doquiera asomaba el encanto del romanticismo en el campo, en el monte, en el cielo, en el lejano, brumoso horizonte, tras del cual suspiraban las olas del Pacífico misterioso. Pero nada tan romántico, en el sentir de Rodolfo Valentino, como el lazo incipiente que ya le estaba atando a aquella morenita que cabalgaba a su lado, joven, hermosa, vivaracha, modesta, cariñosa, dulce...

Tenía Juana 24 años, y, sin embargo, nunca había sido casada, ni parecía tener afi-

Cuatro escenas de la obra que llevó a la fama suprema a Valentino; arriba, con Alice Terry, esposa de Ingram y colaboradora suya en la película y, después, en instantes pintorescos de las parrandas por los barrios bajos de Buenos Aires y en París.

La escena culminante de la vida del protagonista de "Los Cuatro Jinetes", cuando el ruso—transformado en profeta por Ingram—describe la visión de los cuatro caballeros bíblicos.

#5 – 2.

The Four Horsemen of the Apocalypse

173

Los hogares naufragaban por falta de amor. Sólo amándose podían las parejas establecerse firmemente en el proceloso océano social.

Valentino hizo un milagro en el alma de aquella mujer que parecía detestar a los hombres. La hizo interesarse en la poesía, en el amor, en el hogar.

Guardaron silencio durante largo rato, y sus manos jugaban con las yerbas, y sus ojos recorrían la campiña, como si en unas cuantas frases y miradas y caricias se hubiesen dicho ya cuanto sus almas se tenían que decir. De vez en cuando, empero, suspendían el juego aparente y el verdadero meditar, y se miraban fijamente, sondeándose las almas, y rematando el sondeo con sendas sonrisas aprobatorias.

Al fin, convencido Rodolfo de que tenía un poco más que decir, pretendió explanar sus sentimientos y dijo lo mismo que había dicho ya. Habló de su ideal hogareño, de la frialdad sentimental en que ambos estaban viviendo, de la misión elevada que en este mundo tienen el hombre y la mujer.

Suspiraron Juana y Rodolfo.

—¡Qué romántico es todo esto, Rudy!— exclamó la preciosa morenita llena de emoción.

—¡Muy romántico, Juanita! Pero ¿no crees que lo sería mucho más si bajásemos a Santa Ana y nos casáramos ahora mismo?

—No lo digas tan en serio, Rudy, porque corres el riesgo de que te coja la palabra.

—Te lo digo muy en serio, Juanita —repuso ansiosamente Rodolfo Valentino.

Pero a Juana no le pareció bien la idea de bajar a Santa Ana para casarse en forma tan irregular. Prefirió regresar a Hollywood, avisar a los amigos, y casarse, a la vista de todos, al día siguiente, sin prisas ni tapujos de ninguna especie. Quería casarse como Dios manda.

¡Qué muchacha tan buena! Así, así quería él

que fuese su mujercita: que respetase la sagrada institución del matrimonio.

Rodolfo la estrujó entre sus brazos y la colmó de besos de verdad.

En el Hotel Hollywood, donde Juana residía, encontraron a va-

Silvano Balboni, marido de June Mathis y director de cine. A la izquierda, Richard Rowland, peliculero que se oponía a confiar a Valentino y a Alice Terry, por desconocidos entonces, los principales papeles de los "Cuatro Jinetes".

June Mathis, a quien Valentino debió, casi exclusivamente, sus triunfos en el lienzo. Ella sugirió y exigió que el joven actor hiciera el "Julio" de la obra de Blasco.

rios amigos y les comunicaron su propósito de contraer matrimonio al día siguiente. El gerente de la Metro, Maxwell Karger, y su esposa, daban aquella noche una fiesta de despedida en honor del presidente de la misma compañía, Richard Rowland, con motivo del próximo regreso de éste a Nueva York, y propusieron a los novios que adelantaran la boda para aprovechar la reunión convirtiéndola en fiesta nupcial.

Inmediatamente marchó la pareja a Los Angeles en busca de la licencia de matrimonio. Tuvieron que despertar al funcionario que debía expedirla: un tal Sparkes. Después, se fueron a buscar al pastor James I. Myers, de la Iglesia Cristiana de la calle de Broadway (en Los Angeles) y lo condujeron a la casa de Joseph Engel (tesorero de la Metro), situada en la esquina del bulevar Hollywood y la avenida Mariposa, donde se celebró la boda poco des-

pués de la medianoche, o sea el día 5 de noviembre.

En seguida, cenaron, bailaron y bebieron los novios y sus amigos. Bebieron, sobre todo. Rodolfo tuvo buen cuidado de que, según la costumbre europea, se hicieran las copas añicos, para estar bien seguro de que su dicha conyugal duraría muchos años: tantos como fuesen los pedazos en que se había roto el cristal.

Duró la fiesta nupcial hasta las dos de la madrugada.

Pocas horas después, Juana Acker abandonaba a su flamante esposo Rodolfo Valentino.

Se habían ido los dos, después de la fiesta, al apartamento que Juana ocupaba en el Hollywood Hotel. En aquella misma mañana, seis horas después de haberse celebrado la boda, Juana entró al cuarto de la señora Karger, que había contribuido a adelantar la fecha de la unión, y le confesó, sin ambajes ni rodeos, que sentía haber contraído matrimonio, que había cometido un gran error, y que no estaba segura de poder continuar

#5 -3.

Left to Right: June Mathis, Richard Rowland & Silvano Balboni

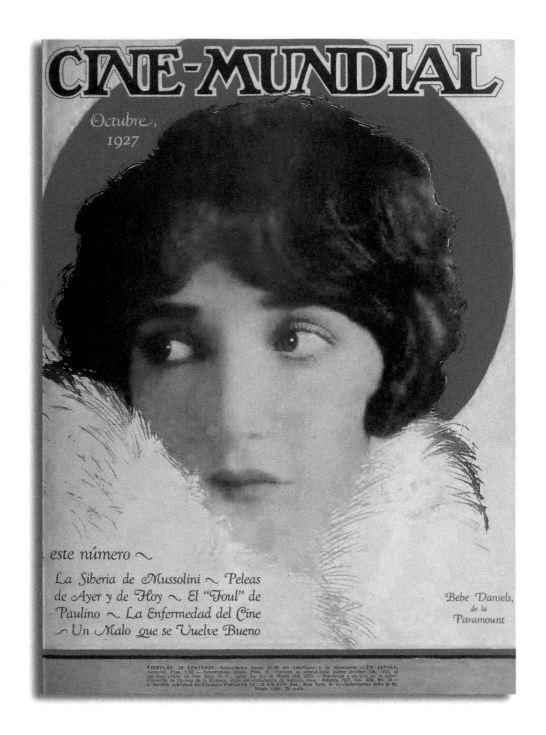

Installment # 6 – October 1927.

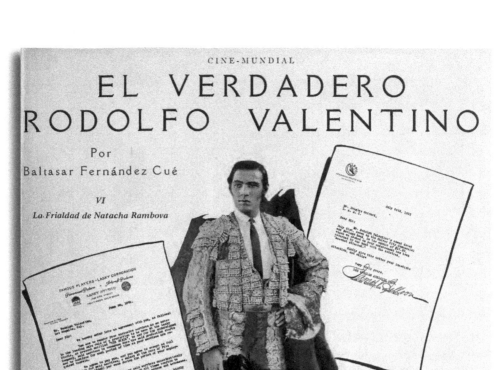

EL VERDADERO RODOLFO VALENTINO

Por
Baltasar Fernández Cué

VI

La Frialdad de Natacha Rambova

El contrato entre la compañía Paramount y Valentino, que dió origen a subsecuentes diferencias entre aquella y éste y a un pleito como resultado del cual se decidió el aumento de sueldo al actor.

Carta que explica que el cheque de Valentino es nulo por "embargo de cuenta".

NATACHA RAMBOVA era la directora artística de Alla Nazimova cuando Rodolfo la vió por primera vez en los estudios de la Metró. La artista rusa proyectaba, a la sazón, llevar a la pantalla la famosa obra de Pierre Louys, "Afrodita"; y en estos planes tenía como colaboradora a su íntima amiga.

Desde el primer momento, Natacha llamó la atención del artista italiano, si bien en una forma que tenía que ver mucho más con la curiosidad que con la admiración. Según solía declarar él después, en la intimidad, aquella camarada de la Nazimova le pareció, a primera vista, demasiado masculina. Su ropa tenía cierto aire varonil. Sus zapatos también parecían de hombre. En su mismo comportamiento, nada se veía en que se delatara el alma de la mujer. A pesar de todo esto, aquella hembra hombruna dejaba una impre-

sión extraña, y atraía con misterioso magnetismo.

Lo que menos se imaginaba Rodolfo en aquellos momentos era la índole del misterio que se ocultaba dentro de aquella mujer ahombrada, de rostro impasible, que no parecía tener interés en mirar ni a un lado ni a otro. A lo sumo, conocería la sugestiva relación que la ligaba a la no menos extraordinaria Madame Nazimova: habría oído, tal vez, alguna de las cuchufletas que corrían por los estudios de Hollywood a propósito de la íntima amistad que unía a entrambas mujeres extrañas, como habían corrido, en otro tiempo, en relación con la misma Nazimova y Jean Acker; porque, en realidad, la Rambova venía a ser, en el afecto de la bailarina rusa, la sucesora de la primera esposa de Rodolfo Valentino.

Pero, aunque lo ignorase por aquel enton-

Durante sus apuros profesionales y conyugales, el astro cinematográfico — fotografiado aquí en su papel de protagonista en "Sangre y Arena" — sufrió el embargo de su cuenta corriente en el Banco. Este cheque de Rodolfo en favor de Douglas Gerrard fué devuelto a éste, sin pagar, porque los depósitos bancarios de su amigo estaban a disposición de un juzgado.

ces, tras la frialdad de esfinge de la hijastra del perfumero multimillonario, Richard Hudnut, había un pasado novelesco, que no sólo servía para imponer al semblante aquella sapiente expresión de indiferencia, sino también para atraer a los hombres con su arte peculiar.

El nombre original de Natacha Rambova era Winifred Shaughnessy. Su padre, ya difunto al conocerla Valentino, había sido el coronel M. Shaughnessy. Su madre, la encopetada señora Edgar de Wolfe, perteneciente a la alta sociedad neoyorquina, y casada

#6 – 1.

Valentino's contract & check returned for lack of funds

#6 – 2.

Above: *Rudolph Valentino in The Conquering Power*
Below: *With Agnes Ayres in The Sheik*

de 1922 y que tantos trastornos había de acarrearle.

En tales condiciones de prosperidad y de enamoramiento, Rodolfo no podía menos que pensar en la formación del hogar con que soñaba desde hacía tantos años. Si no se casó en seguida fué porque aún no había podido desligarse legalmente de su primera esposa. No lo logró, como ya se ha visto en el capítulo anterior, sino hasta el 10 de enero de 1922; y aun entonces lo alcanzó en tal forma, que todavía tendría que esperar todo un año para que el divorcio llegase a ser efectivo y pudiese él contraer matrimonio con otra mujer.

Entretanto, Rodolfo y Natacha se adaptaron a las circunstancias según su leal saber y entender, lo mismo que lo habían hecho antes del fallo referido; porque ya entonces se les veía tan íntimamente ligados, que en el juicio de divorcio salió a relucir una señorita Winifred Shaughnessy, quien, como se recordará, no era otra que Natacha Rambova.

Buscando algún modo de resolver el problema amoroso que tanto los preocupaba, llegaron a averiguar que lo usual en casos semejantes era trasladarse a territorio mejicano para contraer matrimonio de acuerdo con una ley más liberal. Cuantas consultas hicieron para cerciorarse de la legalidad del procedimiento resultaron satisfactorias.

Así es que el día 13 de mayo de 1922 llegaron en un automóvil a la casa de D. Otto Moller, alcalde de Mexicali, Rodolfo, Natacha, la doctora Floretta Mansfield White y Douglas Gerrard.

Una escena de "Morán el Marinero", con Dorothy Dalton, que dió origen al primer lío con Paramount, porque Valentino, en su opinión, no resultaba la estrella máxima de la cinta sino el "primer galán" de Dorothy.

Con los brazos abiertos los recibió el representante de aquella población, quien en seguida dictó órdenes para que la boda fuese celebrada como correspondía al ya famoso peliculero Rodolfo Valentino. Todavía allí Rodolfo y Natacha preguntaron a diversos funcionarios si sería legal en California la ceremonia celebrada en Mexicali; y no hubo uno que no les contestase satisfactoriamente.

Se bebió champaña desde la llegada. Vino el juez Tolentino Sandoval. Se trajo una orquesta. Se trajo también la banda del gobierno. Algazara general.

Mediante las frías frases de la ley, Rodolfo y Natacha fueron declarados marido y mujer; tras lo cual inició la pareja su unión oficial con el consabido beso lleno de amor.

La banda tocó una marcha nupcial, que fué acompañada con el tintineo de las copas de champaña con que los circunstantes brindaban por la eterna dicha de los desposados.

Los novios recibieron las felicitaciones de los principales funcionarios de la población, incluso el gobernador. Y bellas señoritas vinieron a traer ramos de flores a la novia. Hubo después un gran banquete, y discursos en (*Cont. en la pág. 827*)

Natacha Rambova, segunda consorte de Valentino, que se apellida, por adopción, Shaughnnessy, De Wolfe y Hudnut.

acababa de adaptar, el joven artista se atrevió ya a pedir un aumento de $100 a la semana. Después de mucho discutir con Rex Ingram — con quien jamás pudo hacer buenas migas — sólo consiguió que le dieran $400 semanarios. Pero en su fuero interno se iba arraigando ya la consciencia del éxito; y esto, por sí solo, bastaba para llenarle de felicidad.

Terminado "El Poder Conquistador", vió Rodolfo que el importante papel que le había asignado su gran amiga June Mathis había sido considerablemente recortado. Abandonó entonces los estudios de la Metro, y se fué a los de la Famous Players-Lasky para hacer "El Caíd" con un sueldo de $500 a la semana. En la siguiente película — "Morán el marinero" — fué ascendido a $700. Luego, al ser escriturado para "Amor Triunfante", llegó a los $1000, a condición de seguir prestando sus servicios, por ese mismo sueldo, durante un plazo opcional para la empresa y obligatorio para él. Según lo convenido de palabra, después de "Amor Triunfante" haría "Sangre y Arena" en España y bajo la dirección de George Fitzmaurice. Estas condiciones, sin embargo, fueron excluidas del contrato que firmó el 22 de enero

OCTUBRE, 1927

PÁGINA 796

#6 – 4.

Natacha Rambova
Below: *Rudolph Valentino with Dorothy Dalton*

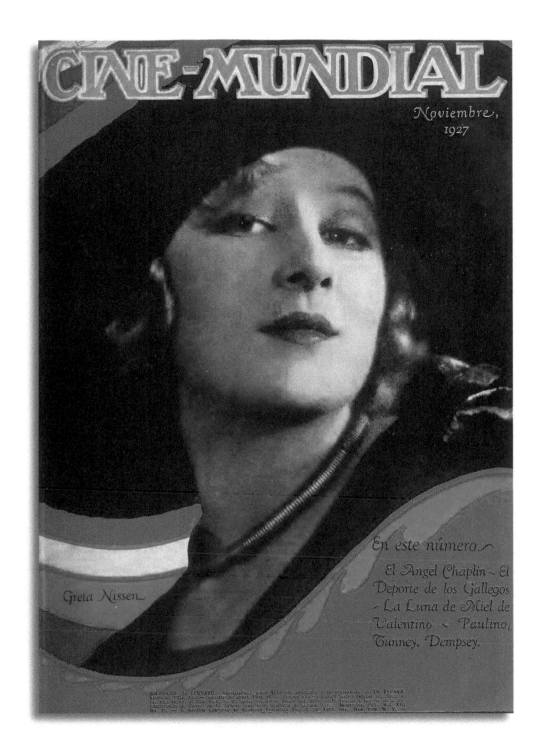

Installment # 7 – November 1927.

EL VERDADERO
RODOLFO VALENTINO

Por Baltasar Fernández Cué

VII
Luna de miel

POCO antes de que Rodolfo y Natacha contrajeran matrimonio en Crown Point (Indiana), se conocieron el artista y Samuel George Ullman, hombre de negocios, que estaba destinado a representar un papel de gran transcendencia en la vida de Rodolfo Valentino. Hallábase Ullman, a la sazón, relacionado con la empresa explotadora de la famosa arcilla "Mineralava", que tanto se anunciaba por aquellos tiempos como un medio eficacísimo en el embellecimiento del cutis.

Sabía el negociante Ullman que Rodolfo Valentino se encontraba abrumado por deudas y responsabilidades, y desalentado ante las dificultades que le rodeaban y le impedían su desenvolvimiento profesional y económico. El triunfo legal de la Paramount le ataba de manos, puesto que, por mandato judicial, se le vedaba el ejercicio de su profesión de actor, lo mismo en la escena silenciosa que en la hablada. A pesar de la posición social a que su fama artística le había elevado, tampoco podía ofrecer a su novia el regalo que hasta las más humildes parejas suelen disfrutar cuando se casan: el consabido viaje de bodas. Y encima de todo eso, tenía un abogado que cobraba nada menos que dos mil quinientos dólares a la semana por la dirección jurídica de semejante fracaso.

En tan lamentable estado de cosas, la imaginación de Rodolfo Valentino, que ya llevaba diez años amoldándose a los hábitos prácticos de los norteamericanos, sólo halló un

En su último viaje a la tierra natal, el malogrado actor en una instantánea frente al Arco de Tito en Roma. La minuta que se reproduce a la izquierda con un autógrafo de Valentino, es de una comida a bordo del "Aquitania" cuando él y su mujer se dirigían a Europa.

recurso digno de su alma de artista: hacer versos.

He aquí lo que él mismo dice en el prólogo de su libro "Ensueños" ("Day Dreams"), publicado poco después, en el mismo año de 1923:

"PREFACIO

A ti, lector benévolo, deseo decir unas palabras de aviso antes de que leas el contenido de este tomo. No soy ni poeta ni erudito. Por ende, no encontrarás aquí ni poemas ni prosa. Solamente sueños — ensueños —: un poco de romanticismo, un poco de sentimentalismo, un poco de filosofía, no estudiada, sino adquirida mediante la constante observación del más grande de los maestros: Naturaleza. Mientras permanecí ocioso, no por mi gusto, sino por hallarme impedido, por la fuerza, para cultivar el cam-

#7 – 1.

Valentino in Rome, 1923

180

Rodolfo con Emil Jannings en el jardín de la Villa Borghese, en Roma.

S. George Ullman, apoderado de Valentino hasta la muerte de éste.

po de mi predilecta actividad efectiva, me entregué a los sueños para olvidar el fastidio de la lucha mundana y el aburrimiento de las fórmulas pedantes de los jurisperitos. Seré dichoso, en verdad, si mis ENSUEÑOS te ocasionan tanto goce en leerlos, como a mí al escribirlos. — **Rudolph Valentino.** — Nueva York, 29 de mayo de 1923.

Sus composiciones son, según dice él mismo en una de ellas, "rimas ultramodernas", y van dedicadas, en conjunto, "A J. C. N. G.; mis amigos de aquí y de allí", sin perjuicio de que muchas de ellas lleven dedicatorias individuales no menos misteriosas que aquella general.

He aquí, traducidas a humilde prosa, algunas de esas rimas ultramodernas:

"A M.

La serenata de mil años ha, el canto de unos labios silenciosos, viven por siempre en el cristal de hogaño, do vémoslos reflejarse con sólo apartar las telarañas de la fe vacilante."

"TU

Tus ojos. Tus ojos: místicos charcos de hermosa luz. Bruna y aurina la color intensa; y, con todo, claro ámbar. Sin la sombra de un ceño. De hondura sin fin, do mis sentidos se ahogan. Tus ojos. Tus labios. Tus labios: mellizos pétalos de seda, de una rosa bañada de rocío. Altar del corazón, donde el ardiente anhelo amoroso adora sin temor. Crisol de las pasiones. La rosa enmascarada. Tus labios. Tu beso. Tu beso: una llama del fuego pasional. Un sello sensitivo que Amor imprime en el deseo. Fragancia del cariño. A veces, ¡ay!, hallo en tu beso amargura exquisita."

"MORFINA

Soy la ingrata Morfina. Me ofreces la co-

pa rebosante de tu Vida. Sedienta estoy, y bebo tu energía hasta colmarme, hasta apurar la copa. Entonces, satisfecha, nada me importas ya. Tiro la copa, la casco bajo el pie, sello su suerte, y sigo mi jornada".

"ESPEJISMO

¡Oh, Dicha!: tú nos aguardas un poco más allá, un poco más allá. Dónde, no lo sabemos; ni cómo habremos de hallarte. Solamente sabemos que aguardas, que aguardas un poco más allá."

"TRES GENERACIONES DE BESOS

Los besos de una madre traen bendición

amorosa desde el corazón mismo del Cielo. Bendición amorosa, su preciada caricia com pendía toda nuestra felicidad. Mientras n hemos besado la boca de la compañera d nuestro espíritu, nunca sabemos que el amo ha llegado a la meta. Divina caricia, im peras hasta que un beso de niño nos resulta más dulce aún. Ese amado capullo — que e el rostro del niño — parécenos que es dond se recrea el amor. Y un millón de besos all reposan en tierno éxtasis. Si yo tuviese qu escoger un solo beso cada día, "¡Oh, qué di lema!", exclamaría yo. Empero, escogería e ósculo de un niño, porque: ¿no comprendéis —en tan sabia elección lograría los tres."

Mientras Rodolfo resolvía tan bellamente los arduos problemas que le impedían desen volverse en la vida terrena, otra imaginación más práctica le forjaba otra solución que, sin ser precisamente tan espiritual, podía también aspirar al honor de ser calificada d ultramoderna.

Cuenta Ullman en su interesante, aunque parcial y *egocéntrica* obra titulada "Valentino tal como yo lo conocí", que, relacionando él las conveniencias de la empresa "Minerala va" con la situación en que se hallaban Valentino y la Rambova al conocerlos él, dió con una idea original, que le pareció mag nífica tanto para sacar de apuros a la pare ja, como para hacer una enorme propaganda de la arcilla embellecedora del cutis.

Recordó Ullman que Rodolfo era, antes que otra cosa, un famoso bailarín, y que no otra era la profesión original de la Rambova. Se cercioró de que el fallo judicial, que le prohibía a Rodolfo ganarse la vida como actor, no le impedía, ni expresa ni implícitamente, volver a ser bailarín. Rodolfo y Natacha podrían, pues, preparar un programa de bailes atractivos, recorrer los teatros de los Estados Unidos, y obtener mucho más provecho que cualquiera otra pareja de bailarines. Y si, al tiempo que hicieran un extenso recorrido, se prestaban a anunciar la

#7 – 2.

Above: *Valentino & Emil Jannings*
Below: *S. George Ullman*

181

#7 – 4.

Valentino in The Son of the Sheik, Monsieur Beaucaire *& the* Sainted Devil

182

En este número:
La Primera Novia de Simón
Bolívar - La Cuna del Cine - El
Marido de Estelle Taylor - El
Sentimentalismo de un Dictador.

Diciembre
1927

Marian
Nixon

Installment # 8 – December 1927.

EL VERDADERO RODOLFO VALENTINO

Por Baltasar Fernández Cué

VIII

Otro Fracaso Matrimonial

APENAS llegaron Rodolfo y Natacha a Nueva York se pusieron a filmar la obra "Monsieur Beaucaire". La voluntad de la pareja reinaba suprema en aquellos trabajos. Lo cual equivale a decir que era Natacha quien mandaba. Ahora bien: Natacha no tenía experiencia alguna ni como directora ni como productora de películas. Lo único en que había tenido alguna práctica era la dirección artística, es decir lo relativo a decoraciones, indumentaria, mueblaje, etc. Era, pues, frecuente que sus ideas, observaciones y órdenes no fuesen todo lo pertinentes que habría convenido que fueran. Los subalternos se veían entonces en un aprieto para expo-

que desempeñaba, que solían notarse en las actividades de su vida privada ciertos rasgos característicos de aquellos personajes. Durante la filmación de "Monsieur Beaucaire", la cortesanía versallesca de que hace gala el noble protagonista inspiraba la conducta de Valentino en la vida real y, sumándose a su natural disposición sumisa ante la dama, hacía aun más profunda la constante pleitesía del gran amante de la pantalla a su altiva consorte. Esta, por su parte, recibía el homenaje como algo que le era debido. Por fortuna, Natacha comprendía que le faltaban aún conocimientos para imponerse cuanto ella hubiera querido. De manera que se extralimitaba lo menos posible, y

Una singular escena de "El Aguila", que interpretó Valentino en las postrimerías de su existencia.

ner su criterio, mejor documentado, ante un temperamento como el de la dueña y señora del artista que actuaba como estrella. Y si de tales divergencias surgía algún argumento, Rodolfo le daba invariablemente la razón a Natacha. Gozaba él con ese homenaje constante a su esposa, lo mismo en los trabajos profesionales que en lo más íntimo del hogar. Era característico de él el posesionarse de tal modo de los papeles

procuraba, más bien, aprovecharse de la situación en su carácter de aprendiz. De ahí el que la película pudiera terminarse en forma presentable. Terminada la cinta "Monsieur Beaucaire", hicieron una más para la misma Paramount: "El Diablo Santificado", en la cual Natacha, con más experiencia ya, pretendió imponer su voluntad con más fuerza que en la obra anterior. Pero en "El Diablo Santificado" no tenía que habérselas con Bebe

#8 – 1.

The Eagle

184

Daniels, cuyo carácter se prestaba para caminar en armonía. Rodolfo tenía como primera actriz nada menos que a la voluntariosa Jetta Goudal, con quien Natacha tuvo pronto un choque tan serio, que dió por resultado el que la vehemente artista francesa fuese substituída por la hermosa madrileña Helena D'Algy.

Lo que ocurriera entre Natacha y la Goudal ha sido causa de no pocas especulaciones. Quién dice que fué todo ocasionado por celos de la primera; y acaso haya sido Jetta Goudal quien más contribuyera a propalar esta especie. Quién atribuye el disgusto al intolerable derroche con que Jetta pretendió resolver el problema de su elegante indumentaria. Acaso contribuyeran ambos motivos por igual. Y por si eso no hubiera bastado, aun quedaba en reserva para facilitar la explicación, la evidente incompatibilidad entre la soberbia de Natacha y el genio de Jetta Goudal, quien, como es bien sabido en Hollywood, es rara la película en que ella toma parte, en que no tenga alguna desavenencia, por lo menos, con el director.

El caso es que la película se terminó y que Natacha, convencida ya de que, gracias a su talento y cultura, y a la experiencia que acababa de adquirir, era una consumada directora de películas, comenzó a forjar grandes planes de los superfilms que, según ella soñaba, habían de influir sobremanera en la evolución del arte peliculero, y de colocarla a ella a la altura de los magnates de Hollywood.

Ya no pensaba en Rodolfo tanto como antes, a no ser considerándolo como instrumento que la ayudaría a alcanzar sus fines. Siempre, claro está, se había considerado superior a él. Pero ahora, al ver sus propias facultades tan cabalmente desarrolladas, tenía muchos más motivos para enorgullecerse de tal superioridad. Lo que necesitaba era demostrársela al público. Y, al fin, le ha-

Tres escenas de "El Aguila", que Rodolfo hi____ para Artistas Unidos con la colaboración ____ Vilma Banky.

gran película. La compañía había autoriza___ que se invirtiese en ella alrededor de med___ millón de dólares; pero la fantasía de Nat___ cha forjaba proyectos que no podrían rea___ zarse con adecuada brillantez por menos ___ un millón.

A fin de hacer la obra con más propieda___ Natacha y Rodolfo se fueron a España a e___ paparse en el ambiente morisco y a adqui___ indumentaria y muebles dignos de la enorr___ película en proyecto. Cuarenta mil dólar___ les dió la empresa para desempeñar e___ misión.

Llegaron a Europa en agosto de 1924, vi___ jando como príncipes. Compraban cuanto ___ les antojaba; y se les antojaba casi cuan___ veían. Sobre todo, a Natacha; lo cual e___ todavía más decisivo que si se le antojaba ___ Valentino. Sólo en perros gastaron un ___ neral. Uno de ellos — un insignificante p___ rrillo — les costó nada menos que mil q___ nientos dólares.

Pasaron otra agradable temporada en ___ castillo Juan-les-Pins con la madre y el p___ drastro de Natacha. Y fué entonces cua___ do la esposa de Valentino conoció a su cuñado Alberto, ya que és___ fué al castillo a la sazón para devolverle a su hermano la visita q___ el año anterior le había hecho en Campobasso.

En aquellos momentos, Rodolfo era dichoso. Quería a su espo___ y a la familia de ésta. Era querido por ellos. Triunfaba en los E___ tados Unidos como nadie lo hubiera imaginado. Después de d___ años de alejamiento del cine, las películas que acababa de hac___ demostraron que gozaba allá de una popularidad enorme. Le aug___ raba esto grandes ganancias; y con ellas podría realizar los proye___ tos fantásticos que, en los ratos de ensoñación, se le ocurrían. T___ dos, por supuesto, enderezados a entronizar dignamente la majest___ de su dueña y señora: la reina Natacha.

Sin embargo, cuenta Alberto Guglielmi Valentino que, durante l___ charlas íntimas que los dos hermanos solían disfrutar en aquell___ días tan felices, Rodolfo le habló de su vida americana, contánd___ los episodios más salientes de su carrera de bailarín y de pelícu___ y entre éstos, evocó emocionado la memoria de aquella beldad su___ americana de quien se enamorara durante su primera etapa neoyo___ quina, y confesó que aquella mujer, Blanca, era la que más hab___ amado en toda su vida.

bia llegado ya una ocasión propicia.

De acuerdo con sus compromisos, después de terminar las dos películas de la Paramount, tendría Rodolfo que dedicarse a las de la Ritz Carlton Pictures, que, como ya he dicho, era la misma empresa recatada tras un disfraz.

Según el contrato correspondiente, Rodolfo estaba facultado para escoger las obras que había de filmar. Por consiguiente, Natacha escogió una de su propia cosecha: "El Halcón Encapuchado", que trataba de la época de los moros en España. Iba a ser ésta una

#8 – 2.

El as de la galantería cinematográfica resuelve el problema que tuvo perplejo a París, ofreciendo dos manzanas a la belleza encarnada por Nita Naldi y Gertrude Olmsted, sus colaboradoras en "Cobra".

Después de tantos preparativos para filmar "El Halcón Encapuchado", y de gastar mucho más de los $40,000 autorizados, y de haberse dejado la barba Valentino, como lo requería el protagonista de

De izquierda a derecha, Clarence Brown, director de la cinta "El Águila"; Vilma Banky, la hermosa húngara; Enrique de Meneses, escritor español; Rodolfo Valentino y Federico Beltrán Massés, pintor hispano.

El director Clarence Brown, el fotógrafo Dev Jennings y el intérprete principal Valentino, durante la filmación de "El Águila".

En el mes de septiembre, se fueron a España, Rodolfo, su esposa y su suegra. Estuvieron en Madrid, en Sevilla y en Granada. Husmearon por doquiera en busca de lo que necesitaban: ambiente, ropa, muebles, armas, alhajas. Gastaron un dineral en objetos antiguos, en realidad o en apariencia. Los anticuarios españoles, y los falsificadores de antigüedades se pusieron las botas. En mantillas, mantones y objetos de marfil, gastaron una fortuna. Huelga decir que cada prenda que compraban tenía su historia, que, andando el tiempo, solía repetir, muy satisfecho, Rodolfo Valentino a sus visitantes cuando, según su afición, los hacía recorrer el interesante museo que era su mansión de Beverly Hills. A la seguridad con que hablaba el *cicerone* avezado a repetir de coro las explicaciones que da a los turistas sucesivos, Rodolfo agregaba la ufanía de poseedor de aquellas prendas relacionadas con tan antiguos personajes. A lo mejor, habían sido hechas poco antes de llegar él a Madrid o a Sevilla.

Entre los primores que trajo de España, y que lució más de una vez en Cinelandia, figuraba un magnífico traje de luces que, según le había jurado el ropavejero que se lo vendiera, había pertenecido a un amigo íntimo del torero en que se inspiró Blasco Ibáñez para crear el Gallardo de "Sangre y Arena".

la obra de su mujer, llegaron a Nueva York, alquilaron por largo tiempo un *apartment* carísimo en Park Avenue, y... so pretexto de que en los estudios de Long Island no había lugar adecuado para filmar una película tan magna como "El Halcón Encapuchado", tuvieron que trasladarse en seguida a Hollywood, donde, a poco, se les dijo que era necesario aplazar la filmación de dicha enorme cinta, a fin de hacer otra de menos pretensiones, escogida por la empresa, no obstante lo pactado, y titulada "Cobra", como la obra de teatro de donde era tomada.

Comenzaba ya a dar resultados el mangoneo de Natacha Rambova. Se hizo "Cobra" bajo la dictadura de la esposa del astro. Y terminados los trabajos correspondientes, se fué la pareja a descansar una temporada en Palm Springs, de triste memoria, por haber sido allí donde habían tenido que separarse al verse él acusado de biga-

#8 -3.
Above: *Nita Naldi, Valentino & Gertrude Olmstead in Cobra*
Left: *Clarence Brown, Vilma Banky, Enrique de Menses, Valentino & Beltran-Masses*
Right: *Clarence Brown, D. Jennings & Valentino in The Eagle*

Installment #9 – January 1928.

EL VERDADERO RODOLFO VALENTINO

Por Baltasar Fernández Cué

IX

Lo de Pola y otras menudencias

ANTES de irse Rodolfo a Europa a gestionar su último divorcio, había iniciado ya sus famosas y diversamente interpretadas relaciones con la tan voluble como vehemente Pola Negri. Siendo tan conocidos los incidentes a que dió lugar esta última aventura amorosa del gran conquistador, es difícil aportar algo nuevo que con ella se relacione; pero, por otra parte, podría parecer deficiente y parcial este relato si en él se omitiera lo concerniente a la amante más famosa que tuvo el personaje biografiado.

Para resolver el dilema con cierta novedad, y también sin correr el riesgo de que se me acuse de repetir mis propios artículos —publicados algunos de ellos en CINE-MUNDIAL, y conocidos, en consecuencia, por los lectores— voy a dejar la palabra a dos mujeres latinas, que se han dignado documentarme en forma no menos interesante que inusitada.

La primera es una de las numerosas admiradoras de Valentino, que me han distinguido con más o menos finas cartas motiva-

Rodolfo Valentino en una caracterización y en una escena de su postrera película "El Hijo del Caíd" (The Son of the Sheik)

das por mis escritos acerca del difunto artista. Se trata de una franca vecina de Buenos Aires que, algún tiempo antes de que CINE-MUNDIAL comenzara la publicación de estos capítulos, leyó otros trabajos míos en una de las revistas en que he descrito fiel y desinteresadamente escenas de las relaciones de Rodolfo Valentino y Pola Negri, que yo mismo presencié y que, andando un poco el tiempo, creí oportuno publicar, porque el triste desenlace de mi malogrado amigo venía a darles, a más de interés especial, un color románti-

#9 -1.

The Son of the Sheik

188

co que las hacía, a mis ojos, más dignas de publicación.
La epístola que me llegó de Buenos Aires se conoce que
está hecha por persona que no tiene motivos para saber
que cuando se le asigna a un periodista la misión de ha-
blar acerca de un tema determinado, no tiene la obligación
de decir cuanto sabe, ni es siempre discreto el que
trate de decirlo, ni conviene que mezcle a lo pertinente
datos que nada tienen que ver con aquel tema. Son éstos privilegios de otras gentes, entre las que reconozco
que se halla la chica de Buenos Aires que, entre las interesantes observaciones que hace acerca de Pola y Rodolfo,
cree prudente distinguirme esbozando, a su modo, no sólo
mi supuesto carácter moral, sino también mi patente fiso-
nomía física. A pesar de esto, dicha muchacha, que a
todas luces es rival de Pola Negri, expone una versión
de los amores de ésta con Rodolfo, que, cualesquiera que
sean los defectos que se le señalen, es una muy aproxi-
mada representación de lo que innúmeras personas creen
respecto de la última aventura galante de Rudy.

(Las palabras subrayadas venían en inglés en el original. Aparte de esta ligera modificación y la supresión de

*El fallecido actor, con Vilma Banky, en un momento de la
cinta "El Hijo del Caíd", en que ambos colaboraron, y a la
izquierda en la cautividad que le impone el tema de la misma
producción.*

un par de renglones ofensivos para una tercera persona,
la carta ha sido respetada hasta en su ortografía.)

"Buenos Aires, enero 10 de 1926.

Sr. Baltasar Fernández Cué

New York

.....he leído con bastante fastidio la "interview" con Pola Negri, y créame
que no he podido menos que enviarle estas líneas en nombre del honor y en
memoria del querido Rudy.

No vaya a creer Ud. que ahora ya que el divino y amado Negrito no vive
Ud. con ese modo de hacer propaganda va a decir lo que le parece, ¡no! ¡eso
nunca! porqué todavía han quedado en el mundo algunas almas que lo han
querido de corazón, lo quieren y lo querrán, y que lo defenderán aún a costa
de sus vidas; una de esas soy yo que no permitiré que el dinero de esa mujer
dado para esta propaganda, y las mentiras suyas se propaguen por el mundo,
destruyendo la reputación de que goza y la delicadeza que él poseía como nin-
gún hombre... ¡Como Ud. (bueno Ud. no lo conoció como yo conocí a mi
Rodolfito) se ha atrevido a poner esa mujer como novia del Negro adorado!
¡Cómo tuvo la audacia de inventar lo que él jamás pensó y hasta lo último
negó su casamiento, pues él aspiraba a otra clase de chica que lo hiciera feliz,
pues si hubiese sido como usted dice no hubiese tenido reflejado en su semblante la tristeza que lo invadía, por no haber encontrado un amor puro y sincero que le hubiese hecho conocer las delicias del hogar, que él tanto se
lamentaba de no poseerla; pues todas esas que hacían alarde de cariño, eran

mentiras, pues lo que ansiaban esas estúpidas era su fama, su dinero y su nombre por encima de todo.

Le pido, porqué no saca una "interview" de esa artista dando a conocer con más detalles la patada tan espantosa que le dió Charlie Chaplin que después de ser su novia la dejó con las ganas, a pesar de haber hecho público, como ahora hace con Rudy, que era el único hombre que amó; ¿Y el pintor donde lo dejó?

Esa "interview" la quisiera conocer pues ha de ser interesantísima, pues se trata de personas que viven; y déjese de profanar la memoria del muerto tan llorado, tan amado por las que lo han sabido llorar y amar. Por qué esa mujer dice tanto lo ha querido, se le esfumaron como por encanto todos los cariños, cuando supo que a la adorada Polita o Polititita le dejó en el testamento una cuarta de narices; ¡qué gracioso!; ¡qué cariño tan sincero!; ¡como ambicionaba la fama, el dinero, la belleza!; pero Dios no permitió que esa mujer llegase a envolverlo, como quería, con su astucia de idiota, para que le diera el nombre, que le negó el célebre é inteligente Charlie Chaplin.

Me extraña que ...... se venda por la publicidad y fama que Politita para aumentar el poco favor del público, se vale de un idiota como Ud. y así ella queda ante los ojos del mundo, célebre; pero la gente no es tan imbécil como Ud. para tragar semejante píldorita; y esos lloriqueos de falsa, cubierta de crespones y sostenida, naturalmente, por el sexo fuerte, dió mucho que reír, pues yo felizmente presencié esa triste ceremonia, y salí desconcertada, pues no eran ritos religiosos, sino una récláme y una comedia, en qué salían ganando los que se titulaban novia, amigos, etc., etc.

¿Por qué no sacó en esa revista la primera entrevista, cuando mi adorado Negrito y Pibe tesoro vivía? ¿por qué ¡ay! de miedo al castañazo y le rompiera esa fachada que tiene de torta frita y la dejase "Knock-out" para toda su vida—; ¡qué cobardía!

Cuide, entiéndalo bien, de honrar la memoria del que fué en vida el más perfecto de los caba-

Valentino y Pola Negri, él de torero y ella de gitana, durante sus amoríos en la vida real. Este retrato está dedicado al autor por ambos intérpretes cinematográficos.

lleros, y acuérdese que aquí hay chicas dignas de defender su nombre y su honor que vale más que todas las ambiciones y riquezas mundanas.

Creo que tendrá dosis para todo el resto de su vida, y antes de escribir una infamia, se corta la mano, y no se venda por el dinero.

Le envío a Ud. y a todos los falsos mi compasión, lástima es lo que merece la gente envenenada y un "secante" como usted."

Algunas de las apreciaciones adversas al amor de Pola Negri, que contiene la carta de la franca corresponsal bonaerense, han sido reforzadas posteriormente, tanto por la nueva pasión y el nuevo casamiento de la hoy princesa Sergio M'Divani como por otros incidentes que la Prensa ha ido sucesivamente dando a conocer; pero hay, por lo menos, dos errores no poco divulgados, que es muy fácil desvanecer.

En primer lugar, era un mito la fabulosa riqueza de Rodolfo Valentino. Si sus herederos llegan, al fin, a recibir algo en virtud de los derechos que les concede el testamento, será porque la muerte prematura del artista vino a dar ocasión para que rindieran mayores utilidades las películas en que figuraba él, en dos de las cuales correspondía a Rodolfo una considerable participación en los beneficios. Y Pola conocía bien la escasez de recursos de su amante, toda vez que, según se ha publicado también, ella misma tuvo que facilitarle una fuerte suma para continuar las obras dispendiosas de la casa que edificó en Beverly Hills.

En cuanto al buen nombre que se cree que ella buscaba al ligarse amorosamente a Rodolfo Valentino, los siguientes documentos

Lelio de Ranieri esculpiendo el busto de su compatriota Valentino, de quien fué amigo personal.

#9 -4.

Rudolph Valentino & Pola Negri

190

En este número:

¿Quién hace la música
yanqui? ~ Novarro se con-
fiesa ~ El último capítulo de
la vida de Valentino.

Installment # 10 – February 1928.

#10 – 1.

The last photograph of Rudolph Valentino.
Taken in the offices of the Strand Theater in New York City a few days before his fatal illness. August, 1926.

desolador el vivir mirando el pasado cuando el porvenir no nos brinda esperanza. Hazme el favor de cuidar las fotografías de Rodolfo. El me ha ayudado de muchas maneras sin saberlo. He tenido muchos momentos admirables, y tengo mucho que contarte; pero con la muerte de Rodolfo se ha desvanecido el último resto de mi valor. En 1922 Rodolfo me ayudó a seguir adelante. Me habló de su propio sufrimiento"... No hay nada en esa carta que autorice la suposición de que hubiera entre ellos relación de amor mutuo o relación reciente de cualquiera otra índole.

De todas las andanzas de Rodolfo durante su última estancia en Europa, sólo una nos revela algo de lo que iba escondido en el fondo de su corazón. Aunque Rodolfo no pertenecía ya a la familia de los Hudnut, la mamá y el padrastro de Natacha le invitaron a pasar con ellos, en el castillo de Juan-les Pins, las Navidades de 1925 (Natacha había regresado a Nueva York). Valentino no quiso pasar aquellas fiestas en la casa en que había hallado "los días más felices de su vida." Habrían sido demasiado amargas para él. Pero aceptó la invitación para los primeros días del año. Y fué, en efecto, a hacer una breve, pero cariñosa visita a sus suegros, durante la cual no dejó, ni por un momento, de estar dominado por la más profunda tristeza; se pasaba largos ratos sentado a solas en la alcoba de Natacha, y solía

El Hospital Policlínico de Nueva York, en una de cuyas camas murió el as de la galantería cinematográfica, cuando le sonreían mejor la fortuna, la juventud y el porvenir.

El cadáver del renombrado actor al ser sacado del Hospital Policlínico para su embalsamamiento en la agencia funeraria donde fué expuesto al público durante varios días.

La presidencia del duelo de Valentino, al salir el féretro de la Agencia de Pompas Fúnebres de Campbell en Nueva York. 1: Adolph Zukor, presidente de la Paramount; 2: Marcus Loew, dueño de la Metro-Goldwyn y fallecido desde entonces; 3: el presidente de First National, McGuirk; 4: Nicholas Schenck, actual presidente de Metro-Goldwyn y, junto a él, asomando apenas la cabeza, su hermano Joseph, marido de Norma Talmadge y actual gerente de United Artists; 5: el finado Hiram Abrams, presidente entonces de la misma casa; 6: Richard Rowland, administrador general de la casa First National; 7: Sidney Kent, gerente de la Paramount; 8: Abraham Warner, de Warner Brothers.

después acercarse a su ex-suegra, arrodillarse mansamente a sus pies, apoyar la cabeza en su regazo, y llorar como un niño.

Las orgías, los amoríos, las declaraciones aparentemente despreocupadas, todo cuanto Rodolfo manifestó públicamente en Europa queda eclipsado por ese detalle silencioso de su vida íntima, cuando uno busca lo que había en el alma del famoso "Caíd." El estrépito de las bacanales tenía tal vez la vana misión de acallar el mudo, pero formidable sentimiento que, aun después del divorcio, sobrevivía en el corazón. Sin embargo, Rodolfo se empeñaba en ser un hombre libre, y volvió de aquella casa al mundo, a las mujeres, al placer.

Para llenar el vacío que había quedado en su propia casa, para dar a ésta más ambiente de hogar, convenció, a duras penas, a su hermano y a su cuñada de que se viniesen, con su hijo Jean, a vivir todos juntos, como una buena familia, en Hollywood. Fué para él una gran satisfacción el conseguir lo que para sus familiares, avezados a una vida tan

FEBRERO, 1928

#10 – 2.

193

Baltasar Fernández Cué termina la biografía de Valentino en este número. En el próximo, iniciará una documentada serie de intimidades cine-matrimoniales tan interesante e inédita como los capítulos que hoy concluye.

Al día siguiente de salir Rodolfo, emprendieron también la marcha, rumbo a Nueva York y a Europa, Alberto, Ada y el pequeño Jean.

Rodolfo se detuvo un día en San Francisco, donde fué muy agasajado, sobre todo, por el alcalde Rolph. Luego, siguió su viaje hacia el este.

Fué entonces cuando, en las breves horas que se detuvo en la ciudad de Chicago para cambiar de tren, llegó a sus manos el famoso artículo titulado "Brochas para polvos color de rosa", publicado en "The Chicago Tribune" y dado ya a conocer en el capítulo anterior.

El tal artículo era injusto, en extremo, porque Rodolfo Valentino no solamente era varonil, sino que como tal se había hecho famoso en la pantalla y fuera de (Cont. en la pág. 178)

Pola Negri, en medio y sostenida por George Ullman y por la esposa de éste, al salir de la capilla de la Agencia de Pompas Fúnebres de Campbell, en Nueva York, donde estaba expuesto el cadáver de su novio.

días antes en Los Angeles con buen éxito artístico y pecuniario, pero con la mala suerte de que Rodolfo, al descender del escenario, resbalara y se cayese al piso de la orquesta, haciéndose una herida en la frente, cuya huella era aún visible el día de la marcha a Nueva York. Pola acompañó a Rodolfo hasta el tren.

Como se ve, no le preocupaba a la artista la superstición, según la cual es de mal agüero presenciar la marcha de un ser amado, como tampoco le había preocupado algunas se-

manas antes el que fuésemos trece los comensales en el banquete que ella misma y Rodolfo dieron en el Ambassador Hotel después de celebrarse la boda de Mae Murray y el príncipe David M'Divani en la iglesia del Buen Pastor, de Beverly Hills.

Pero, por muy despreciables que sean las supersticiones, el hecho curioso es que, a los pocos meses de celebrado el banquete de los trece, murió el más fuerte de todos ellos; y a las pocas semanas de despedir a Pola a su amado, falleció el despedido.

La losa que cubre el nicho donde están las cenizas de Rodolfo Valentino.

#10 – 6.

Beatrice Ullman, Pola Negri & S. George Ullman

194

June 27, 1926
Mae Murray's Wedding

Left to Right: *Elizabeth Stark, Pola Negri, Charles Eyton, Rudolph Valentino Kathleen Williams, Mae Murray & Husband David Mdivani, Manuel Reachi, Agnes Ayres, Alberto Guglielmi Valentino, Balatasar Cué, Maguerite Namara M. Lord.*

Baltasar Cué, in formal portrait and below after arrest in Spain by pro-Franco forces

Index

For Further Reading

The Viale Industria Pubblicazioni
Rudolph Valentino & Natacha Rambova Library

All books are available on Amazon and other online book selling venues

In English:

Affairs Valentino - Special Edition, *by Evelyn Zumaya,* 2013

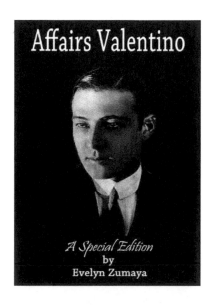

Evelyn Zumaya's discovery of unpublished court documents and a lost memoir written by Rudolph Valentino's close friend and business manager George Ullman became the basis for her ground-breaking book, *Affairs Valentino*. *Affairs Valentino* challenges the currently held version of the silent film icon's personality, professional life and business affairs. Rich with new anecdotes and never-before-revealed details of Valentino's personal finances and his relationships with family, colleagues, friends and lovers, *Affairs Valentino* is a dramatically different story of Valentino's life than the one that has been repeated for decades. *Affairs Valentino* stands as the ultimate and documented true story of Rudolph Valentino.

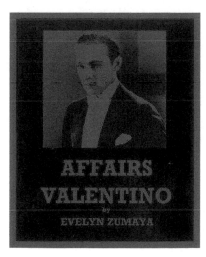

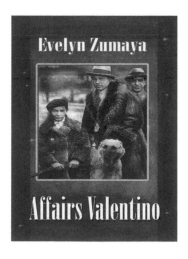

First Edition (out of print) by *The Rudolph Valentino Society,* 2011

Second Edition (out of print), 2013

The S. George Ullman Memoir *by S. George Ullman*, 2014

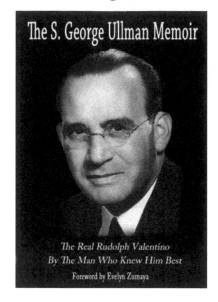

In the days following the sudden death of Rudolph Valentino in 1926, his business manager and closest friend, George Ullman published a book titled, *Valentino As I Knew Him*. Before his own death in 1975, Ullman wrote a second memoir about his life "behind-the-scenes" with Rudy. This memoir is a treasure trove of new anecdotes and information about the movie star's personal and business affairs. Lamentably, Ullman was, and still is, targeted by a few detractors who have aggressively misrepresented his story for decades. It was only after the recent discovery of Ullman's 1975 memoir, that an investigation was conducted into these allegations and documents uncovered which at last revealed the detailed truth about this iconic pioneer in celebrity management. This first publication of *The S. George Ullman Memoir* is accompanied by the entire transcript of Ullman's 1926, *Valentino As I Knew Him*.

Beyond Valentino - The Madam Valentino Addendum *by Michael Morris with Evelyn Zumaya*, 2017

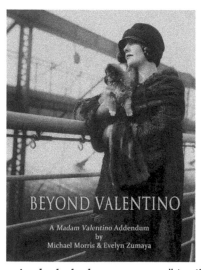

In 1991, Michael Morris published his iconic biography of Natacha Rambova, *Madam Valentino*. He subsequently continued his research, gaining worldwide recognition as the leading Rambova scholar. As his Rambova collection grew, he made the decision to open his archive and share ancillary material he did not include in *Madam Valentino*. With the collaboration of co-author, Evelyn Zumaya, the *Madam Valentino Addendum* was realized.

In this, his "final tribute to Rambova", Michael Morris showcases Rambova's written works, her Egyptological scholarship and her study of myth, symbolism and comparative religion. He has included her essay, "Arriba España", excerpts from her unpublished manuscripts and the story of the discovery of a cache of never-before-published photographs and artifacts. Rambova's contemporaries, as well as her intimate circle of associates are profiled, creating an informed and visual glimpse into her later life as well as her esoteric pursuits. This addendum also includes the enlightening contributions of several renowned scholars, who through their respective fields of expertise delve deeper into the life and times of Natacha Rambova.

The Affairs Valentino Companion Guide *by Evelyn Zumaya, 2013*

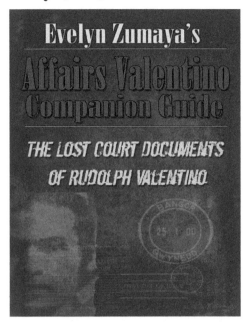

The case file of Rudolph Valentino's probate court records has been missing from its lawful location in the Los Angeles County Hall of Records for decades. With no access to these documents, those endeavoring to tell the tale of the lengthy settlement of the movie star's estate have relied upon surmise and speculation unsupported by facts and figures. As a result, this aspect of Rudolph Valentino's life story has remained a fractionalized, meager and inaccurate account. This would change when Valentino biographer, Evelyn Zumaya conducted a search for the missing archive.

Zumaya discovered that the entire original case file had been stolen. After a lengthy investigation, she located more than one thousand hand-copied pages of this missing file. As the first Valentino biographer to access these records, Zumaya based her book *Affairs Valentino* upon this discovery. The wealth of new information divulged in these court records inspired ground-breaking directions in her research, culminating in her creation of the most accurate and documented account of Valentino's business and personal affairs.

In this *Companion Guide*, Zumaya shares the Valentino documents which are most relevant in documenting her work.

Astral Affairs Rambova *by Evelyn Zumaya*

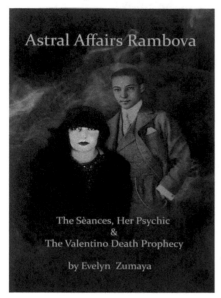

In August of 1925, silent film icon Rudolph Valentino and his second wife Natacha Rambova separated. In the weeks following their highly-publicized separation, Natacha Rambova sought refuge in spiritualism and the occult. She attended séances, studied theosophy and made the acquaintance of a deep-trance medium and psychic, George Wehner. Although George Wehner would become Rambova's constant companion until 1930, he has been, to date, a mere footnote in Rambova's life story. *Astral Affairs Rambova* broadens the context of this time in Rambova's life and delves into her relationship with Wehner.

George Wehner would infamously prophesize Rudolph Valentino's death in a séance held with Rambova and her family in their chateau on the French Riviera. This prophesy would take place only a few days before Valentino died and the psychic would write an account of this séance in detail some years later. *Astral Affairs Rambova* is based upon his account and on Wehner's own autobiography, *A Curious Life,* published in 1929, in which he reveals his relationship with Rambova and her family.

The Infancy of the Myth *by Aurelio Miccoli, 2014*

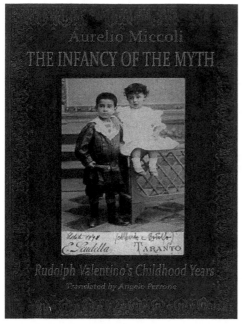

Silent film star, Rudolph Valentino, spent the first nine years of his life in Castellaneta, a small city in southeastern Italy. This is the story of his Castellaneta years, a detailed, authoritative account of his essential familial, cultural, historical and even geographical influences. Author and native of Castellaneta, Aurelio Miccoli reveals "Rodolfo", as a curious yet difficult boy and daydreamer. His narrative is rich with the presence of the actual characters and places of Valentino's childhood days. With Miccoli's first hand familiarity with Castellaneta and his lifetime researching all available archives and locales, he has created a highly detailed, factual depiction of flora, fauna, streets and local history, all illustrated with full color photographs. *The Infancy of the Myth* is a scholarly study, an entertaining tale and a pictorial journey portraying the earliest events and influences of a little boy who became one of the world's most idolized screen icons.

Daydreams *by Rudolph Valentino, 2013*

When silent film icon Rudolph Valentino penned this book of poetry in 1923, he was waging a one man strike against his studio demanding higher quality production standards for his films. While he struggled to find a solution to this employment impasse, he delved into spiritualism and wrote his *Daydreams* poems. Shortly after Valentino's sudden death in 1926, his ex-wife, Natacha Rambova claimed her husband was adept at receiving messages from the astral plane via automatic writing. She also alleged he did not write the *Daydreams* poems, but instead transcribed them while in a trance, channeling them from his own spirit guides and deceased poets. The mystery of the true authorship of Valentino's fascinating "psychic" poems remains unsolved and continues to be the subject of discussion for Valentino's many ardent admirers.

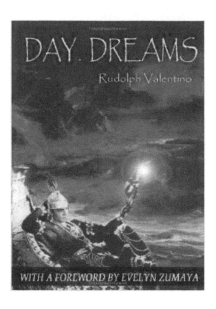

First Edition (out of print) published by PVG Publishing, 2010

In Italian:

L'Affare Valentino *di Evelyn Zumaya, 2014*

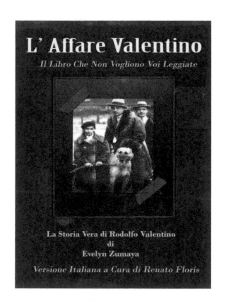

La prima biografia in italiano di Rodolfo Valentino. Le Stelle e i Divi di Hollywood sono ben conosciuti anche per gli scandali che riescono a generare e la Stella del cinema muto Rodolfo Valentino non si discosta da questa tradizione. La Zumaya ha investito ben 15 anni in accurate ricerche sia sulla vita di Valentino sia all'interno della ristretta cerchia di chi gli era vicino, in modo particolare sul ruolo avuto dal suo caro amico ed amministatore-agente, George Ullman. L'innovativo lavoro svolto dalla Zumaya ridisegna drasticamente la storia di Valentino e rivela segreti esplosivi. Il lavoro della Zumaya è al 100% basato su fatti reali ed è supportato dalla scoperta di circa 400 pagine di documenti mai visti prima, relativi sia alla vita finanziaria sia alla vita personale di Valentino. Il fulcro di questo nuovo archivio è l'ancora non pubblicato diario di George Ullman, in cui egli racconta dei suoi rapporti con Valentino. L'archivio è completato da altri interessanti documenti, mai visti prima. Grazie a tutte queste nuove informazioni la Zumaya ha, finalmente, ricostruito il vero ritratto di Rodolfo Valentino ovvero dell'Uomo oltre al Mito.

L'Infancia del Mito- Il Bambino Rodolfo Valentino *di Aurelio Miccoli, 2014*

Il Mito del cinema muto Rodolfo Valentino, trascorse i primi nove anni della propria vita nella cittadina pugliese di Castellaneta. Qui si narra la storia dei suoi anni castellanetani; un dettagliato e autorevole racconto di quanto la sua famiglia, la cultura del periodo, gli eventi storici e l'ambiente lo abbiano influenzato. L'autore di questo libro è un concittadino di Valentino essendo anche lui nato e cresciuto a Castellaneta, Aurelio Miccoli, e ci svela un "Rodolfo" bambino curioso anche se non semplice e un gran sognatore ad occhi aperti. Questo splendido e accurato racconto è arricchito dalla presenza di personaggi reali che hanno affollato l'infanzia di Valentino. Grazie alla sua familiarità con Castellaneta e la sua approfondita ricerca in tutti gli archivi locali disponibili, Aurelio Miccoli ha descritto un ambiente molto dettagliato riguardo alla storia locale, alle strade, alla fauna, la flora e la cultura dell'epoca; il tutto supportato da coloratissime immagini. "L'infanzia del Mito" è uno studio accademico, nonché un racconto divertente dei primi eventi e delle influenze su di un ragazzino che è diventato una delle icone dello schermo più idolatrate del mondo.

The image on the back cover of this book is the last photograph taken of Rudolph Valentino. He sat for the photograph in the office of the Strand Theater in New York City just a few days before he fell fatally ill.

This book's cover design was an artistic collaboration. I thank the London Archivist for their graphic expertise and conceptual vision and Lucero Rabaudi for his artistry and technical ability in creating the final artwork.

CPSIA information can be obtained
at www.ICGtesting.com
Printed in the USA
BVHW022155190519
548718BV00038B/890/P